Above the Battle

To Jean, whom I met at Penshurst all those years ago,
for putting up with all the paper lying around.

Lyell Munro as 2nd Lieutenant in 1941.

Above the Battle

An Air Observation Post Pilot at War

Ronald Lyell Munro

Pen & Sword
AVIATION

First published in Great Britain in 2016 by
Pen & Sword Aviation
an imprint of
Pen & Sword Books Ltd
47 Church Street
Barnsley
South Yorkshire
S70 2AS

ISBN 978 1 47387 275 2

Typeset in Ehrhardt by
Mac Style Ltd, Bridlington, East Yorkshire
Printed and bound in the UK by CPI Group (UK) Ltd,
Croydon, CRO 4YY

Pen & Sword Books Ltd incorporates the imprints of Pen & Sword
Archaeology, Atlas, Aviation, Battleground, Discovery, Family
History, History, Maritime, Military, Naval, Politics, Railways, Select,
Transport, True Crime, and Fiction, Frontline Books, Leo Cooper,
Praetorian Press, Seaforth Publishing and Wharncliffe.

For a complete list of Pen & Sword titles please contact
PEN & SWORD BOOKS LIMITED
47 Church Street, Barnsley, South Yorkshire, S70 2AS, England
E-mail: enquiries@pen-and-sword.co.uk
Website: www.pen-and-sword.co.uk

Contents

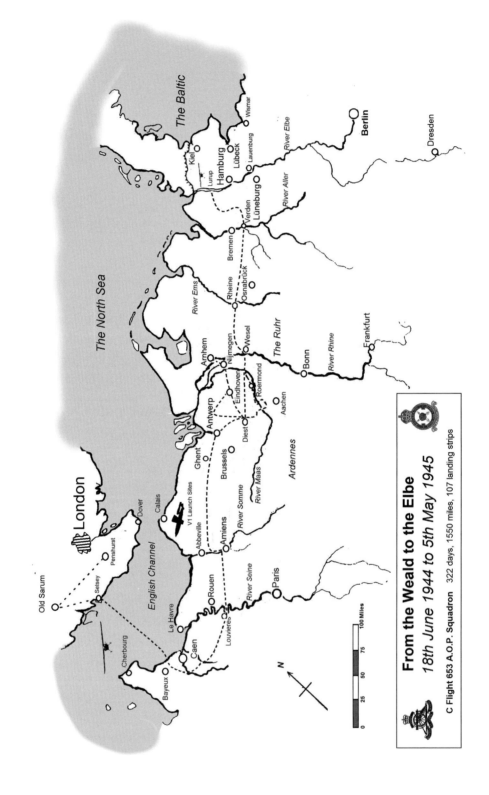

From the Weald to the Elbe

18th June 1944 to 5th May 1945

C Flight 653 A.O.P. Squadron   322 days, 1550 miles, 107 landing strips

List of Maps

Introduction

This is the story of an Air Observation Post (AOP) pilot's war in Europe. It is one of only two full accounts by British and Commonwealth pilots known to be in existence and, unless we are very lucky, there will be no more.

AOP pilots were the controlling eyes of the artillery and could direct devastating firepower onto the enemy formations over which they flew. They were expert gunners and pilots with the unorthodox flying skills their work demanded. The aircraft which had the characteristics needed for the role were Taylorcraft Austers; slow, unarmed and unarmoured, often flown so low that a parachute offered no chance of escape should things go wrong. From bitter experience, the enemy soon learned to dread their presence in the skies above the battlefield. German soldiers knew that an incautious movement, a puff of smoke or a chance flash of sunlight from a truck windscreen could bring tons of steel and high explosives raining down on them from the guns controlled by the pilot of the little monoplane circling like a buzzard, not far above them.

Usually flying alone, without fighter escort or radar warnings, an unwary AOP pilot was a sitting duck for enemy fighters. Like their Royal Flying Corps and Royal Naval Air Service predecessors of the First World War, they had to be constantly alert to what was happening in the skies around them as they directed the fire of the guns onto targets on the ground. Closing at over 250mph, an attacking Messerschmitt ME 109 or FW 190 left little or no time for indecision. Reactions had to be instinctive and evasive action instant. Failure was fatal.

Flying at low altitude made them easy targets for ground and anti-aircraft fire from the guns of an enemy keen to shoot them down before they could accomplish their mission. They were even at risk from the guns that they controlled. The intensity of artillery fire meant that, all too often, the path of the outgoing shells crossed the flight path of returning aircraft. Sometimes, the pilot's luck ran out and they were shot down by their own guns.

Thanks to their unobtrusive role, with the noise of their aircraft engines drowned by the din of the guns, they were scarcely noticed by those on their own side, and in accounts of the battles in the long hard fight for Europe's freedom their contribution is mentioned only in passing or, more often, not mentioned at all.

One of those AOP pilots was Captain Lyell Munro MBE. He first wrote about his experiences many years afterwards, partly for his children and partly because he wanted to make sure that what he and his comrades of 653 AOP Squadron achieved would not be forgotten. Only he and another pilot, Major Andrew Lyell of 658 AOP Squadron,[1] have told their stories and now none survive.

Lyell's own account starts in April 1943, on the day he arrived for duty at an airfield in wartime England; it ends three years later amidst the ruins of a defeated Germany. It is drawn from the memories, diaries and the active encouragement of his friends and former fellow pilots. From the start, his intention was not simply to record his own exploits: he wanted to pay tribute to his comrades in the Squadron who he hoped would read it. He therefore left out much that he considered to be too personal or which might bring back memories that were best forgotten.

When the first draft was sent years ago to the chosen publishers, they pointed out that, good story as it was, it needed more. They suggested he add something about himself and his post war life, including how the book came to be.

Lyell began to make the additions to his book but his time ran out and he did not complete them. After his death in 2002, his children and his nephew, Squadron Leader Alan Munro RAF (Retd), decided to finish the job. To give the full story, we have added material that provides both the beginning and end of his story and also adds much else that he wrote at the time of the main events. The opening part of the book includes a very early record of his experiences, possibly started as a journal. Much of this writing precedes *Above the Battle* and gives his immediate and personal impression of his flying training, his first experience of combat and above all what it felt like to be an AOP pilot. To read it is to hear Lyell's voice as a thoughtful and determined young man preparing for a very great and highly dangerous adventure.

The second part is the manuscript as he wrote it. Many years have passed since then and it is very likely that today's readership will not share the knowledge or experiences he took for granted. Wherever it seemed possible that today's reader might find references obscure or puzzling we have added explanatory footnotes. We have also added excerpts from letters written by him to his fiancée Jean. They add a sense of his feelings at the time as well as throwing light on one or two incidents that the original manuscript glosses over.

The final part, taken from Lyell's letters, family history and the recollections of his children and his nephew, tells of Lyell's career after the war and in later life.

Whilst completing the story, we have been guided by Lyell's wish that this book should be as much about his comrades as about himself. On the flyleaf of the original manuscript, he wrote this quotation from another veteran who fought across the same landscapes, long ago:

"If you ask why I wrote these observations, it was because I loved my comrades: if why I published them, know it was for my friends."[2]

Lyell, his comrades and his friends are gone; but their story lives on.

Notes

1. Lyell, Major Andrew. *Memoirs of an Air Observation Post Officer*, Picton Publishing, Chippenham, 1985.
2. Monro, General Robert, *Account of Mackay's Regiment's service in Germany during the Thirty Years War*, 1637.

Foreword to the Original Manuscript

This account of 'C' Flight's activities between 1 April 1943, (when I joined the Flight) to 5 May 1945 (when the German army in NW Germany surrendered) is based on my present recollection of them, on the notes I made after the war ended, my log books and on the 'C' Flight War Diary.

I have read some of the more accessible literature on the campaign in NW Europe; that has helped me to put our doings in the wider perspective of the Allied strategy (or the lack of it at times).

What impressed me was the matter-of-fact way the British soldier went into battle against an enemy who had occupied almost the whole of Northern Europe for the previous four years and was well prepared to defend its coastline from the North Cape to the Pyrenees against just such an invasion as was begun on D-Day, 6 June 1944.

As for 'C' Flight, I can only say that if one had to go to war, one could not have done so with a better bunch of people, and I have pleasant memories of all of them. War is always a horrible business, but it can and does bring out much that is admirable among men who have to share their lives in adversity. In that respect, as in many others, 'C' Flight was a very lucky Flight, and I was lucky to have been part of it for so long.

Lyell Munro
20 January 1990

With this foreword Lyell Munro introduced his story of the wartime experiences of himself and his 'C' Flight comrades-at-arms. Now, over a quarter of a century later, and with the help of Laura Hirst and her colleagues at Pen and Sword, we are delighted that the book that he always wanted to have published has finally arrived.

For most of his subsequent life Lyell put the war years behind him and looked forward towards a better future. Consequently for us, his children and his nephew, the research and exploration involved in preparing this story for publication has taken us into a family past about which we had only a vague understanding. Since Lyell's death fourteen years ago, the letters and diaries that he very carefully preserved have given us a window into the lives of both himself and Jean during those most fearful times when the dread prospect of defeat hung over the country and when victory was never certain. It was as if at last we ourselves shared and could imagine in some degree, their experience of the war that dramatically shaped their futures and indeed the future of generations.

We have done our best to bring you their story. We hope we have done it well.

Alan Munro
Jim Munro
Neil Munro
Robert Munro

Chapter 1

In the Beginning

On a Sunday, almost three months after the end of the First World War, James and Rose Munro's second child was born. The date was 9 February 1919 and he was given the names Ronald Lyell. His unusual second name was the surname of his father's best man and close friend who was killed during the Battle of the Somme. They already had a son, Alan, and were later to have a daughter, Mary Rose.

James and Rose Munro were Scots: James was born in Logie and Rose in Perth. James was a graduate of Edinburgh University and first worked in the forestry department at Aberdeen University before spending a year at

James and Rose with Lyell and elder brother Alan in 1919.

Tharandt in Saxony studying forest entomology under Dr Karl Escherich.[1]* Although he was elected to a scholarship at Imperial College, the First World War broke out shortly afterwards; so instead he was commissioned as a captain in the Royal Army Medical Corps and sent to the Western Front.

During one of the many attacks and counter attacks which marked the early phases of the Battle of the Somme, James was wounded and posted as missing for some days before he was found in No Man's Land and brought back into the British lines. He was invalided out of the army in the autumn of 1916 and joined an entomological research team at Cambridge where he spent the rest of the war researching ways of controlling the spread of trench fever – a disease transmitted among the troops in France by lice and fleas. After the War, his work for the Forestry Commission took him far afield including a trip to British Columbia in 1923. His family accompanied him on some of the trips to Europe and particularly to Germany where he had made numerous friends. He always returned from his travels with many stories about what he had seen and the people he had met, as well as an inexhaustible fund of jokes and limericks that his children loved. In 1926, with a firmly established reputation as a distinguished entomologist, he joined the faculty of Imperial College as Assistant Professor and became Professor of Entomology in 1930. In 1934 the Entomology and Zoology departments at Imperial College were united and he became Professor of Zoology and Applied Entomology, holding this post until his retirement in 1953.

Lyell, Alan and Rose, grew up in the calm and prosperity of academic life, first in Oxford and then at the Imperial College research station founded by their father at Silwood Park. Holidays were spent with their grandparents in Scotland where they learnt to sail, canoe and rock climb. It was a happy and secure childhood, which Lyell tried hard to recreate for his own family many years later. In September 1926, Lyell's education began at the Dragon School that had been founded in 1877 as the Oxford Preparatory School by a group of Oxford University dons for their own children. The Lynam family

---

* It was a sad irony that, as early as 1921, Dr Escherich would become one of the first followers of Adolf Hitler.

ran the Dragon School for many years during which it reflected their own unconventional approach to education, as they believed that children should enjoy school and learn to understand the world around them. Its teaching methods encouraged originality and unorthodox thinking – something that later came to characterise Lyell's approach to life as it did many of his schoolfellows, such as Leonard Cheshire VC.

In 1933 he won a scholarship to Repton, a public school (only for boys back then) with a high academic reputation; it had a well-established Officer Cadet Training Unit (OCTU), which all its pupils were expected to join. The uniforms were of the British Army but with Repton buttons, badges and belt buckles. The Repton OCTU had a good reputation and was a strong selling point in attracting new pupils, especially from families with a tradition of military service. As a cadet, Lyell reached the rank of Corporal and gained an 'A' certificate, which was regarded as a preliminary qualification for officer rank if he ever joined the Territorial Army. His very few surviving school reports suggest that he had already begun to develop a streak of stubborn independence and a reluctance to accept what he was told without question. He was definitely not a follower, and later on he was to show little or no patience with those who blindly accepted situations and instructions that he saw as being unreasonable or impractical. In 1938 he left Repton and went up to Oriel College Oxford as an undergraduate to study economics.

In the world outside the calm of academic Oxford, the rise of Fascism in Italy, Spain and Germany was beginning to threaten the uneasy peace that had existed over most of Europe for nearly twenty years. German expansion into Austria and Czechoslovakia had brought about the discredited 1938 Munich Agreement under which Britain and France had accepted German occupation of the Czech territory of the Sudetenland. The pact gave Britain and France a little more time to re-arm but it was only a brief respite from a worsening international situation. Britain began to prepare for war and in January 1939 the Military Training Act was passed: all men aged between 20 and 21 were required to register for service in the 'Militia', a term covering all the branches of the Armed Forces. Lyell's twentieth birthday was in February so he registered and waited for the bureaucratic wheels to turn. His brother Alan had already gone up to

Oxford and joined the University Air Squadron, which was linked to the RAF Volunteer Reserve. Lyell enthusiastically took part in the political and other activities of Oxford students and became first a contributor to the student newspaper *Isis* and then the editor of the University Liberal Society newsletter, *The Oxford Guardian*.[2] He also seems to have enjoyed a long and passionate argument in print with the Chairman of the local Communist party. From the articles that survive, it is clear that he had little or no time for the policies being followed by the Conservative government of Neville Chamberlain. In an editorial published on 6 February 1939, he described Chamberlain as 'senile and inept' and his government being '*long bankrupt of any positive plans for either peace or victory,*' adding:

> *We must have men with a sense of the historic occasion and who can communicate that sense of urgent necessity and enthusiasm to the whole nation. At present the Government is a brake on the spirit of the country which is ready to serve if shown where service is needed and if voluntary effort is not stifled by rotten bureaucracy.*[3]

As the 1930s came to an end, many people in Britain had gradually come to understand that what had first been thought of as being only exaggerated rumours of atrocities, mass deportations and imprisonments in Germany and the occupied territories were brutal fact. There was a growing refugee presence in Oxford as German, Austrian and Czech academics sought shelter from the German Government's increasingly harsh reaction to political dissent. But time was running out and from the tone of the articles and letters in these small, roughly printed newsletters, Lyell and his contemporaries knew it.

Nowadays, when first hand memories of the Second War are fading and those times seem remote, it is hard to put ourselves in that generation's shoes. For those who lived through it, the First World War was likely to have been a dark and traumatic experience. For their children growing up in its shadow, there were apparently no illusions about what renewal of war with Germany would mean. Veterans of the 'Great War' and the memorials in almost every village and town were ever-present reminders of the price that would be paid.

Alan Munro senior, c.1941.

On 1 September 1939, Germany invaded Poland and Britain and France declared war. Lyell's brother Alan was now a trainee pilot in the RAF Volunteer Reserve, and on 4 September he married Alison. They used a curtain ring for a wedding band and the ceremony was witnessed by the churchwarden and a passer-by. Their marriage was to last for 18 months before Alan was killed in July 1941. About a month later Alison gave birth to their son[4] whom she named after him.

The excitement and patriotic fervour with which an earlier generation had greeted the declaration of war in August 1914 was not repeated. Instead there was a matter-of-fact acceptance of what had happened – coupled with personal excitement and apprehension – but no rejoicing. In one of his last articles for the magazine *The Oxford Guardian*, Lyell wrote:

When we went down at the end of last term … no one could have conceived the tremendous eruption in our lives that has taken place so suddenly. Like so many we have seen our careers melt like wax in front of us, we have seen our immediate future cut down to the limits of a calling up notice, we have seen friends swallowed up in the maw of Army and Air Force and we have seen the University itself turn into one vast recruiting depot. While we have a deep conviction that we are engaged in a just war, if there be such a thing, we feel a little upset, a little cynical and very ready to criticise.[5]

In November 1939, Lyell joined the Royal Artillery as a gunner. At this very early stage of the war, recruits were still able to choose which branch of the armed forces to join and to specify which corps. It was, therefore, almost certainly Lyell's decision to become an artilleryman. He never explained why, but he was technically adept, good at mathematics and physics and, as it later turned out, keen to fly. He was also an individualist who his OCT commander described in his final assessment report as having, 'plenty of initiative and enthusiasm and who thinks for himself.'[6]

Lyell's educational qualifications also fitted him for the RAF, and it seems that he may have had second thoughts about the Artillery because, in June 1940, he applied for a commission in the RAF through the University Joint Recruiting Board. Why he did this we do not know. It may have been because the frontline fighting was in the skies over Britain and he felt that he was needed more in the RAF than in the Army. In the event, the Board referred him to the Air Ministry and warned him that even if there were vacancies in the RAF, he would have to get the War Office to agree to release him from the Army. If successful, he would have to approach the Board for further assessment before re-applying to the Air Ministry. This glimpse into a maze of bureaucracy seems to have put Lyell off going further. Another factor that might have played a part in his staying in the Army was a War Office decision in late 1939 to set up airborne Artillery Observation Posts using light aircraft piloted by Artillery officers.

Notes

1. *The people lexicon to the Third Reich. Who was what before and after,* 1945 ISBN 3596160480. German foresters were of high status and 'frequently called upon as local dignitaries'. Regarded by the Nazis as influential figures, foresters were often inducted into weltanschauliche schulungs lager – ideological training camps. (*How Green Were the Nazis?: Nature, Environment, and Nation in the Third Reich* By Franz-Josef Brüggemeier, Mark Cioc, Thomas Zeller).
2. The Oxford Guardian was the newspaper of the Oxford University Liberal Club. It was launched in 1935 by future Prime Minister Harold Wilson, future MP Frank Byers and Raymond Walton. From 'Friends of the Oxford University Liberal Club'.
3. Munro RL, *The Oxford Guardian Vol .V No.3*, Oxford University Liberal Club, February 6 1939.
4. Squadron Leader Alan Munro (retired).
5. Munro R.L., *The University and War,* University Supplement to The Oxford Guardian, October 1939.
6. *Commanding Officer's remarks*, L.Delahaye, Lt Colonel RA, 122nd OCT Unit RA, 22 April 1941.

Chapter 2

The Birth of the AOP Squadrons

The original Observation Posts were simply Gunners who had climbed the nearest tree, hill, steeple or other high point from which they could see the enemy lines in enough detail to identify targets for their batteries and control the fire. During the nineteenth century, the United States and European armies had experimented with balloons and man-carrying kites, but it was development of military flight and reliable wireless communications during the First World War that made it possible to use aircraft for observation and to control the guns. By the end of the War, experience had proved that, to be effective and accurate, massed artillery needed data that only an observer in an aircraft could supply. It had also shown that using balloons and dirigibles as Observation Posts was no longer effective. They were too vulnerable to fighter attack and the support train required meant that they could not keep up with a rapidly moving army.

During the last years of the First World War and over the ensuing two decades, the original view of the aircraft as an observation platform was replaced by the concept of the aircraft as an offensive weapon. Aircraft designers therefore focussed on aircraft to fill fighter, bomber or transport roles and the RAF had no aircraft suitable for air reconnaissance and artillery co-operation over a modern battlefield. When the Second World War began, the only aircraft available was the Westland Lysander, conceived in 1939 as an armed Army co-operation, all-purpose aircraft. Although the designers spent a lot of time discovering what RAF pilots wanted, there is no evidence that they approached the Army for its views. The result was an aircraft that was too fast for spotting purposes, but too slow and un-manoeuvrable to out fly modern monoplane fighters. Worse still, it was big and heavy (2.5 tons with a 50ft wingspan) which meant that, although it could land in a very small field, it was almost impossible to conceal quickly and tended to bog down if the ground was soft. Even if a suitable aircraft had existed, the kind of pilots produced through RAF training tended to be temperamentally unsuited to the role of an Artillery Observer. In addition, as it was policy for pilots to move on after a three-year tour of duty, they had no real opportunity to acquire the specialised skills which artillery observation and control required.

In September 1939, a detachment of the RAF Advanced Air Striking Force accompanied the British Expeditionary Force to France. It included four squadrons of Lysanders with a fifth joining in early 1940. The Lysanders' role was to be as light bombers and artillery spotters, but no one had anticipated just how vulnerable they would be when attacked by modern, heavily armed fighters such as the Messerschmitt ME 109 and the FW190. By the time this was discovered, the RAF had lost air superiority and no longer had the resources to provide the protective escorts needed to allow the Lysanders to operate.

In his journal, Lyell later wrote:

In the recent past Army cooperation had been a somewhat unlucky, unwanted branch of air warfare. The crippling losses of Lysander Squadrons in France in 1940[1] [118 shot down out of a total of 175 aircraft deployed with 120 aircrew lost or captured] had not been forgotten. Since that time air observation of artillery fire by the RAF had been perfunctory and hopelessly ineffective. It was left to a few enthusiastic artillerymen to get back to the first principles on which early gunner pilots like Dickson[2] in 1911 had relied. It was the gunner who came first, not the pilot. Experience had shown that it was practically impossible to take a pilot and to train him to become a gunner. If air observation of artillery were to be effective then gunners would have to train to be pilots.[3]

A small but influential group of artillerymen had been developing their own ideas about what was needed and were pressing for the Army to acquire its own aircraft. In 1934, the Royal Artillery Flying Club had been founded and quickly became a forum for producing and discussing ideas about the uses of aircraft on the battlefield. Its first president was Brigadier HRS Massy RA, its secretary was Captain Charles Bazeley RA and among its members was Major Jack Parham RA. All three were enthusiastic supporters of the idea of

Army flying and were to play a leading part in its development and acceptance by the military Establishment. In their opinion, the Artillery Observation Post squadrons should be highly specialised artillery observation and control units – the aerial eyes of the gunners. The pilots would be trained gunners, flying from small front line airstrips or even fields and using radiotelephony to communicate with the batteries under their control. The aircraft itself had to be highly manoeuvrable, capable of flying low enough and slowly enough to allow observation.

For some time the idea of creating an independent air service for the Artillery was strongly opposed by the RAF High Command but, in late 1939, the Army won grudging agreement to be allowed preliminary tests using various light aircraft and an autogyro. These tests identified the Taylor Model D – later to be called the Auster – as one of the most suitable, the other being the Stinson Vigilant. Both of these aircraft were American designs, although the Auster was already manufactured in the UK under licence. In February 1940, D Flight, the first Air Observation Post (AOP) Unit of the RAF, was established under the command of Charles Bazeley, now a Major, and by April it had moved across the Channel to the French artillery ranges at Mailly to begin a series of tests and trials in liaison with the French Army.

It is possible – even probable – that Lyell had some inkling of these developments, but he still had to gain the skills of an artilleryman before he stood any chance of successfully applying to be an AOP pilot.

Auster Taylorcraft C.2: the RAF version of Model D.

In Europe, the strategic situation deteriorated rapidly. By the end of October 1939 Poland had fallen and Germany and Russia had signed a pact dividing that unhappy country between them. An uneasy six-month lull followed, which the British press nicknamed the 'Phony War' and then, on 9 April 1940, Germany attacked Denmark and Norway. By 6.00 am that day Denmark had surrendered rather than face the obliteration of its capital by German bombers. The terrible example of Guernica and other horrors inflicted during the Spanish Civil war were powerful incentives to co-operate with a ruthless invader. Norwegian troops assisted by British, French and Free Polish reinforcements held out until the 10 June, although Free Norwegian armed forces based in Britain continued fighting until Germany surrendered in 1945.

After the declaration of war in September 1939, 316,000 British troops had been sent to France to form an expeditionary force under the command of the French. It included artillery, tanks and a detachment of the RAF Advanced Air Striking Force. So far it had been asked to do little but consolidate its position and wait, but on the 10 May 1940, Hitler launched a massive attack through Belgium, Holland and Luxembourg. The speed and unexpectedness of the assault gained it the name *blitzkreig* or 'the lightning war' and it was overwhelming. Above north-west Europe the Luftwaffe had total control of the skies and its dive-bombers ably supported the Wehrmacht's ground forces, the tanks, self-propelled artillery and motorised infantry. The German forces quickly overcame (or simply by-passed) the static defences of Belgium and France. By 15 May, Holland had been forced to surrender and the French Second and Ninth armies had been routed at Sedan by German forces under Field Marshal Gerd von Rundstedt. On 20 May when Amiens fell, British forces were in great danger of being cut off from the coast and trapped. By 26 May, the ports of Boulogne and Calais were in German hands, in spite of British reinforcements to their garrisons.

A day later, Belgium surrendered and British troops, with remnants of the French and Belgian Armies, fell back on Dunkirk. A mass evacuation, Operation Dynamo, was begun and by the 4 June when Dunkirk finally fell, 338,000 British, French and Belgian troops had been evacuated, although they left behind 41,000 prisoners and most of their vehicles, artillery and weapons. Operation Ariel evacuated another 190,000 from ports in the South of France. Italy seized the opportunity to declare war on France and Britain and on the 27 June, France finally surrendered leaving Britain, its Empire and a few allies, such as Greece, as the only nations in arms opposing Germany. By July 1940, the Luftwaffe's first mass air raids on British airfields, ports and docks were under way and the Battle of Britain had begun. The debate concerning the future of AOP had almost been resolved. D Flight, the only AOP flight in existence, had been about to undertake the last, vital phase of the training programme, which was to engage real German targets. However, the German attack proved to be too rapid and the training programme had to be abandoned when the French supporting artillery retreated back to its operational area. D Flight was ordered to return to the UK and then to disband. Its commander, Major Bazeley, obeyed the first part of the order and managed to bring the flight back to Old Sarum airfield on 20 May 1940 with all its aircraft and ground equipment, which was something of an achievement. He had no intention of obeying the second part however, and the new location was carefully chosen to be out of sight, and hopefully out of mind, of the RAF Command until the Army could negotiate RAF agreement to the Flight's continued existence.[4] The RAF, preoccupied though it was with the Battle of Britain, found time to argue that the appalling casualties suffered by Air Co-operation Lysanders proved that light aircraft such as the Taylorcraft Auster could never operate in the presence of modern fighters such as the Messerschmitt 109.

In 1939, the RAF had set up No. 22 (Army Co-operation) Group which, in December 1940, became the Air Co-operation Command. Using Lysanders and a mix of Army and RAF personnel, its squadrons were intended to specialise in tactical reconnaissance, supply dropping and air defence training.[5] This meant, the RAF argued, that a separate Army Air Observation group was unnecessary and a waste of very scarce resources. It took a direct intervention from the Chief of the Imperial General Staff, General Sir Allan Brooke, then Commander in Chief Home Forces and a fierce opponent of the RAF's ideas on co-operation, to overcome this and assure the AOP's future.

By August 1942, three RAF Air OP squadrons, 651, 653 and 654, had been formed. Pilots, drivers, and signallers were Royal Artillery and squadron adjutants, technical staff and equipment officers came from the RAF. The squadrons started off with DH2 Tiger Moths, but were soon issued with the Taylorcraft Auster Mk I. The Auster had been very much a second choice, but the first batch of the preferred aircraft, the Stinson Vigilant, had arrived from the USA packed under several hundred tons of cheese, which squashed flat all but two or three. Tested against the surviving Vigilants, the Auster was found to be smaller, lighter, more manoeuvrable and generally better suited to the work of Air OP; 'So', as one historian commented, 'it all ended happily'.[6]

Notes

1. 118 shot down out of a total of 175 aircraft deployed with 120 aircrew lost or captured.
2. Captain Bertram Dickson RA, the first British Army officer to demonstrate the role of aircraft in military reconnaissance during the 1910 Army manoeuvres.
3. R.L. Munro, Unpublished diaries (1942–47).
4. Farrar-Hockley, General Sir Anthony, *The Army in the Air*, Alan Sutton Publishing, 1994.
5. Delve, Ken. *The Source Book of the RAF*. Shrewsbury, Shropshire, UK: Airlife Publishing Ltd., 1994. ISBN 1-85310-451-5.
6. *The Eye in the Air*; Peter Mead, (1983).

Chapter 3

The Making of an AOP Pilot

In August 1940, Lyell arrived at Bulford to join 4th Field Training Regiment Royal Artillery to train as a Gunner. Unfortunately during the evacuation of British troops from France at Dunkirk and the Mediterranean coast the month before, the British Expeditionary Force had lost most of its vehicles, guns and equipment. Britain also faced the prospect of invasion at any minute so priority for supplies of weapons and equipment was given to the troops preparing to defend Britain and the armies fighting in Norway, Greece and North Africa. Those newly recruited, like Lyell, found themselves making do with whatever weapons, equipment and uniforms were left. Nevertheless, he and his fellow recruits were able to learn the basics of gun drill and individual skills such as driving. His 'A' rating as a cadet in Repton's OCTU meant that he was automatically earmarked as potential officer material so when he successfully completed his initial training at Bulford he was posted to 122nd Royal Artillery OCTU at Larkhill, where he arrived on 10 October 1940.

The RA OCTUs taught potential Artillery officers basic military skills and the specialist skills they would need to command artillery in the field. The average course took six months, after which the trainee officer joined his regiment for intensive training as an artillery officer. Lyell seems to have enjoyed his time in training, although he and his fellow trainees were only too aware of the horrors of the Luftwaffe attacks on London. From their quarters, they could see the night sky glowing red above London as its docks and warehouses blazed.

In April 1941, Lyell, now a second Lieutenant, was posted to the 128th (Highland) Field Regiment (Territorial Army) Royal Artillery that was based at Rosmarkie in Rosshire. Although the 128th had not gone to France in 1940, a few of its officers and men were veterans from the 51st Highland Division who had survived its destruction in the bitter rearguard fighting at St Valery, and made their way back to Britain via the South of France. They had seen at first hand the effects of German air superiority and tactics and no doubt they passed lessons drawn from their experiences on to the newcomers. The artillery ranges were deep in the Highlands and the local lairds were hospitable to Lyell and his comrades. Whisky – by this time a rare luxury in England – was freely available and Lyell's stories of his time in Scotland hinted at wild parties, of jousting with stag head trophies and of appalling hangovers.

Even at this early stage of his military career, Lyell was looking for something more challenging. In August 1941, four months after arriving at Rosmarkie, he applied for a transfer to Anti Aircraft Command as an Integrated Fire Controller or IFC. This was a highly technical job requiring some scientific background. Although recommended by no less a person than his father's friend and former schoolmate, the radar pioneer Sir Robert Watson Watt, his application was apparently unsuccessful. This was probably because he did not have the scientific qualifications required. In September 1941 he was detached to attend further training at Woolwich and, in January 1942, he was transferred to the 170th Field Regiment that was training at Hamilton in Lanarkshire. The 170th was a brand new regiment formed only a month earlier so even inexperienced officers were welcomed with open arms. Lanarkshire was a coal-mining county, and malnutrition and poverty were rife in the grimy towns and villages where the miners and their families lived. Lyell had never before travelled to this part of Scotland and he often recalled his shock at seeing children going barefoot in the depths of winter and by the dirt and misery in which they lived. It made a deep impression on him especially when later, he saw the infinitely better conditions enjoyed by miners in Holland.

Lyell training in Lanarkshire, 1942.

Lyell had no intention of spending the rest of the war in an Artillery Field Regiment. He wanted to fly and he was determined to seize what looked like a golden opportunity offered by the creation of the new AOP squadrons so he promptly applied to join the new arm of the Artillery and was accepted.

In October 1942, he was promoted to full Lieutenant and arrived at Panshanger flying school to join eleven other would-be pilots. The course lasted for three months and training was on DH2 Tiger Moth aircraft. RAF instructors taught flying and navigation, although for administrative purposes the trainees came under the control of the de Havilland Company, who ran the school.

The airfield had originally been intended as a decoy field to divert German bombers from the de Havilland plant at Hatfield.

The training was intensive and the failure rate was high, a fact that Lyell's account does not mention. In action, the pilots would reconnoitre and identify targets for the artillery. They would also give the firing co-ordinates and orders which would bring the guns onto the target, make corrections as the shells landed and identify and shift fire to new targets as the old ones were eliminated.

Besides doing their job as observers and controllers of the guns they also had to keep a constant watch for enemy aircraft. Their opponents quickly learned to dread the arrival of an AOP in the skies above the battlefield and would make every effort to ensure that the aircraft was shot down before its gunner pilot had a chance to do his deadly work.

To survive and be effective, they had to be both unorthodox and expert, combining the alertness of a pilot alone in a hostile sky with the complex skills of an artillery observer able to direct the fire of the guns onto whatever presented itself as a target and destroy it. The aircraft they flew were unarmed and unarmoured; their main defence against fighter attack was their aircraft's manoeuvrability and paradoxically its slowness. Lyell said he and his friends learned very quickly that if they were bounced by German fighters, their best defence was to find the nearest clump of trees, get as close to it as possible and circle it very slowly. The stalling speeds of the main German fighters, the Messerschmitt Me 109 and the FW 190, were too high to allow them to stay on the Auster's tail in a turn and, provided he had time to see it coming, a good AOP pilot could use this advantage to evade a straight forward strafing attack. This aerial agility was a crucial asset in the struggle to survive.

Lyell described this stage of his career as a pilot in a journal that he kept intermittently between October 1942 and June 1944. The entries, which are not dated, precede and overlap the early events in *Above the Battle* and are a very immediate and personal account of his training, his first experience of combat and what it meant to him to be an AOP pilot. What follows is taken from the journal without editing:[1]

It is not difficult to feel depressed. One is constantly being reminded of the unique qualities which one should possess before one may learn to fly: it is only in moments of optimism that one believes that one possesses them. When the sky outside is not only grey but moving rapidly across the aerodrome just above the control-tower roof, & the only sign of life is a mackintoshed airman inspecting the pickets of the aircraft in sweeping rain, the whole future becomes oddly circumscribed. It contains at any rate no promise of clear aerial perspectives, soaring ascents into the blue & far-seen landfalls across sparkling waters.

For one thing the intense concentration of cigarette smoke in the flying-room is a depressant. The impossibility of holding gloves, helmet, maps & parachute off the wet and dirty floor is an irritant. The pointless conversation or inexpressive silences among ones companions are equally intolerable. Everyone is, in any case, waiting for news. Either flying is OFF, scrubbed and a wash-out, or else the Met. Office says it is clearing rapidly from west & the aircraft will soon be pushed out of the puddles ready for starting by groups of angry airmen.

Meanwhile, one waits. One plays poker aimlessly or one tries to read ones lecture notes. More often one just sits watching the clouds for the sign of a chink. Somehow one survives; but one never gets inured to the boredom & the anxious expectation of a lift in the cloud. The process of becoming an airman works through many devious channels and the hours of waiting on the leisurely progress of a cold front across one's aerodrome are perhaps not to be omitted from the true and only effective formula.

The mass of megalopolitan man has little real contact with the weather (from which I beg to exclude the clear blue skies of the south or tropical countries). The minority, such as farmers, seafaring men and so forth, alone watch the sky for change with any real concern. Airmen live beside the treacherous physics of hot and cold, damp or dry and in time the constant habit of critical inspection of wind and cloud seems to set a man a little apart. As in other ways, one lives one's days with other sanctions.

Is it over clever to detect the process at work even during days which are expressly and by command 'non-flying'? Indeed it may be that the hours of waiting accentuate the airman's isolation from normal ways of livelihood and his acceptance of sanctions which apply to him alone.

But flying is, one should admit, a positive course of action; the attitude or posture of 'getting airborne when the weather lifts' is not, however much it may instruct the soul. One feels a fool of course, in the old-fashioned bird-man equipment: too many clothes on the ground and too few at ten thousand. One may wear three pairs of gloves, simultaneously, of course: one pair silk, one pair woollen and one pair leather gauntlets. This makes the holding of maps difficult. It also makes the mind curiously dull at first: one's mind matches the clumsiness of the fingers in a kind of stupid sympathy.

There are also several layers of clothing round the body and a pair of boots like an elephant's feet. To crown the actual vestments is the traditional helmet, which has the deliberate purpose of excluding all sound except what is canalised down a narrow speaking tube. This might be thought enough, but that one's personality and capacity may be finally crushed, a parachute is compulsory wear. This provides an extra weight, harnessed to the body in such a way that forward motion in a straight line is just possible. On arriving at the aircraft, a final buckling up between the legs is necessary which raise considerable forebodings as to what will happen to one's manly person should one actually have to use the parachute.

One's last minutes, as they are now clearly seen to be, are spent strapping up and locking the little doors in the side of the fuselage –they will open again during the flight – plugging in the curiously named Gosport Speaking Tube and wondering how soon one's goggles will mist up. A patient airman starts the ritual of prop swinging. Either, the engine fires, and goes on running, or a second, alternative litany must be intoned. If the engine starts first time, it is no thanks to you. If it doesn't, you are left in no doubt as to your responsibility, which if not criminal is vexatious and tortuous.

One does get started eventually: everything happens fast, until a final jolt gives the aircraft a chance to lift and soar. After a quick glance round, one notices trees sweeping past below and then the ground becomes a more untidy and intractable version of some part of one's map, if only one could sort out which part. One has meanwhile escaped from it. It is a different element. However dramatic other sides of one's flight may be, there is no other so drastic and impressive. The climb out of Midland murk, through thousands of feet of wet, grey cloud, with nothing but instruments to watch except the thin streams of rain across the windows and wings: that is the moment of wonder, when the gloom suddenly brightens and brightens until one bursts out in a silver plain of endless rolling cloud with an intense blue above and cold pure air to bear one into it. But however wonderful and unfailingly delightful such ascents may be, it is the last jolt that gets the aircraft airborne that is always impressive and ominous beyond any other. It is the sensible snapping of an ancient natural tie which, if you felt it at all, you will always experience with some wonder and satisfaction.

Life under training follows a curiously flat yet intricate pattern: there is always something to be done and there are many significant points – key lessons successfully completed, a first solo, as memorable, at least in awkwardness, as a first kiss, a dangerously bad landing: but it is a pattern and one only remembers it as a whole. I still merely accept in retrospect as I did at the time, that it is remarkable to try to shoot pheasant with a twelve-bore from the back seat of a taxiing Tiger Moth, but that our instructors should do so on still autumn evenings was only part of the pattern of conduct and no isolated eccentricity. At the time, it appeared not unreasonable to fill a pocket with nuts and ball-bearings and drop them with mock-precision from several thousand feet onto the local glass houses. I still feel that under the circumstances it was not unreasonable. It is not to be unexpected or wondered at that others disagreed.

Such crudeness and harshness of conduct were mere external signs of the development of a highly trained and specialised type of individual – the pilot. The final product was robust and sturdy rather than delicate or subtle: perhaps it had need to be. At any rate we were not disposed to criticise our attitude to life too closely however closely we might criticise each other's landings. We hung together in public however much we might quarrel in private.

So it went on: spins, left and right hand turns, re-starting engine in flight – an extremely unpopular exercise – cross-wind landings, forced landings, and, with some reticence, aerobatics. These were indulged in during the later part of the course but our internal system of etiquette forbade anyone to say much about his efforts. My own slow rolls suffered from the fact that my instructor also did not like doing rolls. After a vicious spin out of a demonstration (which nearly prised me out of the cockpit) a slower spin through cloud nearly landed us onto a Luton roof. With this final demonstration we tacitly agreed to learn other things. In any case, true inverted flight entails all the mud, grit and dust in the cockpit – as well as one's maps – falling out past one's face. Unexpected and unpleasant when it happens. I learned however, the simple loop and the not so simple half-roll off the top of the loop and with practice I could execute them accurately and well. Aerobatics were made a little tedious because the Tiger lost so much height in performing them and was so slow to regain it.

The Tiger was a direct descendant of the 1914–18 machine. It was made partly of wood; it had two wings instead of the more fashionable one; it had much character and no vices; it never flattered but it usually forgave. If you could fly a Tiger well, you could fly anything – the difference between a Tiger and a Spitfire was mostly therefore cockpit drill and the question of adjusting the mind to a different order of speeds, time and distance.

On these rather shabby machines we staggered off the ground, scrambled up to 3,000 feet and at this safe height, did our best to master the intricate simplicity of flight. Either we sat dumbly obedient behind our desperate instructors (mine was a Canadian ex-mountie, Flt. Lt. E. (Ted) Scolville, RCAF, with a patient pessimism which once a month exploded into withering invective) or we sat tensely alone wishing for two more pairs of eyes and a spare hand, while the horizon dipped and tilted and the airspeed began to fall off alarmingly. Worst of all was the curt command "Get under the hood" just before take-off. A small canvas contraption of hoops would pull over one's head from behind and fasten insecurely down. Within, all was black: darkness unnatural and curiously tangible, made darker by various gleaming slivers of light admitted through chinks in the hood.

This was indeed an alarming method of torture. Intense, usually excessive, concentration was coupled to lack of skill and gave a feeling of complete

DH.82A Tiger Moth with the blind canopy in place.

bewilderment. It was up to you with a vengeance. The dials and needles were allies of the intractable aircraft. There are few acts of greater faith than to ignore the evidence of one's senses and stake everything (including perhaps one's neck) on the improbable, seemingly irrational, behaviour of dumb instruments. But it was so; the aircraft appeared at one moment to be climbing – yet the altimeter and speed indicator would infallibly collude to indicate a shallow dive. The senses might shout that the aircraft was turning steeply to the left; the turn indicator and compass would deny it. In the end one's senses had to be distrusted: the needles never lie – that way lays salvation, sometimes quite literally.

It was in any case a joy merely to open the hood, to let the light in and to gaze around at the unfamiliar world. In the full light of day those twitchings and veerings of the dials that had seemed so ominous and alarming under the hood are discovered to be the mere accompaniments of normal passage through the air. What the mind read as the start of some drastic change of altitude or the symptom of a massive, possibly uncontrollable disequilibrium were by daylight seen to be the mere adjustment of the aircraft to a gentle lifting current or a slight easing of the controls beneath the pilot's glove.

Thus the days were spent, waiting and watching, interrupted by more and more venturesome sallies into the indifferent, ever-changing sky. All the while each pupil forgot his private struggle against despair, incompetence and timidity, while the instructors tried to make something of their intricate routine – something less than friendship by necessity, for the sake of discipline – yet something more than mere pedagogery. So is it to be wondered at, that these grassy fields, now mostly abandoned or returned to farmland, should feel like consecrated ground to those who laboured thus in them?

The next move was out of the foggy dormitories of London to Salisbury Plain. It was raining when we arrived. Our quarters were temporary and apparently only available at all as a result of vast schemes of brilliant improvisation, achieved at great trouble to all concerned. We need not expect to enjoy them long.

In January 1943, Lyell and his fellow trainees moved on to the final stage of training and joined No.15 Air OP course. This was a two-month course at No.

No. 15 AOP course. Lyell back row, 2nd from left.

Old Sarum Airfield in 1943. Auster aircraft on apron.

43 Operational Training Unit (OTU) at Old Sarum airfield near Salisbury. Training was delivered by experienced Air OP pilots using Austers because the specialised type of flying demanded by AOP work required behaviour such as low flying and landing in confined spaces which would have outraged most RAF instructors. However, the chief emphasis was on gunnery. To qualify, a trainee not only had to fly well but had also to demonstrate that they could conduct a shoot effectively from the air. The two skills did not always go together and some trainees washed out at this stage.

> *Inertia being what it is, we remained there undisturbed for the duration of our training. Perhaps the effort of removal was not to be contemplated or if contemplated, was found to be too costly.*
>
> *Training was on rather less formal lines. The aircraft were fewer and more varied. There were one or two Tigers, a Piper and sundry Taylorcrafts. These last two types were mainly impressed* [taken over by the Army] *and the Piper in particular could not be made to look very military. It was furnished like a well-appointed American sedan, but its performance was poor. Most of its energy was absorbed in producing a very loud hum from the*

tastefully varnished, laminated propeller. Given enough time and room it would eventually become airborne but it was a gentleman's aircraft and one felt quite pleased to fly it for a change. The Taylorcrafts were also noisy but took off with agility. They had no wing flaps but they did have wheel brakes and were basically suitable for the work of basic training. A neat mounting for the necessary wireless set had been devised.

Owing to the fact that my instructor was courting his future wife, a Signals Officer, WAAF, I had at first some difficulty in getting any flying. Having satisfied himself that I was not exceptionally likely to damage an aircraft, he eventually allowed me to fly when and where I wanted. By choice I preferred Tiger flying; most people preferred Taylorcrafts, so there was usually an aircraft available whenever I wanted one. I never regretted the extra hours I spent flying this type: it was hardly glamorous and only dangerous through one's own incompetence or folly. It was instead an ideal training instrument and I was able to make the most of it. Life was a good deal easier. We were, for one thing, over the first and stiffest hurdle. We were potential pilots at least and we were treated as such.[2]

Trainee setting off in an Auster at Old Sarum in 1943.

At this stage in his flying career, Lyell was already showing every sign of enjoying the freelance and unorthodox approach to flying which the Army encouraged in its AOP pilots. Sacred tenets of the RAF rule-book were routinely broken with pilots indulging in low flying, unorthodox manoeuvring and landing wherever there was enough space to put down an Auster. Lyell believed that their freedom to 'get on with it' made him and his fellow pilots closer to the pioneers of the RFC than to the pilots of the RAF – something he obviously found very much to his liking.

His initial training was over and Lyell was posted to 653 RAF AOP Squadron where he takes up the story.

Notes

1. R.L. Munro, Unpublished Diaries, 1942–44.
2. R.L. Munro, Untitled memoir, 1947.

Chapter 4

The Calm Before the Storm

Training with 'C' Flight in England

April 1943–June 1944

On 10 April 1943 I arrived at Penshurst Airfield in Kent and joined 653 Squadron as an AOP pilot. Despite the name, the airfield was three miles to the north of Penshurst in a small hamlet called Chiddingstone Causeway, a fairly recent development that had evolved around the railway station serving Penshurst. In it there was a pub aptly called the 'Bat and Ball'* and a modest workshop that made cricket gear together with tennis-racket frames of ash from local coppices. The nearest town was Tonbridge and well to the north was the chalk ridge of the North Downs. The railway ran almost due west or east for the 40 miles between Redhill and Ashford, and made a useful navigational feature for pilots. Where it passed the hamlet it went through a cutting, so Chiddingstone Causeway was a quiet spot, apart from the song of numerous nightingales during the hot summer nights.

The Mess and admin buildings were in a large Victorian house called Knotley Hall, 'standing in its own grounds', with various Nissen huts tacked on. Earlier it had been a Dr Barnardo's home and it now made an ideal Air Observation Post Squadron Headquarters. The airfield lay just across the road, a large area of grassland with the watch-office and one or two other

---

* The nearest pub, built in grand Victorian style, is the 'Little Brown Jug' opposite the railway station. The 'Bat and Ball', about a mile away, was less formal and the editors are sure Lyell would have preferred the latter! Unfortunately, it closed in 2010.

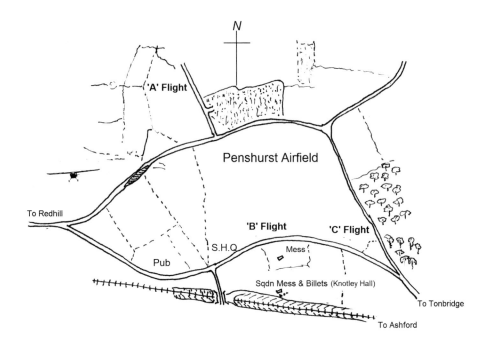

Knotley Hall, years later.

huts. It was level, with low boundaries, and large enough even for an RAF Wing-commander to land in. [In 1938 pilots were requested not to land there as it had been converted to a polo pitch and re-turfed![1] In 1988, when I revisited it, it appeared virtually unchanged.] We understood that it had been a relief airfield for Croydon, which was then London's main airport. Being below the North Downs it did not suffer much from low-cloud and fog and when Croydon was fog-bound the old Imperial Airways 'Hannibals' could trundle in to Penshurst, off-load their passengers onto the Southern Railway at the station and speed them off to Victoria Station. Its latest occupant, 653 Squadron, had been formed on 20 June 1942 at Old Sarum, when Tetley Jones was appointed commanding officer. Soon afterwards, on 1 July, it moved to Farnborough, and then on again to Penshurst a month or so later.

'Penshurst', as everybody called Knotley Hall/Chiddingstone Causeway, remained the headquarters for the Squadron until we left for Normandy in June 1944. It was a happy enough station, although flights spent a great deal of their time away on detached training or exercises with their infantry divisions. Under Tetley Jones' slightly remote style of leadership it all seemed to work out satisfactorily, while Bobby Brown was one of the most efficient and kindliest of adjutants, so unlike some I had suffered under.

The unusual feature of an Air Operation Post Squadron, when compared with most Army units (or indeed RAF units), was that there was almost no commissioned rank structure. On those rare occasions when all the flights homed in, whether for night flying, some other form of pilot training or on a squadron basis, it was officers from wall to wall, most of whom were captains. Command (as opposed to control and administrative overview) was rarely exercised on a squadron basis, nor did it need to be. A problem could have arisen at flight level although I cannot recall a situation where one ever did. Once again, it was the flight commander's own style of leadership that made the flight what it was, for better or worse, and not the exercise of a superior rank.

The second marked peculiarity was the mix of Royal Artillery and Royal Air Force non-commissioned officers and other ranks. The nature of this unusual combination meant it took longer to evolve into an efficient organisation. There were perfectly good reasons why the airmen should be exclusively responsible for repair and maintenance of the aircraft; they were accountable to the Warrant Officer (Engineer) RAF at Squadron Headquarters for professional standards. Whilst there was no physical reason why the airman should not also drive a vehicle, dig his slit trench, and take part in ground defence of the landing-ground those were not duties that he joined the RAF to do, nor was he trained to do them. Add to that the natural feeling that the Auster was not a 'proper' aircraft and also that the Army required higher standards of discipline, smartness and self-reliance than your average maintenance unit, then there were bound to be problems and misfits. Long before the end of the day most of them had been resolved by common sense and compromise between involved parties.

I am sure the fact that the rank structure was so simple, and that almost all officers were pilots, enabled discipline to evolve from within the flights, rather than to have it continually imposed from above.

Once I had done the round of introductions and generally been booked into the Squadron, I was told that I would be joining 'C' Flight as a section pilot. The Flight Commander was Tony Knight; Freddie Riding and Bill Huntington were two of the other pilots, along with Peter Newman. Newman I was told had been having a little trouble with stampeding sheep on Romney Marsh, and a length of telephone wire wrapped round the legs of the undercarriage bore witness to some excessively low flying. I gathered it was chiefly a matter of damage to the feelings of the farmer, who had been placated by an offer of compensation. Nevertheless, it was a sobering thought as only weeks before another Squadron pilot had struck a balloon cable near Weybridge with fatal results *(Squadron diary: 12 March – Captain Whitson crashed on returning to Penshurst* [from exercise 'Spartan'] *by fouling balloon cable at Weybridge. Captain Whitson killed. A/C write-off)*. Both Tony Knight and Peter Newman moved on fairly soon –Tony to command 'B' Flight, and thence to 658 Squadron on its formation at the end of April, and Peter, to another new squadron. Freddie Riding took over command of 'C' Flight, and whatever success 'C' Flight achieved between Normandy and the Elbe was due to his energy and enthusiasm during months of training and preparation in the UK. The great lesson Freddie taught me was to keep the Flight landing-ground as close to the battle as possible. Morale, efficiency, and of course response times, were all at their highest when everyone in the

Flight could feel himself involved in whatever operation was under way. At Squadron Headquarters Jock Scott was Squadron Captain, and Bobbie Brown the RAF Adjutant. Frank Ellis was the Equipment Officer.

The Squadron was equipped with the Mark III version of Auster that it had received in March 1943. It had an excellent take-off and initial climb, but I found it difficult to land it short without slamming it onto the ground. The reason for this difficulty was that it was nose-heavy and the tail had needed to be weighted to compensate. This soon began to show in tailskid breakages and failure of the bolts at the bottom of the undercarriage legs. Even so, it had good visibility compared with the Mark I and a much better climb. I don't remember flying the variant with the perspex rear dome for the observer. It was said that this inverted chamber-pot feature was why people (other than Auster pilots) sometimes called Austers 'Pissers'. Ingenious folk-mythology this may be but I have found no alternative explanation.

[Editor: The dome was an experimental feature on MkIII Austers. It was abandoned when it proved disastrous and the OC, Major Tetley Jones, left this account of the matter:

I also lost a flight commander, one of my best friends; the Air Force were always having ideas on how to improve our planes, mostly making them too heavy or clumsy. One was that we should carry an observer as the American's did, seated looking backwards above the pilot's back in a small plastic bubble. He, as a flight commander went off with another pilot to test both visibility and manoeuvrability against a fighter plane's simulated attack. He ended up diving into the ground with both of them burnt to a cinder. I had the unpleasant job of identifying them. We believe that the observer was pushed against the pilot during a diving evasion – one of the standard methods of escape from a fighter – or that the bubble blanked the tail and lost the pilot control. A bad idea.

Or as reported by 653 Squadron Diary:

10 May 1943: Auster Mk III allotted for trail [sic] of Astrodome. Mob. Vehicle return in accordance with A.C.I. 2376/42 rendered. C.O. and

Captain Scott took aircraft to Fairlop for evasive action trials. In a result it was considered that this fitment was not desirable. Major Ballard and Captain Benson took off to repeat the trials, the aircraft struck a tree during evasive action and both were fataly [sic] *injured. Mob. Major deficiencies return rendered. 22 May: OC attended Major Ballard's funeral at Hornchurch.*]

For communications, voice wireless was used. The aircraft had the usual No 19 set[2] mounted in the rear on the starboard side, where the observer or passenger would otherwise be. To enable 'netting' (tuning into the agreed working frequency of the unit) four locking screws on the tuning dial were released and the dial then turned to find a pre-arranged 'tuning and netting call' made at maximum strength from a ground set. Once the dial was set to the correct frequency the locking screws could be re-tightened, taking care not to displace the tuning. The transmission side was then similarly harmonised. Even when carefully netted to the working frequency the wireless's performance was really little more than adequate.

The procedure was simple enough carried out from a firm position on the ground but netting the wireless whilst flying in tactical conditions (that is, while low-flying within as small an area as possible) was extremely difficult

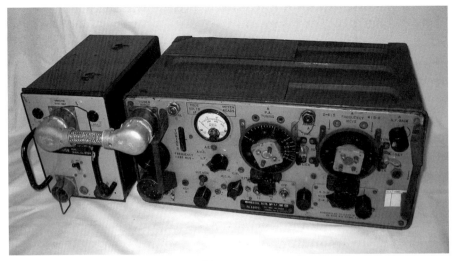

Pye Wireless set No19 MkIII (with amplifier).

and all too hazardous. In practice it meant getting a penny out of one's pocket (without undoing one's harness), reaching back to feel for the correct tuning knob, then using the penny to slacken off four separate locking screws. Once tuned in to the netting-call from the ground set, the screws had to be retightened and the reception checked. This performance had then to be repeated for the transmit side of the set, to ensure that the set would transmit on the same frequency. Given that low flying was already a sufficiently risky activity, the distraction of tuning a radio at the same time was a last resort, reserved for essential cases when there was no opportunity of landing to make the adjustment more easily while relatively safe on firm ground.

'The less you fly, the less you want to' was a piece of advice one of the Hatfield instructors had let fall. That was fine by us: aircraft were to be our personal transport, to be flown wherever and whenever necessary. Such hours of practice, rushing round Salisbury Plain and parts of Dorset with one hand on the throttle and a keen eye for power-wires, or lowering the aircraft into fields so small that after landing the possibility of ever taking off again seemed remote. They served to enable a solitary artillery officer to accompany a regiment of guns into action and to observe their fire and to control it whenever necessary at a few moments notice. It was not only necessary to fly, and fly well in a specialized and unorthodox fashion, but, critically, to observe fire from the air and master the technique of controlling it. The rules of airmanship were to be observed, but not as taboos – merely as logical aids to enable happy landings. It was, in any case, impossible to mend one breach in the wall – low flying (almost a blasphemy to the RAF) was not only permitted and encouraged, it was compulsory. It was a part of the training and essential to operation in action; it was part of the whole technique. It became, instead of a thrilling and illicit joy, a rather interesting experiment to do steep turns round the Woodhenge beech clumps, or do long cross-countries on the deck.

Experience had shown that it was practically impossible to take a pilot and to train him to become a gunner. For effective air observation of artillery, gunners would have to train to be pilots. After much debate, this idea had been accepted. Hence the spectacle of a solitary light aircraft climbing, turning and diving over a troop of artillery, while far off on a bare chalk down, scanty puffs of shell smoke would appear and immediately dissolve.

Once the mobility of aircraft and ground crews can be achieved, providing the traditional but desperately hard 'Ubiquity' of the Royal Artillery motto,[3] it only remained to perfect the technique of observation and fire control. First of all, there must be complete mastery of the aircraft, so that it becomes a mere mobile observatory. It is not easy to see a shell burst on the ground a mile away unless you know where to expect it. It is not easy to visualise the correction needed to straddle the target with the next round. Even from a stable observation post on the ground this can seem an unlikely skill to acquire. On a windy day, in an unstable aircraft with a map tucked under one's thigh and a handful of controls to cope with, it can be so difficult it seems ridiculous. The aircraft must be got into the air and in sight of the target; it must arrive there as soon as possible. The wireless has to be working without temperament or hesitation and when the business of ranging begins, you must devise a pattern of flying which will result in the aircraft reaching a point in space from which, just before each shell is due to land, the target is clearly visible. As soon as the shell is seen to burst you take the aircraft to just above ground level while radioing the necessary correction to the gunners. Then there is a lull while the guns are re-laid during which operation the aircraft remains concealed by flying low and fast among whatever cover is available. Once the guns are ready again you give the order to fire and pull the aircraft straight up into the sky, ready for another observation.

You can look out of the windscreen or watch through the side windows or, if you like, backwards through the roof. With real co-ordination between aircraft, pilot and guns, a rapid climb up to the necessary point in space, a quick look for the bursting shell and a stall turn is all that is needed. It looks simple, like most good tricks, but a lot of rehearsal is required to make it become so. From the days of training to the shot fired in anger is a strangely short step. The enormous concentration in technique both in artillery work and airmanship made the introduction of a third party – the enemy – almost a formality or anti-climax. In the event, the massive act of invasion overshadowed everything else. Years of training made it impossible for us to doubt that we could fail to destroy whatever German units would oppose us. It was the physical possibility of the act of invasion that was to occupy all our attention.

The unit to which 653 Squadron was attached was British Second Army XII Corps, commanded by Lieutenant General Neil Ritchie. Its shoulder flash, an oak, ash, and thorn in an oval, was designed in 1940, when the corps was raised under Major-General Sir A.F.A.N. Thorne. It was intended to link the name of its commander with the Oak, the Ash and the Thorn taken from Rudyard Kipling's *Puck of Pook's Hill* set in the Corps' home county of Sussex.

XII Corps was made up of three infantry divisions – 59th Staffordshire Infantry, whose shoulder-flash was a pithead winding gear, 53rd Welsh (a red 'W') and 43rd Wessex Division (a Wyvern). The first two divisions had our 'A' and 'B' Flights allotted to them for training, and we, in 'C' flight, had the Wessex Division whose men were drawn mainly from the west of England. Only later did we appreciate how lucky we were to have trained with Wessex Division, as will become clear. The Divisional Commander was Major General 'Butch' Thomas, who knew what he wanted from the troops under his command, and how to get it. The Commander Royal Artillery (CRA) was Brigadier 'Bill' Heath, and again we could not have been more fortunate in our CRA.[4]

Lyell's Oak, Ash and Thorn badge.

Group around Geoff Burgess' Auster in Kent, probably Autumn 1943. Left to right: A.C. Lewis, F.M.E.; Unknown A.C.; Geoff Burgess; Unknown; Freddie Riding; Bill Huntington.

The training pattern for the rest of 1943 was made up of moves by the whole Flight to landing-grounds in Kent. We spent most of our time operating from Ickham. Splendid names like Hunger Hatch, Biddenden, Frittenden, Lashenden, Elham and Lasham appeared in the log-book as we learned to land and take-off in the very small fields characteristic of Kent in those days – usually bordered by hedges growing out of steep banks. We went off with the Division to Larkhill for shoots – including a massive XII Corps artillery practice called Exercise 'Fortescue' [on 26 June to 30 June, it also included night-flying exercises – Sqdn Diary]. We also did much shooting on the South Downs at Friston, near Eastbourne, where we used an 83 Group strip on a headland of the Downs overlooking the Channel – it was near the Birling Gap, a dip in the land used to advantage by German aircraft doing hit-and-run raids on the coastal towns. The Spitfires on the strip were carrying out low level sweeps over Northern France (known as 'Rhubarbs'), shooting up trains and otherwise doing as much damage as possible to communications and radar stations. As I listened in to the Squadron net on one sweep, one Spitfire went off the air and was reported by another pilot as disappearing into a cloud of dust as it hit the ground. In the Army we were largely insulated from the steady drain of casualties being borne by the RAF day after day in these operations, and of course from the massive bomber raids, many of which in the light of hindsight consumed such enormous resources for so little effect [e.g. the so-called 'Battle of Berlin': in the words of the official RAF history 'in an operational sense the Battle of Berlin was more than a failure, it was a defeat']. These casual contacts with the reality of the war, as the RAF was fighting it, made us try harder.

We were, of course, often back at Penshurst for Squadron training. Night flying was a particular speciality, involving Squadron Headquarters (mostly Jock Scott) in a good deal of planning with the RAF (so we wouldn't get shot down by them) and a final nail-biting decision on the night whether it was 'on' or 'off'. (My recollection is that it was more often 'off' than 'on', which allowed the pilots to celebrate in the mess). Preparation of the flight-path (according to wind) consisted of getting ready dozens of little tin cans filled with paraffin with wicks stuck in top. These were known as 'goose-neck' flares, a low-technology invention which went right back to the early days. The main disadvantage was the considerable time and manpower it took to set up flight-paths using such methods.

Having decided that night flying was 'on', the pilots lucky enough to be chosen to perform were given the RAF letters and colours of the day. Pilots, on being challenged, were expected to flash the letters in Morse on the navigation-lights, or as a last resort fire two or three Verey cartridges of the right colours in the correct sequence. The pilot would be in touch by wireless with his own flying control and the landing-ground, but of course due to having a different sort of wireless set, he had no personal contact with RAF flying control in the same area. The general idea was for pilots to do one or two take-offs and landings, fly around for a bit away from the circuit and avoid getting lost. One also got a parachute, although no one had, so far as we knew, succeeded in bailing-out of an Auster, least of all in the dark.

On one of these happy-go-lucky nights, Mike Pritchard-Davies did get lost. After flying around in the dark for nearly an hour, he decided to look for a suitably large and treeless area in order to attempt a landing. He found what he considered a reasonable field and he did a dummy run. He then went round again and landed successfully. After securing the aircraft as best he could in darkness he spent the night in a farmhouse. When he returned in the morning he was shocked to see a line of power-cables running right across the field, and realised that somehow he had landed beneath them unscathed. With characteristic determination he took off and returned to Penshurst as if very little had happened. (One of the dangers of leaving unattended Austers in fields was that cows liked to eat the fabric off the fuselage).

Navigation was clearly a challenge to be met if night flying was to play any useful part in Air Observation Post operations. Tetley Jones set to and devised a simple rectangular aerial-array, which could be rotated so as to maximise a radio-signal sent out by an aircraft in flight, thus enabling a bearing to be measured from the landing-ground to the aircraft. The reciprocal of the bearing was obviously the course that would lead the aircraft home. It was, in fact, a simple radio-goniometer and gave promising results. The idea however was not pursued and I later found out that it had been tried and found wanting back in the early days. Interference or unsuitable terrain could lead to errors of up to 180 degrees.

However, despite these drawbacks, we did manage to achieve a significant amount of successful night cross-country flying. On one occasion I went due south towards the South Downs and saw the whole of Sussex lying dark beneath me. There was a small moon, a light breeze and very little cloud, so a compass-course was sufficient to get me out and back to the flare path without difficulty. Less well organised was a trip east along the railway towards Ashford. The railway tracks showed up well and some way ahead I could see what looked like the white tail light of another aircraft. So I pressed on in pursuit, but after about twenty minutes the light remained a long way ahead. It also seemed to be climbing and had turned a bluish colour, which did not seem quite right so I decided to turn back. As I turned, it suddenly occurred to me that the 'aircraft' I thought I had been chasing was actually the planet Jupiter.

Later on we went down to Friston to do a night shoot on the range. The night I went up it was broad moonlight as I flew over Glyndebourne, with the farm-roads gleaming white as they threaded through the Downs. My target was a small wood in a valley and I engaged it satisfactorily; the shell-burst showed up well from the ranging rounds, which were petrol-filled. We had shown that we could direct fire from the air at night, but I wondered whether it would ever be of practical use in the field, and as far as I know it never was used. Nevertheless, learning to fend for myself after dark was valuable experience that significantly increased my self-confidence.

Throughout this busy period of pilot training our ground crews had settled down after a lot of transfers in and out, and cross-postings within the Squadron, particularly on the RAF side. Corporal Wood, a regular, began to pull the airmen together while Bombardier Cookson on the M.T. side and Bombardier Naylor on the signals got these vital areas functioning smoothly. But we couldn't seem to get a good Sergeant/Q. and this remained a weak link until after we had arrived in France.

At the beginning of September 1943 we took part in an ad hoc exercise that proved a crucial stage in creating a close-knit Royal Artillery and RAF unit. We were supporting a crossing of the Medway just south of where there is now a motorway bridge carrying traffic on the M2. In hindsight, I suspect it was a simulation of crossing the River Seine at Vernon or thereabouts. We had to occupy a landing ground near Detling and then, as a further part of our training, dig in the aircraft and get our own slit trenches dug before dawn the next morning. Everyone got stuck in with a will and made a first class job of it. We were feeling pleased with ourselves when a staff car rolled up unexpectedly and a senior RAF officer got out and introduced himself as the commander of 83 Group (I think this was Air Vice-Marshal J. Whitworth-Jones).[5] On inspecting our efforts he insisted that we could not possibly have dug ourselves in overnight and accused us of having sent an advance party in the day before! He also urged us to abandon voice communication from aircraft to ground (R/T) in favour of Morse (W/T). He had apparently been brought up on this during the last war.

We were greatly surprised by his suggestion and did not attempt to explain to this very senior RAF figure that a reversion to W/T would destroy the whole ethos of Air OP and take us back to the bad old days when Army cooperation had been the unwanted, unlucky branch of air warfare (the crippling losses of Lysander Squadrons in France in 1940 had also not been forgotten).

It was already established by early gunner pilots, like Dickson in 1911, that effective air observation of artillery needed gunner pilots contributing as an extension of the Corps' artillery capability rather than replacing ground observation. They would operate under the command of the CCRA rather than within an RAF structure and would be integrated with the other artillery units in the Corps.[6] Altogether, we were very happy to see the back of the Air Vice-Marshal who was the first and the last senior RAF visitor we ever had to the Flight.

The rest of 1943 passed quickly by with plenty of movement to keep us happy – shoots down at Friston and Larkhill, and in September a major Corps exercise, Operation 'Blackcock. It took place on the North Yorkshire Moors with 43rd Division, 15th Scottish and 11th Armoured. 653 Squadron provided three aircraft that set off on September 17, piloted by Captain Riding, Captain Huntington and myself. At the same time a ground party took vehicles and equipment. The combined convoy spent one night at Royston, Cambridgeshire and then another just south of Doncaster before arriving at York (Clifton Aerodrome).[7] We later moved to an Advanced Landing Ground (or ALG) at Thornton-le-Clay (with permission from the land-owner!) from which we operated for purposes of the exercise. The three Divisions with whom we were taking part later played a heroic part in the battle of Normandy, both during 'Operation Epsom' and also the subsequent defence of the Odon river-crossings and the Scottish Corridor, when the German Panzer attack that was intended to destroy the Normandy beachhead was itself destroyed instead.

We found we were well able to play our part in these exercises, whether in disciplined road-movement, rapid occupation of landing-grounds, radio communications or maintaining the serviceability of the aircraft. Meanwhile, back in Kent we practised low flying, cross-country at low altitude, and landing in small fields. We were encouraged to land on almost any field, or corner thereof, which might be sufficiently level and unobstructed. The technique was to keep the aircraft flying at minimum speed, hauling it along by vigorous use of the engine. The very second the engine slowed down, the aircraft would rapidly sink and it was the objective to achieve the final descent onto the limited space available as quickly and gently as possible. The difficulty was to hit the right point between letting the aircraft fall out of one's hands in a heavy stall and motoring gracefully into the far hedge at about six inches above the ground. Extra refinement is needed to do this trick over the tops of elm trees on a gusty day, but it came with practice.

There were less orthodox talents: we found that supplies of mushrooms for breakfast could be assured if two or three aircraft made a joint evening sortie in search, mushrooms being highly visible from the air. Once they were spotted, a pilot would land his aircraft to pick them while the others would continue the search and then do the same. However, it was more in the spirit of scientific experiment that compelled one pilot to accompany the afternoon express from London, along several miles of its route into Salisbury at window-level. When the engine driver or fireman threw a piece of coal at him the day was made.

I also found time to set up two unofficial flight records. Corporal Wood (our great guide and mentor on all things technical) and I were discussing how high an Auster could go with a normal load and without use of the mixture control (which was wired back to rich mixture for low altitude flying). We set off together and climbed up through the smog (smelling of stale biscuits, for some reason) into the bright clear air above. We climbed more and more laboriously until we reached a record height of 12,000 ft,[8] at which point we heard a loud bang. Bearing in mind that we had no parachutes, we looked around anxiously to see what had happened. The engine was still running happily and responding to the throttle. There was no smoke and all the instruments were normal, but we agreed to pack it in and call it a day. On the way down – it takes a long time to lose 12,000 ft – I noticed that my window was split from side to side. The perspex, which was riveted to the frame, had contracted in the low temperature and had simply parted from corner to corner, for want of any other way to release the tension. This explained the bang.

There were mainly two things that I learned from this trip. The first was that without a parachute, a pilot observing at more than 3,000 ft had little chance of survival if the aircraft caught fire, from whatever cause, and so the lower the height at which one operated, the less the risk in that respect.

The second was that in NW Europe there was little benefit in observing from above 3,000 ft, the reason being the existence of the 'temperature inversion' that tended to begin at that height. This acts as a lid and the smoky, warm moist air is prevented from rising any further. The result is a layer of thickening smog, which makes observation more and more difficult, particularly if one is observing the ground obliquely through it, as would normally be the case.

My other record was to fly backwards over Tunbridge Wells. I chose a nice windy day, got up to 5,000 ft, headed into wind and put down the landing-flap, while maintaining height with the throttle and dropping the air speed as low as I could, until I was moving slowly backwards relative to the ground. It took nearly half-an-hour to complete the trip, which I like to think would qualify for the Guinness Book of Records if carried out today (balloons don't count). I don't think I learned anything from that experience; except that Tunbridge Wells was not as narrow as I'd thought.

To round off the year, in December 1943, we had a grand Squadron outing to the West Country, the object being to fly the Bristol Channel.[9]

Bearing in mind that our training was intended to prepare us to play our part in the invasion of Europe, we should obviously have to cross the Channel and make a landfall on whatever piece of the French coast the assault forces had managed to secure. It was likely to be no more than a beachhead, with very little margin for navigational error on either side. Earlier on in our training Tetley Jones had devised an exercise which involved flying towards a 'coastline' represented simply by a line on the map. To simulate the Channel, all features on the approach side of the line were blacked out. Although a useful paper illustration, the early scheme was just too artificial to be of practical use as flying training. The excursion to the Bristol Channel however turned out to be a real success in the end, despite a rather shaky start. It seems to me to demonstrate the spirit of Air Observation Post.

The idea was for all three flights to proceed independently to an RAF station near Taunton in Somerset with the rather apt name of Weston Zoyland. We would stage at Old Sarum to enable lunch and petrol to be taken aboard and on to Weston Zoyland, a reasonable day's journey. 'C' Flight took off from Penshurst, led by Bill Huntington who was acting as flight commander in Freddie Riding's absence. As we flew west, up the railway towards Redhill, patches of ground mist began to appear. Then the mist turned into low cloud, with higher cloud stretching beyond as far as we could see. The meteorological forecast we had before we took off was

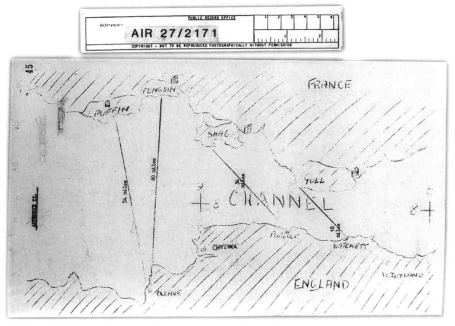

Exercise Seabird, the successful practice Channel Crossing.

quite evidently no longer accurate. Although we had our wireless-sets on and could speak to each other, the technology of the day meant we could not speak to RAF ground-control and ask for a more recent forecast. Bill, in his role as flight commander, made the decision that we should continue in formation and climb above cloud-level. As Bill continued to press on, and we had reached about 2,000 ft, it was apparent that everything to the west was covered in cloud. It all looked beautiful in the sunshine, but where did the cloud end?

Eventually it was decided to pack it in and go back; undoubtedly the right thing to do in the circumstances. However, at the same time, Bill decided to exercise his powers of command by calling for the flight to 'follow me' as he dived into the clouds. We were, at that moment, somewhere over Box Hill with nearby Leith Hill at just under 1,000 ft high; both were likely to be under low cloud, if not actually in it. Whilst we might wonder when Bill would pull out of the dive and level off, 'ours was not to reason why', but to keep in formation as best we could and wait for his manoeuvre.

As far as I was concerned, it never came. Suddenly I saw a church spire flash past the aircraft window. The ground, with houses and trees, was scarcely visible through the dull fog, and between the ground and the low cloud was only 100 ft of airspace; I could only hope there were no more churches or chimney-stacks in my path. As I was sorting things out and allowing the compass to calm down, I heard something above me and saw a pair of wheels pass overhead and disappear into the mist. They belonged to the aircraft of one of our newly joined pilots, who was with 'C' Flight for the trip. Then I noticed Geoff Burgess, who was very much my 'half-section', flying along nearby and joined him. Things were looking difficult, with a bank of dense mist that seemed to be rolling over the ground in front of us. It was starting to seem that all we could do was to climb out until we broke through the cloud above and then set course back for Penshurst. Then we would have the unenviable prospect of letting down through low cloud without knowing exactly where we were – a well-known recipe for disaster. However, as luck would have it, a sudden break in the mist revealed a runway in front of us. It had wheelbarrows and cement mixers on it so we just banged down on the grass beside it and then tried to work out where on earth we were.

It turned out that we had broken through the cloud over Dorking and the strip where we had landed was Gatwick. There was no sign of anyone else, but later we heard that Bill had put down in the middle of the local fireworks factory (now Schermuly's), which certainly scared the management. I don't remember where our young recruit went, but I bore him no ill will for the near miss, and he got down safely, to his great credit.

We tied down the aircraft with the help of the local RAF people and got a lift to a nice hotel. Not only were they able to put us up for the night but they would also accept a cheque the next morning – by no means usual practice in those days. On returning to the airfield we set off for Old Sarum with a promise of good visibility. As we taxied in we saw another Auster arriving and the pilot turned out to be Bill Huntington, so we went into the mess for lunch together. Bill had hardly passed the door when the eagle-eyed mess secretary spotted his floppy suede flying-boots and told him he was not allowed in the mess in flying-clothing. Bill, never the smartest of officers, went out, removed his boots and re-entered barefoot. When common sense eventually won he was allowed to put on his boots again and join us at the table.

As the low cloud remained over Weston Zoyland, we stayed on for the night and it was another two days before we could get through, by which time everyone else had turned up safe and sound. Letter home, written a few days later:

RAF Station,
Weston Zoyland,
Somerset
14.xii.43

After a struggle we have got here where it's a bit colder than Siberia. We spent two days at Salisbury in a fog & now there's another one here. Goodness knows when we shall see Penshurst again at this rate. We should be back by the 17th if we can get some weather. So I shall be seeing you some day.

The idea then was that we should all move on to a landing ground near Bridgwater, and from there, set off individually across the Bristol Channel to Nash Point, just west of Cardiff, where we had another landing-ground near the village (as it was then) of Llantwit Major. We had a radio link to both landing grounds, a map with courses and distance carefully worked out, and a Mae West lifejacket in case of trouble. We also made a precautionary visit to the swimming baths at Taunton, where we were given a chance to try the Mae West in real water. Keen swimmers like Jack Bandy were well to the fore, but I preferred to trust my navigation and did not volunteer. The Mae West had some interesting gadgets. It could be blown up with a little CO_2 sparklet bottle by pulling a tab, or by mouth, in what may be properly called a breast pocket. On the left side, it had a small hot water bottle that was filled with magnesium powder or such like, which heated up in contact with salt water and was supposed to keep hypothermia at bay. It also had a block of fluorescent compound in another pocket, which turned the surrounding water an eerie greeny-yellow colour visible from a distance even in rough water. Of course someone jumped in with his block of dye still in the jacket, and the swimming bath water turned yellow from end to end, which was not in the programme.

On the eleventh, the fog that had enveloped Weston Zoyland cleared just sufficiently for us to put on our Mae Wests and fly low across the Bristol Channel. Trust in one's navigation was indeed important; just a small error in a Westerly direction would mean the South coast of Wales was missed and the next stop was Ireland or even America. On arrival we found what turned out to be an exceedingly bad landing-ground the other side – the Squadron Diary recorded one smashed under carriage, on Captain Buckley's aircraft.

We drank a cup of tea and put some petrol in the tank and returned. By this time the remnants of the great fog that had held us up so long had formed into a grey mist. Flying back towards the sun at 1,000 ft, there was no sign of the horizon; nothing outside the aircraft was visible except the silver sea below; and this only directly below, where the waves crawled. Otherwise the aircraft was moving (although one's senses had no real evidence of this) within a pearl grey globe without a single break or stain. To all intents we were flying blind with our eyes open. On the dashboard the needles hardly quivered. It was as if evidence of change in time and space had been suddenly abolished. Only the waves sliding silently below and the steady sweep of the second-hand across the clock face deprived us of immortality.

There was however an exception. One member of our flight had for some reason now forgotten, taken over my aircraft for the trip. Halfway back the engine began to run rough. It kept going until the land appeared and continued to run long enough to land the aircraft on top of the nearest cliff. There are few more trying experiences: to all but the bravest (or perhaps least sensitive) there is no worse sound than a sick engine over the sea. A mere catch, a minute falter, becomes a symptom, one imagines, of an early and complete dissolution. There may be some who wish to add to their experiences and stock of anecdotes by landing in a wintry sea, but most people prefer to keep flying and to hell with fame. Each aircraft was equipped with a dinghy for such events but really any pilot trying to push a dinghy out of his door at sea level would end up in the sea by himself. Luckily a combination of will power and good fortune kept the aircraft going and the interesting experiment of ditching an Auster was never carried out.

In the end the exercise had worked out perfectly; we hoped it would be just like that on the day, (it wasn't), but nevertheless exercise 'Seabird' did wonders for our confidence. It was wound up with a pleasant celebration at the County Hotel in Taunton and with the singing of traditional songs, to everyone's satisfaction, including the landlord's.

Soon after, following a less eventful flight back from the West Country, 'C' Flight returned to Penshurst just before Christmas.

By now we had settled down into one very happy team – Frank 'Butch' Pritchard, the Flight's tame Rhodesian was a great organiser and expert card player; Geoff Burgess, from just south of Hadrian's Wall, was a man who did not suffer fools gladly, whatever their rank; Bill Huntington, easy-going and quite unflappable, and Freddie Riding, in command of the Flight. Freddie had seen action in France in 1940 before and during the Dunkirk evacuation, and his pride had suffered accordingly. He was passionately determined to get back into the ring and it so happened that 'C' Flight was his means to do so. It followed quite logically that 'C' Flight had to be as efficient as Freddie could make it in the service of whatever divisional artillery we might be appointed to support. Our landing-grounds were, for instance, to be within the gun area, as close to the forward areas as possible; we did not simply move with the battle, but lived with it too. Whatever 'C' Flight achieved between Normandy and the Elbe was founded on Freddie's insistence, during these days of training, that we should identify ourselves with the forward troops, and be seen by them accordingly.

We had a very good Christmas (it lasted until well into January, when exhaustion set in). The mess at Knotley Hall was the centre of conviviality, with numerous visitors; the gunners and airmen were well in with local families and had their feet under the table in many households nearby. On 18 December we had our official Christmas party in Mess. A group of WRNS came over from Chatham (where Don Falkland-Cary's wife was serving) and some of the VAD nurses came from the military hospital at Penshurst. One of them was a girl called Jean, who became my wife three years later.

Christmas dinner was in the best tradition, served to the men in the dining hall by the officers. For the married men it must often have been a time of memories of absent families, but everyone seemed to enjoy what we all felt was likely to be the last time we would celebrate Christmas and the New Year together this side of the Channel. The intensive training that we had done in 1943 had shown us that we were a small part of the great military organisation that was preparing us for the 1944 invasion of Europe for which we had waited so long. Two subjects that were never the topic of discussion were the possibility of failure or the odds on individual survival. Indeed the years of training made it impossible for us to doubt that we could fail to destroy whatever German units would oppose us.

On 14 January we were all brought back to military reality by Tetley Jones, who told us we were going to be on parade, with aircraft drawn up in lines and pilots and aircrew in attendance, so that a distinguished visitor (we had not invented VIPs at that time) could present the Squadron with an aircraft. It was to commemorate a gunner officer named Dickson, who had apparently carried out a sortie during military manoeuvres at Larkhill in 1910. The exploit had enabled Dickson to report information of 'enemy' troop movements, to the discomfiture of the opposition. The money to pay for this aircraft had been generously provided by his sister, Mrs Winifred Gordon, in support of the war effort. She was living in Switzerland, so Mrs Richard Law, wife of the War Office Minister, was deputising for her. It all went off well, Tetley Jones doing a nice demonstration take-off and landing, and we adjourned for lunch. Dickson was, we learned, one of that small

Auster-3-NJ838-Dickson Pioneer presentation ceremony, 14 January 1944.

CO 653 Squadron, Major Tetley Jones, Mrs Law and 'Dickson Pioneer'.

Major Tetley Jones in the first 'Dickson Pioneer'.

group of individuals who pioneered the use of aircraft for civil and military purposes. He did so despite official indifference[10] and is said to be the first British Serviceman to qualify as a pilot (at Mourmelon near Reims, 10 April 1910). Dickson himself never lived to see his efforts come to fruition in the Royal Flying Corps' operations in the 1914–18 War; he was badly injured in the first aerial collision at Turin in autumn 1910, and died in 1913. Had he lived, he would surely have made a distinctive contribution to the history of flying in Britain; as it is, he is remembered as the pioneer of the Air OP.

The presentation aircraft, named 'Dickson Pioneer 1911–1943' was handed over to 'C' Flight, and I was told to take it on. As it turned out, this was an Auster Mk. III, NJ 838, and within a month the Squadron was being re-equipped with the Mk. IV; by the beginning of March, NJ 838 was withdrawn from 'C' Flight, and I took over MT 169, which was duly named 'Dickson Pioneer'. I flew this aircraft from then on until the German Army surrender in 1945. The only damage it sustained during its time with me was one or two bullet-holes in the fabric covering, and I think it was being flown by Harry Eastgate when the leading metal spar under one wing got a nasty hole through it. A yellow Wyvern, the emblem of 43rd (Wessex) Division, which we supported, was painted on the engine cowling. MT 169 survived the war and was sold out of service.

After the end of the war I prepared an account of the service of this aircraft for Captain Dickson's sister, and she wrote me a kind letter of thanks and enclosed a generous cheque. Unfortunately I never met her, due to my absence abroad after the war, but ground crew and pilot took a pride in her aircraft and I hope that Captain Bertram Dickson will continue to be remembered in the Army Air Corps in years to come.

The tempo of training increased further. On 10 February, Geoff Pollitt relieved Tetley Jones as Squadron Commander on his posting to a Senior Officers' course. We did shoots and exercises with 43rd Division, ferried senior officers about for visits of inspection and conferences, and concentrated on low flying and short landing practice when we were not otherwise committed. My monthly total of flying-hours was about thirty. My particular field regiment was 94th Field, and I found them not only thoroughly professional, but also very likeable. One evening, after a conference at Shoreham, which we attended with the regiment, I found myself with the CO, Lieutenant Colonel Bishell, sitting on the sea wall and looking out over the Channel. We talked about nothing in particular at first, and then he told me he was off on forty-eight hours leave to see his family, and told me about his children having grown up in wartime without him. Being unmarried, I had not really considered that aspect of war and I suddenly realised what a long and miserable business it was for so many ordinary people, by reason of absence and separation if nothing else.

As the pace of events quickened, the Squadron was mobilised, equipment was renewed and brought up to scale, administration and accounting put on an active-service footing, pilots medically examined – and one or two found unfit for service overseas. We took the ground crews off for firing practice (some of them had never fired a rifle before). We brushed up our evasive tactics in the air, but never repeated 'live' training with fighter aircraft, remembering the tragic deaths of two pilots in 655 Squadron.

Also in February, the Auster Mk. IV arrived to replace the Mk. III. The Mk. IV was in most respects easier to handle than the III, particularly when it came to short landings. The undercarriage did not suffer from the weakness of the III, but it was slower in initial climb after take-off and had a longer take-off run.

An essential difference was that the new aircraft was fitted with Lycoming engines in place of the Gipsy Major used in Mk. IIIs and this caused problems of maintenance as well as handling in the air (and in take-off and landing).

Even the seemingly simple operation of propeller swinging gave some trouble. The Mk.IV's Lycoming driven propeller turned in the opposite direction to the Mk. III's propellor. I think it also lacked impulse-start magnetos, so that the engine was liable to fire during a larger arc of the propeller's rotation. A different swinging technique was therefore needed, but our airmen were not advised of this. As a result, my own L.A.C. Allen got one hand hit by the propeller firing unexpectedly quickly, and broke two fingers. He was still unfit for duty by the time the Flight left for Normandy, to my regret.

In December 1943 we had been lucky to avoid a far more radical change in equipment, when a well-meaning minister in the Aircraft Production Ministry, Captain Balfour, Under Secretary of State for Air, visited us to inspect and test an Auster III. Although an amateur pilot then, this gentleman had a distinguished reputation as a former WW1 flying 'ace'. Six days later, on the eighteenth, Captain Balfour returned with a Miles M38 aircraft, which he thought might prove to be the ideal aircraft for Air OP It was a low-wing monoplane, built of wood, with twin rudders and a low-mounted tail plane and had been designed for AOP work. Being low-wing, however, it lacked pendulum-stability and had poor downward visibility when flying level. The tail plane was liable to damage when taxiing in rough grass or taking off on stony surfaces. Its wooden construction meant that all our airframe fitters would have to be retrained or more probably replaced. No doubt it was ideal for weekend jaunts to Le Touquet in peacetime with the girlfriend, but we were not in that line of business. The squadron diary records that 'flight tests were carried out against an Auster Mk. III flown by Captain Scott. The trials proved the great superiority of the Auster take-off'. (At the end of the war General Montgomery accepted the offer of the Miles M38 as his personal light aircraft.)

A rather more useful idea was a kit of three pieces of steel plate, which could be placed under the pilot's feet, under his seat and behind his back. It was comforting to have such protection, but it added critical extra weight, particularly in take-off, and initial climb away.

OC Major Tetley Jones was not impressed by the armour plate which he said which 'added at least 100 lbs' to the weight problem. He described 'setting up a plate at 1,000 ft [distance] and putting a .303 bullet clean through it; this was the height we expected to fly over German rifles: I marked it "fragile" and returned it![11]

Later on we found another use for it: installed in the floors and under the seats of the Jeeps, at a time when we had cause to worry about land mines. Again, it was good for morale and this time did not affect the handling of the vehicle. 'At least', we thought, 'someone is thinking about us'.

One of the results of mobilisation was that Bill Huntington was found unfit for operations overseas and he was replaced by Tom Place who had been with the Squadron since September. Tom had had a varied career, as far as we could gather. Being a good deal older than the rest of us, he tended to take life more soberly. He had apparently spent some time in South Africa sheep farming, and had been at one stage a second pilot with Imperial Airways (the second-pilot did all the flying, the first pilot all the landings and take-offs, according to Tom). Banging in and out of small fields was something he found interesting, but I don't think he ever regarded it as an entirely respectable occupation for a gentleman.

As spring began to change to early summer, troop movements in the Southern Counties became noticeable. The big camps in Sussex began to empty as the Canadians moved out and the main roads to the Channel ports became ever busier. Day after day the sky was filled with bombers, Fortresses and Liberators, climbing up from their bases to join formations heading for various targets in Northern France. These raids were part of the so-called 'Transportation Plan' whereby the French Railway system was being targeted in order to hinder the German response to an invasion as much as possible. German reports confirm the effectiveness of this measure, in contrast to the area bombing of German cities favoured by Air Chief Marshal Harris. The dense pattern of vapour trails they left behind would often spread out until the sun was hidden for the rest of the day with a veil of high thin cloud. As they reached the Channel they began to release a shower of fine aluminium foil or 'chaff' that was designed to confuse the German radar. Small clusters of this would drift down on the wind long after the formations had gone.

Short temporary airstrips consisting of wire mesh laid on top of cocoa-nut fibre matting had been laid all over the Southern Counties, with tented camps beside them. They were occupied by flights of USAF long-range Thunderbolt fighters operating in support of the bombers. The fighters would take off from these tiny strips, two at a time, slightly staggered, heavy with long-range wing tanks and full loads of ammunition. As each became airborne, the pilot would retract the undercarriage and pull up in a steep climbing turn, ready for his buddy to tuck in behind, until the whole flight was heading for rendezvous with the bomber groups high above.

The assembly of these USAF bomber groups was a huge task in itself. On any one morning several different missions might be mounted with hundreds of bombers and fighters taking off from a wide spread of bases all over the South of England to be then brought together within a strict time-frame. The bomb-load and fuel-load carried by the aircraft on a specific mission naturally varied according to the type of target and its distance; there was also the problem in that there might not be enough bomb-sights for each aircraft to have one; aircraft without a sight would have to wait to see the bombs go down from the nearest aircraft with a bomb-sight.

Each mission was given a different series of recognition colours that the leading aircraft fired off as the formation climbed to its appointed height. Aircraft on the same mission would be able to join the formation that was firing the appropriate colours. We met one pilot in a pub who told us about when his aircraft was loaded up for a short-range mission – lots of bombs but not much gas. He said he got the mission colours wrong and joined a formation heading on a long-range mission bound for the depths of Germany with lots of gas and not many bombs. It could happen to anyone no doubt, but he was lucky to get back. Any aircraft dropping out of the box was fair game for German fighters.

On 25 February the Squadron played host for three days to Flying Fortress crew members who had bailed out of their crippled aircraft. Eight survived, but sadly the pilot's parachute failed to open so he did not. They had been on a raid to Regensburg in Bavaria.

The time came for the two final exercises. One called 'Sabre' was with 43rd Division, in which we practised close support of the division during fast movement down a major axis very much as we did in the breakout from the Normandy beachhead. We managed to keep up.

The second one – 'Spes' – turned out to be an embarrassment. It covered the area round Hurstmonceux Castle, and involved 59th (Staffordshire) Division, who were normally looked after by 'A' Flight. We took it on in good faith, but it turned out rather badly, the divisional artillery managing to lose touch with each other and their CRA into the bargain. We ended up flying sorties for the CRA trying to locate the various formations nominally under his command. What the object of the exercise was I don't think we ever knew; tragically the collapse of the command structure was to be repeated in Normandy a few months later during the attack on Caen. It so happened that I was acting as liaison officer with the same divisional artillery when they ground to a standstill yet again. As far as I was concerned, the only difference was that this first time it was an exercise and I was flying an Auster over Sussex; the next time, I was riding a motorbike and the collapse occurred in front of the enemy in Normandy.

On 12 April, Harry Eastgate arrived as a reserve pilot to complete the Flight's establishment. Harry was a Derbyshire man, and he wore a fine black moustache, which contrasted well with Freddie's ginger effort. Before being called up, he had spent a short while in the police force, and had acquired the knack of inducing that uncomfortable feeling most of us have when being interviewed by the law, however clear our consciences. He was, in fact, a kindly and genial soul when you got to know him, and had not enjoyed his time in the force.

The gunners and airmen were also up to strength; Bombardier Cookson had a firm grip on the drivers and our vehicles were well serviced and smartly turned out. Cookson was a Staffordshire man, brought up in the strict Baptist tradition but by no means a prig. He once said to me: 'you know, sir, when I joined the Army I didn't swear and I didn't drink. Now I do both, and I don't really think I'm any the worse for it.'

Bombardier Naylor, who came from Nottingham, also had the signals side under control. We rarely used the field telephone, and depended entirely on radio both on the ground and, obviously, in the air. Keeping the sets serviceable and the batteries healthy was one aspect; we had a good deal of trouble with the multiple quick connectors between set and microphone and earphones. Then the radio truck had to be manned, and aircraft sets tuned and netted on the allotted frequency. Once more we were lucky in having someone in charge with high standards that he was able to pass on to others.

On the aircraft side, Corporal Wood had moved on elsewhere in the Squadron, but his younger brother Stan remained behind. They both came from Marham, I think, in Kent [Editor: probably Marham, Norfolk]; Corporal Wood was a regular, and stood no nonsense from anyone, especially his brother. He was, however, a kindly man at heart and got the best out of the airmen during a period when there was plenty of opportunity for them to grouse about 'not having joined the something Army'. His successor was another regular, Corporal Carter, and with him again we were extremely lucky. The two airmen in my section, Lewis and Baverstock, were both cheerful souls. Lewis was a Lancastrian, quite ready to criticise a sloppy landing or an untidy take-off. I had great confidence in them, and I think I eventually gained theirs, chiefly by not causing them extra work by damaging 'their' aeroplane. We did have a showdown, early on, when I complained about the dirty state of the perspex canopy. This could be kept clean by using 'Sinec' polish, a coarse abrasive paste, which was followed up by a fine polishing paste, applied inside with a damp cloth, always at an awkward angle. Nevertheless, it was essential to keep the whole canopy clean inside and out, not least because any prospect of successful evasive action depended on clear vision towards the rear. Having failed to get much co-operation, I spent an unpleasant hour with the box of polish cleaning the thing myself, and then showed them the result. It worked, but I had to agree it was an unpleasant job. My fingers ached for days.

Soon after Harry Eastgate's arrival we were issued with cans of black fibrous asbestos waterproofing compound, and told what had to be done to waterproof the vehicles. This involved sealing up the electrical system, and various other, less accessible, parts of the vehicle with compound so that it could withstand being driven into several feet of water from the ramp of a landing craft. I think there were also extension hoses for the air-intake and exhaust systems; but I must admit that, since there seemed to be plenty of volunteers, I kept clear of the actual dirty-work as far as I decently could. We were also taken over to a park in Sevenoaks where scrambling nets had been strung up so that people could get an idea of what it might be like to come ashore over the side of a ship. On 24 March all pilots were given a lecture on 'escape' by MI9. This was the organisation that specialised in aiding resistance groups, stranded forces personnel and escaping POWs. One of their tasks was the provision of concealed maps, compasses and other paraphernalia to aid servicemen stuck behind enemy lines.

We were all concentrated on Penshurst for these larks, and had time to spare for excursions in the evening to our favourite pubs. One evening, after a pleasant session in Tunbridge Wells, we crawled into our tents (which were at the back of the Mess) and got our heads down. At what seemed a very early hour we were woken up by a loud rumbling noise overhead, succeeded by several more. Some new sort of bomber was flying low – directly above us and in a northerly direction, so we returned to our slumbers. The next morning we were told that the first V1 flying bomb had landed in South London, and of these there were many more to follow.[12]

In an effort to frustrate these attacks the anti-aircraft defences were re-deployed into the south coast area, and we had our first sight of the new

Tempest fighters in action. It had enough speed to overhaul a V1 flying bomb quite easily, which the Spitfire apparently had not, but there was trouble with over-keen pilots flying in hot pursuit into the anti-aircraft belts. The new proximity-fuses had been introduced to increase the chances of success, but with all these defences the V1s still got through. With London in range of daily rocket bombardment from sites near the coast of France, the invasion of Europe was to be not a moment too soon.

No one in that part of England could any longer doubt that the invasion was, at last, imminent. All over the South Coast the pattern was the same: throbbing air-fields, huge formations of bombers spreading their ice trails across the blue sky by day, and the long-drawn boom of bomber streams by night. On the ground, the whole of one side of Folkestone Road was blackened by the tyres of innumerable vehicles on their way seaward, with no such tracks on the returning side. The presence of US troops was more and more evident; North Sussex was pockmarked with baseball diamonds. There were fields of tents, petrol-dumps and lorry parks and beyond all that, the quiet sea and the French coast.

Ever since the surrender of France we had looked across at the rest of Europe occupied by the Nazis, from Norway to Portugal, and from Spain to the coast of Turkey. The task was, quite simply, to force a lodgement somewhere on the north coast of France and, from that beachhead, achieve the re-conquest of Western Europe.

In April, censorship was imposed on our mail and the squadron MT complement was completed with the arrival of new Jeeps. There remained a few more things to do at Penshurst. We sorted our kit out and somehow or other reduced it to what would go into the back of an Auster. (It was all right for the ground-party, crossing by sea on a LCT, who were, by now, quite comfortably organised in the backs of the 3-tonners. As they said: 'Any fool can be uncomfortable'). At the end of May, I flew down to Larkhill to take part in 'Exercise Glenmore'. As the object of the exercise stated: 'trials will be carried to test various counter-mortar devices, including Air OP on Larkhill Ranges, 24–26 May'. Our job was to discover how best to locate the German mortar positions, and to that end a number of mortar positions had been prepared on the ranges from which captured German mortar bombs could be fired, so we could try to spot them. For my part I

could not see either flash or smoke, even when I knew the exact position
of the mortar, and that was, of course, what made German mortars such a
formidable weapon. As a battle-winner they may not have proved the equal
of the British divisional artillery, but they inflicted terrible casualties on the
British infantry nevertheless.

On 28 May, I persuaded Geoff Burgess to come with me to Croydon and
fly my aircraft back to Penshurst, while I snatched a quick weekend at home.
It so happened that the night before, we had been involved in a rather heavy
session in the mess, and I felt far from bright as we set off over the ridge.
The upshot was that my landing-approach at Croydon erred on the side of
caution. I came in too high and too fast over the main runway, and had to
open up and go round again. I booked in at flying control and shook the dust
of Croydon off my feet as quickly as I could, feeling I had let the side down.
Geoff left me in no doubt that he thought I had.

I made my way back by train in the blackout the next night. When the
train reached Redhill, the compartment emptied, except for a young woman
in black seated in the opposite corner. She got out at the next station, and as
she opened the door to leave she put her hand on my shoulder and said 'good
luck', then stepped down into the darkness. My thoughts were miles away,
and before I could say anything in reply the door slammed and we moved
off down the line.

Notes

1. *Flight*, January 1938.
2. The Squadron Diary shows that both 19 and 22 sets were used. They are similar
   although the 22 set has a shorter range. (see http://www.pyetelecomhistory.
   org/prodhist/military/military.html)
3. 'Ubique', latin for 'everywhere'.
4. Brigadier – later Major General – 'Bill' Heath was also the founder of the
   Larkhill Royal Artillery racecourse.
5. Confirmed by the Squadron Diary. He later became Air Chief Marshal.
6. The arguments for this arrangement are well described in *Unarmed into Battle*
   together with an account of overcoming the resistance to the idea from the
   RAF and Air Ministry.
7. When Lyell revisited fifty years later he found it converted to a retail park and
   housing estate. The 'Minster Inn' that he also remembered from the time had
   changed very little. He was pleased to find an 'Auster Road' on the estate.

8. Raised 10 June 1944 at Hoya to 14,200ft.
9. Squadron Diary, Exercise Seabird: the 'Intention: To practice all pilots in cross-water navigation; selection of A.L.G.'s from photographs and maps; night flying'. The 'enemy will not be represented'.
10. Richard Haldane, Secretary of State for War, who could see 'no future for aeronautics as a branch of military service'.
11. Unpublished account by Major Tetley Jones.
12. The first V1 bomb struck the Mile End, London on the 13 June, 5 days before 'C' Flight left Penshurst for their embarkation area.

Chapter 5

The Storm Breaks

6 June–22 August 1944

The Battle of Normandy 'Overlord'

At last we were preparing to leave our concentration area at Penshurst. Between 28 May and 4 June all the Squadron's vehicles had been waterproofed and loaded with equipment and stores; all the aircraft had been put in to SHQ for 'major' or 'minor' inspections so as to have the maximum period before the next one was due. Like every other Allied aircraft, they had had broad black and white stripes painted on wings and fuselages as recognition marks which even the most trigger happy GI could not mistake. It spoilt the camouflage, however.

Harry Eastgate took over the rear-party of vehicles, which would cross by sea and meet us in Normandy. Meanwhile we passed the time as best we could as we waited for the word 'Go'. On the night of 5 June we received the code word 'Adoration', meaning radio silence was in force and we heard many aircraft passing overhead; we knew then that next morning was 'D-Day'. One of our spare pilots was already assigned to select landing-grounds for the Air OP Squadrons due to land after the invasion *[Squadron diary 9 June: Capt Buckley and 3 ORs left to concentrate at Tunbridge Wells with 12 corps advance party]*.

We all got a personal message from Monty with his best wishes in the battles to come. It stressed that this was a combined sea, land and air operation, and that we were part of a great Allied team under General Eisenhower. It wound up with a rousing quotation from a poem by Montrose, originally addressed to his 'Dear and Only Love':

> He either fears his fate too much
> Or his deserts are small
> That dares not put it to the touch
> To win or lose it all

That certainly summed up the gamble to which the Allied forces were now committed. I wonder, however, if Monty realised the very different and much more delicate manoeuvre to which the gallant Marquis was actually referring.

Of more practical encouragement to us as we waited was the return of our man from the beachhead; he told us that the landings had been a success, with fewer casualties than expected. Nevertheless, much was still to be achieved to expand the beachhead and seize enough ground to accommodate the reinforcements needed for a breakout. All over the South of England, troops were moving into their marshalling areas, where they waited to be ferried over to Normandy. Somehow space must be made for them and the only way to do that was by driving back the German Army. Reports of our AOP squadrons already in action were very encouraging and made us all the more eager to make our own contribution.

As things turned out, our chance to get into action was to be delayed by two factors. First, the assault divisions had failed to exploit the initial

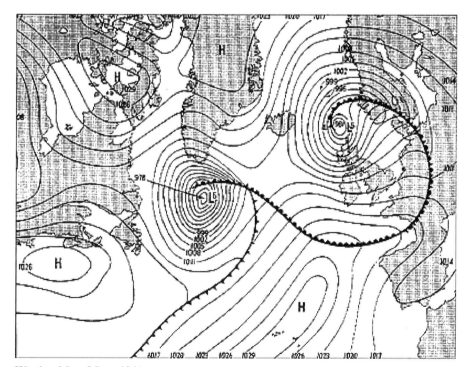

Weather Map, 5 June 1944.

advantage of surprise and push on to gain as much ground as possible. This was compounded by the onset of a north-easterly gale, the heaviest for forty years, which struck the beachhead on 19 June and did not blow itself out until the twenty-second. It considerably disrupted the improvised landing facilities – of the two 'Mulberry' harbours one was abandoned[1] – and further delayed the arrival of troops, equipment and ammunition.

[It was strange that Allied meteorologists, most famously Group Captain John Stagg, were extremely accurate in predicting the narrow window of weather suitable for the beach landings on 6 June, yet failed utterly to predict this storm:

Based on prior episodes, they predicted a lobe of 1,030 millibars pressure would extend north-eastwards from the Azores into the English Channel area, thereby allowing calm seas. Instead this lobe's center paused near southern Ireland while a low-pressure zone moved up from southern France. Consequently, from June 19th through June 22nd near gale force winds blew from the northwest directly down the Channel for 120 miles ... Because the onset of the storm was not predicted, pandemonium reigned throughout the beachheads.*

A recent explanation is that the intense naval activity in the Channel completely altered the water's surface temperature. The action of propellers and of artillery meant the much colder water from the seabed replaced sun-warmed surface water. The unusually steep contrast between the cold Channel and the land either side provided the conditions for the storm to develop.]

Whatever might be going wrong on the other side of the Channel, the order was given on 18 June, for us to move by air to our marshalling area or staging-camp at Old Sarum – familiar ground indeed – while our ground-party, under Harry Eastgate, set off by road for their marshalling area near the port of embarkation. This turned out to be Tilbury, and although they got aboard on the twenty-first, their landing craft was held up in the Thames

---

* *(SEA, SWELL AND SURF FORECASTING FOR D-DAY AND BEYOND THE ANGLO-AMERICAN EFFORT, 1943–1945, Charles C. Bates Lieutenant Colonel, US Air Force ([Retired]).*

Estuary until the twenty-fifth. They eventually landed near Courseulles, dry-shod and without incident, at half-past nine on the morning of the twenty-seventh, arriving at what was to be 'C' Flight's first landing-ground in France by 4 p.m. Slit trenches were dug and vehicles camouflaged before night-fall. The next day was spent in removing the waterproofing compound from the vehicles and generally getting ready for the arrival of the aircraft in the next few days.

The air-party arrived at Old Sarum in rather better order than when we had last called there on our way to Western Zoyland six months earlier. We were placed in a remote corner of the perimeter where we lounged in tents, bored, forgotten and faintly envious. For our recreation we had been thoughtfully provided with a NAAFI marquee and from this point in time, in the interest of security, we were expected to refrain from all communication with the outside world. Nevertheless, having sampled with NAAFI, we spent the next evening at one of the local pubs. Like many other troops assembled in the area we found our departure for Normandy was put off from one day to the next and so we also found we were literally drinking the county dry and having to go further and further afield in Wiltshire in search of refreshment and relaxation. We resorted to hiring a taxi, on a kind of tacit 'no beer, no pay' basis. This worked out quite well, although it was risky since the driver was expected to drink his share.

The daylight hours, of course, were spent on standby in constant expectation of orders to move. The aircraft had to be started up every morning and checked over generally. We had, however, reckoned without the Canadian 84 Group ground party that was billeted elsewhere on the airfield; they carried out a night raid on our aircraft and made off with the flying-helmets, goggles, throat-microphones and earphones, and they even stole the mirrors off the inverted roof-compasses.[2] This meant a dash by road to our Maintenance Unit at Redhill to replace what had been stolen. Had the order to move come through that day, we would have been several aircraft short.

In fact the weather could hardly have been worse for the flight to Normandy, with a succession of cold, windy days with low cloud scudding in from the south-west. Although we were to leave from Selsey Bill, the most southerly point on the South Coast opposite Normandy, the distance over water was barely within the safe endurance of the aircraft. Overloaded as they were with kit, and with a strong south west wind, it was unlikely that they would arrive at all; there was simply no choice but to await some slackening of the adverse south westerlies which had set in after the gale of the nineteenth.

It was thus not until 28 June[3], that we were called for briefing and told to take off for Selsey. After the delays and uncertainty of the past ten days it was a relief to get airborne again and going somewhere; the elation we had all felt on D-Day was now replaced by a wish to get the Channel crossing over and to tackle whatever awaited us in Normandy. We flew off in loose formation and landed at the airstrip amidst the shingle and marram grass of Selsey Bill in time for lunch in the big marquee that catered for birds of passage of all kinds. We allowed ourselves half a pint of beer apiece – on the excuse that we had no idea when and where we would get the other half.

We were called together by RAF flying control and given our briefing for the crossing. We would take off as soon as possible, by flights, and fly in line-ahead as a group, with a Walrus amphibian in front to guide us. As soon as we reached the beaches, the Walrus would break away and leave us to find our landing grounds. A small strip of card was given to us with our courses on it: the first leg of the trip was to be on a course of 183 degrees magnetic, with duration of fifty minutes. That was the point of no return after which

The card with courses to Juno Beach, Normandy.

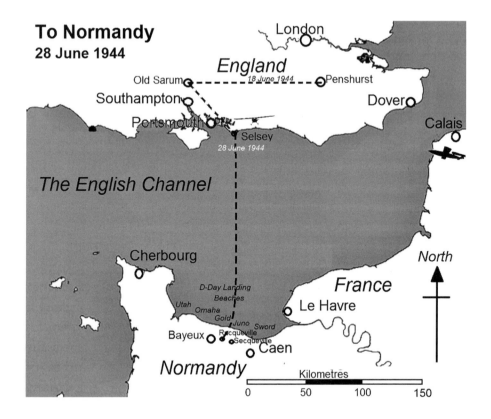

we would turn onto 195 degrees for about twenty minutes, and finish on 209 degrees for the final fifteen minutes, which should take us to the beachhead.

We were also given a double-yellow Verey cartridge, to be fired if challenged by another aircraft. (Most of this briefing was for the benefit of any pilot who was stupid, or unlucky, enough to get cut off from the main body and have to continue on his own, or if the Walrus was put out of action). I was given a rubber dinghy to carry and the post of honour at the rear of the gaggle. This carried with it the title of 'arse-end Charlie' and the responsibility of dropping the dinghy near (but not on) any pilot who might have to ditch. My aircraft was already full of kit, bedding and personal clobber, so the rubber dinghy was almost the last straw.

We took off at a quarter to three, and staggered up to 500 ft where I took up the rear of an irregular line of aircraft. Ahead was the Walrus, flying steadily on course. In between there was an unstable line of erratic Austers, curiously characteristic: although heading on the same course, at the same height and

speed, the aircraft were entirely independent of each other. They wandered
and weaved, and quite early on I thought I had a customer for the dinghy, as
one of the aircraft suddenly lost height and fell out of the line. He climbed up
again, however, and then someone else did the same thing shortly afterwards.
It was the slipstream from the Walrus's huge four-bladed pusher propellor
that was the problem – anyone flying into the blast from it would immediately
lose flying speed and altitude, giving a good imitation of engine trouble. In the
air we were a collection of individuals, beyond a doubt. There was a strong
common discipline, a common object and a common loyalty, but of uniformity
there was none. Underneath us there went a mass of shipping; building up,
reinforcing and returning – most of them – for more. The pattern became
clearer as the coast drew on; it concentrated on an antlike aggregation on the
beaches. Boats of all types cut erratic arcs in the shallows; the only stable points
were the hulks of block-ships, mulberries and wrecks. The beaches themselves
were pulsating with movement, while in the dark interior smoke blew across
and mixed with clouds of yellow dust from airstrips and runways.

On approaching the black smoke, dust and turmoil that marked Juno beach
near Courseulles, the Walrus, having performed its task well in shepherding us

Walrus aircraft, similar to the cross-channel leader.

across the water, turned back and left us to our own devices. There was nothing for it now but to do some rapid map reading and trust one's judgment. I had spent some time beforehand poring over the unfamiliar French maps of the area that we now had to use, colouring in the high ground and trying to pick out features that might help to identify the landing ground. It was not easy. There was no room for anything. The map no longer resembled the ground: villages had no firm outlines and new roads ran across fields that had been turned into camps or tank parks. The whole area was heaving with activity – except in the villages. It all seemed terribly different from our dear old Kentish landscape and of course, there were Germans to be reckoned with.

Freddie, followed by the rest of the Flight, put his nose down and headed off to the east of our landfall. Remembering my experience of follow-my-leader on the way to Weston Zoyland, I decided to find my own way in, and held on. Before I had gone far, I spotted a landing ground with a white 'T'

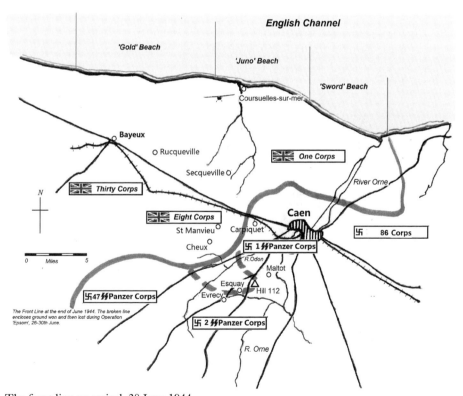

The front line on arrival, 28 June 1944.

marker. It appeared to be rather near the enemy (in fact it was several miles away; at that time we understandably lacked experience of the scale of battle), but I landed beside it on the 'any port in a storm' principle. The rest of the Flight was not to be seen and I taxied in feeling rather lonely. When I found I was on the right landing-ground and was welcomed by Harry Eastgate and the 'C' Flight ground crews I felt happier, and happier still when the rest of the aircraft turned up later on. They had spotted the Squadron HQ strip at Secqueville, had put down there, then flown over after refuelling.

Now it was a matter of getting the aircraft tied down and camouflaged, and settling in to our new accommodation. The basic priorities were to locate a vacant slit trench (as near to one's tent as possible), the cookhouse and the latrines. The actual landing ground was a large meadow, with big poplars along two sides. There were no habitable buildings to occupy, but no dead cows or horses around either. The former inhabitants had taken what possessions they could and fled. There was the constant noise of aircraft, and sporadic gunfire that intensified from time to time but never really died down. After what had been a busy day, I found it helpful to take a walk around the landing ground with Geoff Burgess and unwind. Everything, we had to admit, had gone rather well. Old Sarum (and Old

Captain Munro's flying log – 28 June to Rucqueville (Calvados).

England) seemed a long way off already, and only a few miles to the south was the battleground to which we would be committed within a matter of days – or so we expected.

> *Capt R.L. Munro 653 Sqdn RAF APO*
> *Monday 3rd July 1944*

My Dearest Jean
Thank you very much for your proxy – I will look after her.
The enclosed is what I got on the way and I've just managed to get it away.[4]
Nothing much to report – I'm trying to organise some leave!
> *More soon.*

Meanwhile, the Flight slipped into its familiar routine. One of the first things that had to be done was to scrub off the black and white stripes from the top of the aircraft main planes and fuselages. After that, we somehow felt we were ready again for business, and a great deal less conspicuous from above, which, after all, was where the threat would come from (or so we thought).

As things turned out, we were not to be called on to face the foe in the next few days, thanks to the delay in the building up of 2nd Army caused by the gales of 19–22 June. (This had especially affected those divisions under command of XII Corps, and their supporting troops, of which we formed part. The non-arrival of these troops had prevented the expansion of the beachhead, so that there was simply no room to deploy the forces now arriving).

> *Capt R.L. Munro*
> *C Flight*
> *653 AOP Sqdn RAF*
> *BWEF*
> *July 4th*

My Dearest Jean
Thank you very much for your letters – they seem to arrive if somewhat delayed on the way!
Nothing much to relate on the business side, that isn't censorable. The weather has been foul till today and one keeps a general level of dampness at the best of times.

There is nothing much to see or do outside the official routine: money goes (intentionally) nowhere so we just live on our rations and don't go anywhere. A bottle of reasonable wine is 200fr=£1 [2011: £33.50] so it's not worth spending the stuff. If you care to queue for it you can get a drink in a café but it's all rather wearisome.

I'm glad to say we have nice quiet nights except for the odd shell-fire (ours) which I can sleep through very happily. I suppose you're plagued with buzz-bombs – very dim things! I can't stand them personally.

The countryside here relatively intact – except where fighting has lasted more than a few hours. Then it's either flat or badly cut up.

The few French people I've seen seem a bit dumb but quite genial: no charming women snipers though. Loot (in the shape of Old Masters and jewellery) is also absent to my great disappointment. I had hoped for a few small perquisites at least.

I must stop drivelling, Jean and get this off to you. I'll organise a news service to you if I get disorganised for any length of time. Everything is going very well just now – even the weather, aforementioned.

We were, after all, trying to fit some fifteen armoured and infantry divisions, with their supporting troops plus 83 and 84 Groups Royal Air Force, into an area about the same as that of the Isle of Wight, with a road system which was only just adequate for the local peasant economy never mind an invasion force. There was a main road running across the beachhead from Bayeux in the west towards Caen in the east, plus a few minor roads linking up such villages as had had the misfortune to be caught up in the Liberation. Whatever else the invasion forces needed to meet their needs for mobility was carved out of the countryside by bulldozed tracks, billowing yellow dust in dry weather, and churned up into yellow mud when it rained. There was, in fact, precious little 'room to manoeuvre', and new units were pouring in as fast as the Navy could deliver them.

During the next few days we shook down and started improving the landing strip. We emptied the lorries, finding unsuspected hoards of completely unnecessary materials – such items as a dozen boxes of plastic training grenades, which had clearly outlived their usefulness. The Flight diary records that a tennis court was laid out, and a framework of rules

2 July 1944, view over the Commune of Mathieu, looking across the front line towards Caen, 4km to the south.

hammered out, after vigorous discussion. A bridge-school was formed, to add even more tone to the social scene – '3rd July; rained all day. Capt Burgess made a grand slam. Capt Place made 15 francs' – this in our new, and rather homemade looking, liberation currency notes. A Jeep-load of pilots, led by the flight-commander, made a trip into Bayeaux (still almost intact) – ostensibly in search of baths. As to the future, it was not yet certain.

The news of the battle was good; we were in a kind of halfway house between the forward areas of the beachhead. There were few distractions once one had grown used to the ceaseless thunder of gunfire and the rumble

Encamped near Caen, Normandy in 1944, with shell damage evident.

of aircraft. The main interruptions were variations on these patterns: sudden bursts of aerial cannon fire and the angry scream of aircraft engines from fighters in brief combat.

On 4 July, Freddie Riding set an example by taking Lance Bombardier Windle as rear observer on an information sortie in the Cheux area. The rest of the pilots followed suit, some with observers, others on their own. I preferred to sort things out by myself, as did Geoff Burgess. The point of carrying a rear observer was to have someone in the back to watch out for enemy aircraft, and it says much for the quality of our ground crews that we were never short of volunteers for this duty. Back in England we had always taken our ground crews up for flights as a matter of course when carrying out air-tests, and for air experience, but we had not considered using them as rear observers. This, then, was a new development. We could not give them any sort of flying pay – they never asked for it nor did they have any special training in aircraft recognition. We did give them a badge, to be worn on the left sleeve. It was made from a pilot's flying badge by cutting off one wing, but it was an unofficial designation.

While SHQ and the Flights were settling in after the arrival of the aircraft on 29 June, Operation 'Epsom', the first of three major operations, had already begun with the object of enveloping Caen on its western side, and then swinging east across the River Orne to occupy the higher ground south of the city through which the Caen-Falaise road ran. This was undertaken by VIII Corps, with 15th Scottish, 43rd Wessex and 11th Armoured Divisions under the command of General O'Connor. It had begun on 26 June, the first objective being to force a crossing of the Odon, through which 11th Armoured would pass and make for the River Orne. After an intense artillery bombardment, 15th Scottish made good progress at first, but was then faced with tremendous opposition from 12 SS occupying the villages of Cheux and St Mauvieu [editor's note: The village is Saint-Manvieu and not Saint-Mauvieu as it appeared on WW2 Allied maps.] Having captured the villages, albeit with great losses, two determined counter-attacks by Panzer and infantry divisions were fought off, and heavy casualties inflicted on them by concentrated artillery fire. Rommel's last hopes of driving the British Army into the sea had been decisively defeated.

Capt R.L. Munro
C Flight
653 AOP Sqdn RAF
BLA
17th [July]

My Dearest Jean
Thank you very much for your letters, which arrive far more often than I can compete with.
Your last, incidentally, took only two days.
There's a terrible racket going on just now: it shakes everything up but encourages the old grasshoppers (when there is enough lull to hear them. All

nights are noisy: being two foot below ground (4 ft tonight) I don't worry much whose bangs they are. We got shaken in the daylight not long ago on a road when a FW 190 came along at 0 feet. We got smartly down; my nose was firmly in the dust of the roadside and not even my curiosity induced me to look up at the darned thing. I think he was more scared than us as every one was pooping off at him. The dust here is pretty bad when you've been out. You can beat clouds of it out of your battle dress and a hair-wash is revealing!

Today is a big day: our first bread arrived (instead of biscuits) and our first bottle of beer. I'm saving mine for a blind (the whole bottle at one frantic session).

You may notice the new address: it stands for British Liberating Army. There is a certain amount of caustic humour going around as a result of this change.

Things are a bit flat round here: not as bad as I have seen but ruined. The houses are full of rubble, dust and junk. Most of the walls are holed and battered: there aren't any roofs intact or even vaguely so. Everyone left weeks ago except for the odd cat. It is all pretty bad: north of Caen was worse. I haven't bothered to go there yet: I don't think there's much to see.

The German air force is in a bad way since they lose a steady 2 per raid (always a mere dash in and out). Rather different from the Caen effort.

I still manage to amuse myself, I make the odd shelf for the Jeep* between times and generally potter about in my idle moments. It's the best way of getting time past and things have been pretty good as far as our jobs go.

I read with interest the results of foot drill: I've forgotten what saluting is, to say nothing of the obscurer drills.

I do hope the buzz-bombs are not too persistent: Dover certainly seems a queer place to relapse into quiet. Well I'm trying hard to get 1) some wine; 2) a battery wireless set and 3) a handful of small change. There is nothing small but potty little notes: you shed them like an autumn tree.

I will write to you anon: my next 48 hrs will be rather busy, so I will have a shot after that.

---

* Editor: The alternative use for pilot protection? 'Later on we found another use for it [the steel sheets]: installed in the floors and under the seats of the Jeeps, at a time when we had cause to worry about land mines.'

By the morning of the twenty-eighth, 11th Armoured were moving across the Odon over the bridge, which had been captured intact, and heading for the Orne. On the twenty-ninth, Point 112 was captured after desperate fighting. (As its map-name denotes, Point 112, or Hill 112, is a gently sloping rise with a height of 112 metres. The broad top commands the whole area and has several hedged fields on it with two minor intersecting roads. From the north all this is concealed from view by a shallow false crest, giving complete cover except from the air. Whichever side held Point 112 held the key to the Caen-Falaise plain to the north, and open country to the west, south of Caen).

It was therefore tragic that this prize, gained at such terrible cost by VIII Corps, should be surrendered the next day on the basis of a mistaken intelligence appreciation. The whole of the German armoured strength in Normandy had been drawn into the battle, and decisively defeated. There was nothing left in the kitty, and General Dollmann's death due to stress was the best evidence of the Germans own assessment of their position at that point. General Dempsey thought otherwise and ordered 11th Armoured to withdraw from Point 112, right back behind the River Odon, which had been secured at such heavy cost by 15th Scottish only a few days before. Although the damage done to no less than five Panzer and SS divisions had put paid to any further attempt to drive the British (let alone the US Forces) into the sea, the withdrawal meant that the casualties suffered by 15th Scottish and 43rd Wessex, the two finest infantry divisions in 2nd Army, had not now achieved any substantial gain in ground. Whatever the strategic value of the operation, it was certainly nothing compared to what would have been achieved if its objectives had been resolutely pursued, and hard-won success exploited.

In fact 15th Scottish, who had performed so gallantly throughout, had suffered infantry casualties amounting to half their strength. A single day's losses in one battalion of the Glasgow Highlanders during the battle of Cheux amounted to thirty-four per cent of the officers, and almost twenty-five per cent of the battalion as a whole. (Some days later GOC 15th Scottish received a gift of 180,000 cigarettes for his men from the Field Marshal – 'I hope they will enjoy them'). Both of these divisions continued to fight with distinction throughout the rest of the campaign; 'C' Flight counted it a privilege to fly in support of them in several later battles, including the crossing of the Rhine.

That was the price that 2nd Army was made to pay for playing its part in the Allied strategy for the liberation of Western Europe. One attack after another had to be launched in the 'hinge' area round Caen (so favourable for the type of resolute defence which the German soldier had learnt to mount in Russia, and so favourable to their superiority in armour) in order to draw the Panzer divisions away from the US forces to the west, where

Auster AOP pilots being briefed at 652 Squadron mobile headquarters, July 1944. Courtesy Imperial War Museum.

General Bradley still hesitated to launch his break-out into the heart of France (Operation 'Cobra').

The next of these major operations was called 'Charnwood'. It was mounted by I Corps, with 3rd Canadian Div. on the right, 59th (Staffordshire) in the centre, and 3rd British Division on the left. Its objective was the city of Caen, to be launched from the north, and it would incidentally tidy up Monty's eastern flank. It was preceded by a heavy RAF bombardment, intended to soften up the formidable German defences.

On 5 July, Freddie was called over to see Major Cobley, the CO of 652 Squadron at Plumetot, to see if we could make ourselves useful in this operation in a ground liaison role. As a result it was decided that Butch Pritchard would be attached to 3rd AGRA (the medium gunners), Geoff would go along with the Flight Commander to 652 SHQ and I would be with 59th Division HQ; each would have a Jeep and a wireless-set.

Ground crew of No. 652 (Air Observation Post) Squadron RAF wheel a Taylorcraft Auster AOP Mark IV out of its blast pit at Cresserons, Normandy, for a sortie in support of I Corps operations. *IWM*

The next day I took a jeep over towards the sea and found 652 Squadron Headquarters well below ground level. As the Flight Diary records:

All personnel dug in well as the ALG was under Harassing gun fire from the Boche across the river Orne.

7th (July) – In the early morning the Boche shelled the ALG quite heavily so the day was spent digging well underground.

The aircraft were sunk into crescent shaped emplacements; slit trenches abounded and so did shell holes. We had our section signallers with us, and spent the next two days under sporadic harassing fire from 88mm guns on the east side of the River Orne. One round landed by a slit trench and pushed the side in. The pilot whose refuge it had been was pulled out, unhurt but dazed. When the ambulance arrived he had been well filled with whisky and was removed in a state of trance, returning next day with a headache, which naturally he ascribed to the explosion, and slight deafness. Ron Thompson, from 'B' Flight, was a bit slow in taking cover and got a wound in his foot and an unexpectedly quick return trip to England. (During this period, all casualties were flown back to UK for treatment as a matter of course).

On the evening of the seventh, a stream of RAF heavy bombers came in and began bombing the outskirts of Caen; unfortunately they dropped the bombs well behind the German main defensive positions, which consequently escaped with little damage. The city itself took the brunt of the attack and was devastated, with heavy civilian casualties in the ruins of its northern suburbs. Early next morning a massive artillery attack was launched on the German positions, and the infantry moved forward with every expectation that the defences had been well and truly softened up. Instead, there was strong resistance, particularly from 12 SS Panzer Division who were confronting 59th Division. 3rd British Division managed to reach the built-up area of Caen, where they were halted by the mass of rubble and cratering caused by the bombing; any idea of capturing the bridges over the River Orne was out of the question. 3rd Canadians fought their way over the airfield at Carpiquet and also managed to reach their objective.

59th Division, however, could make little progress against a resolute defence, and they too were faced with a lunar landscape of overlapping bomb-craters, left by the RAF. Each one formed an excellent defensive position and a nightmare for tank-crews. The whole division began to lose cohesion, just as it had back in Sussex on exercise when we had been flying around trying to locate their artillery for them. This time I took to a motorcycle and tried to find who was where, but it was a hopeless task, so I reported what I had found out and returned to base. Although the attack as a whole had been successful, it was once again at the cost of heavy infantry casualties; one battalion of the North Staffords lost twenty-five per cent of its strength in the capture of the heavily defended small hamlet of La Bijude. In hindsight, the use of heavy bombers in this operation had indirectly caused far more difficulty and casualties to the British (and directly to the luckless French inhabitants of Caen) than it did to the Germans. Once again the superior quality of German armour, skilfully sited in defence, was proving a nightmare for the British and Canadian infantry. Our first brief glimpse of battle, and at a respectful distance from the real fighting, gave us much to think about. If this was how France was to be liberated, we thought, there would be nothing left of it in the end.

On the eleventh we were brought closer to reality when we were ordered to take over from one of 652's flights, which were about to begin an operation south west of Caen, and given a tour of the battlefield. Everything had gone so smoothly for us so far that we had still been living in the world of training and exercises; our landing in Normandy, whether by air or sea, had seemed little more than an extension of that. We were now going to find out how we would perform in the face of the enemy.

We moved up on 12 July, to a prepared landing strip at St Mauvieu (sic), a village which had been captured a fortnight before by 15th Scottish, during 'Epsom'. (While we had been kicking our heels at Rucqueville we had seen the survivors of a company of Highland Light Infantry marching back with a piper at their head – they had just been pulled out of the battle). We were delighted to hear that it was 43rd (Wessex) Division whom we were to support, with Bill Heath as our CRA. The operation was named Operation 'Jupiter'; its objective was the recapture of Point 112, with its crucifix on the summit, and two neighbouring villages that had been turned into strong points (Maltot and Esquay). It remained the key to the Normandy battlefield and the great obstacle to any advance towards the Orne and the open country to the south east. The strategic objective was the same – to re-engage the German armoured strength and thus prevent it from being switched to the American sector. 43rd Division was to be supported by two infantry brigades and two independent armoured brigades. East of Caen, another attack (Operation 'Goodwood') was to be launched within a few days.

Our landing-ground at St Manvieu-Norrey, a few kilometres west of Caen was next to a troop of 25 pounders on one side and a Field Dressing Station on the other. We had good oblique photographic cover of the area and good wireless links, thanks to our forward position. On the 13th, the flight went into action for the first time and, as the diary recorded, 'with a swing'. Two shoots were carried out and during one of them I was lucky enough to catch a column

Brigadier 'Bill' Heath CB, DSO, MC, C.R.A.

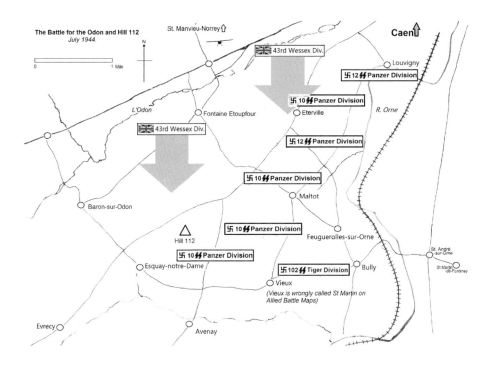

The Battle for the Odon and Hill 112
July 1944.

Auster flying over 25 pounders in Normandy. *IWM*

of vehicles and blow them up. Twelve sorties in all were made, chiefly tactical reconnaissances, or 'Tac/Rs'. LAC Graham was rear observer in seven sorties, LAC Sellicks in two, and AC Lewis in another two.

The need for rear observers was shown the next day, when a swarm of Me 109s took advantage of cloud cover and beat up the beaches and everything else they could see on the way. They were quickly engaged by light and heavy A/A guns and one came down a mile west of the ALG, whilst others were reported destroyed. Ten sorties were flown. Freddie caught a group of vehicles in St Martin [really it was Vieux],[5] with the fire of the whole divisional artillery – known as an 'Uncle Target'. Later, Tom Place registered the point of origin of a smokescreen that was put down to cover an infantry attack.

The next day was much the same – Tac/Rs., regimental targets (Code-named 'Mike' targets), and observation of, smokescreens. Freddie, with Lance Bombardier Windle up, was nearly bounced by three FW 190s. Freddie's temper was not improved by a taxiing accident (not his) that temporarily disabled two aircraft.

Flight Diary (Captain Burgess) *16 July: Captain Place tried to extinguish himself by hitting aircraft 960 violently against aircraft 958 during a take off. He was very annoyed. So was the flight commander. Captain Place showed his annoyance and flew away in 169. The flight commander concealed his annoyance magnificently. Maybe Captain Riding was feeling charitable having just evaded 3 FW190s which made a pass at him over Fontaine-Etoupefour.*

Things did not calm down with nightfall. The Luftwaffe put in a series of determined attacks on the whole beachhead, with Ju 88s chiefly. The A/A response was dramatic, with streams of tracer arcing into the sky in all directions. We all put our tin hats on and cowered into our slit trenches – which seemed to have grown rather shallow. It eventually quietened down until there was only the sound of the intermittent bombardments from our own guns that persisted for the rest of the night.

The next morning, after some light German shelling of our area, we found a number of holes in the upper surfaces of the aircraft, caused by shell-splinters, possibly from our own A/A fire. It was therefore decided to withdraw all aircraft and personnel at nightfall to SHQ's strip and fly in at first light with the minimum of ground crew needed to man the landing-ground during daylight. We were already short of two aircraft due to the taxiing accident, and could not afford to risk losing any more. We also rigged up a field telephone to our neighbouring gunners so that we could take off without being raked by a broadside from our own 25 pounders – however well intended. Nothing could be done about landing across their line of fire, but at least we could try to get off to a good start.

It was about this time that we learned that Captain Watkinson of 'A' Flight and his observer had been hit in mid-air by one of our own shells; both were killed. The fact was that the fire from British weapons of all descriptions was so intense during this period that such an accident was not unexpected.

Author's view of 25pdr gun emplacements, Normandy 1944.

'C' Flight Diary (Captain Pritchard) *17 July: The slight anxiety felt by all pilots over taking off and landing in front of battery of 25pdrs by the runway showed a definite tendency to increase during the day until tonight our practical minded 2 i/c* (Lyell) *decided to visit the GPO in person to come to some arrangement. This has been successfully done.*

The Squadron Diary for that day reports that Capt Watkinson was hit by a 25pdr shell 'while flying low in front of guns'. On 24 July the CCRA gave a directive requiring great care when Austers were close to the gun area. 'Unarmed Into Battle' p.57 mentions that this danger was recognised early in 1944 during the Italian Campaign and 'steps were taken to minimise it'

One pilot, not given to romancing, reported seeing a mortar-bomb turn over at the top of its trajectory and fall away again. The air was full of invisible projectiles rushing on towards the German positions. So long as one was not aware of them, it was not disturbing, but when one had completed a sortie and begun to fly back just above ground level, one had no option but to run the gauntlet of the mass of active weaponry in front of one. The concussion from a battery of field guns firing a round of gun-fire just as one approached was unnerving, to say the least. After one busy day, I caught myself putting off my return to the ALG on the excuse that 'just one more look' at the area would be a good idea.

The battlefield was indeed always worth that extra look. Fighting had now reached the stage when Point 112 was in continual eruption. The commander of Panzer Group West, General Eberbach, had orders that the hill must not be surrendered; the troops entrusted with this task were 10 SS Panzer Division, part of 1 SS Panzer Division and the 102 SS Heavy Tank Battalion – the Tiger tanks. The arrival of reinforcements had been blocked by the launching of Operation 'Goodwood' down the east side of Caen towards the Caen to Falaise road – the same objective as 'Epsom', but on the opposite flank. It was preceded by a massive bombing attack by Bomber Command RAF and the 8th and 9th USAF on the eighteenth (and as far as we were concerned, it stirred up so much dust that despite flying twelve sorties in our two remaining aircraft, only one shoot was possible). This attack by two infantry and two armoured divisions tied up the remaining armoured strength under command of Panzer Group West and gave General Bradley yet more time to mount the US break-out, Operation 'Cobra', without fear of German armoured intervention.

The lower slopes of the hill were dotted with the remains of British tanks, some still smoking; most of them were Sherman tanks. The Sherman, apart from being under-gunned, had the fault of providing inadequate protection for its own ammunition, which tended to detonate inside the tank if it sustained a hit. The effect on the crew can best be left to the imagination. On top of the hill sat a single Tiger tank, which acted as an OP as well as an almost impregnable anti-tank gun emplacement. In the small fields adjoining, surrounded by high hedges, mortar positions and infantry were dug in. It seemed to me that I could not do better than make the lives of these people as difficult as possible, and I made it my business to put this into practice, with some success.

Flight Diary 19 July: Captain Munro found a tank and possible Infantry or Mortar emplacement near Pt 112. He watched it with great patience and persistence. Finally seeing movement there and shooting it up.

To begin with I attacked the mortar area by calling down the concentrated fire of a field regiment. The immediate result was to stop the mortar fire and to set ablaze a half tracked vehicle concealed behind a hedge; it was probably carrying ammunition for the mortar positions nearby. The Tiger tank was then given the same treatment but as field guns[6] are not designed to penetrate solid steel of any great thickness at such a range it only made the tank withdraw slightly and sit tight while I continued to observe. I then saw it fire its 88 mm gun: a cloud of dust sprang up in front of it and almost at once I saw a red ball of fire pass well behind the aircraft. I turned round and flew back and the same thing happened. It was not good shooting. The gunner failed to lay off to allow for the speed of the aircraft – a modest 60–70 mph – but if left unpunished I reckoned it might start a bad precedent, so I returned to the strip and obtained the CRA's consent to shoot a single medium gun (and of course a 'blanked' gun as a kind of tweedledee to fire simultaneously and eliminate any chance of enemy sound-ranging).

After I had re-netted the wireless I set off again and started to engage my target, which was still sitting there, master of all it surveyed.

Flight Diary 20 July: Captain Munro returned to his pet tank, so infuriating it that, losing all self-control, it fired at him using AP. This so annoyed Captain Munro that he got the CRA's permission to destroy the tank and locality. He got a successful concentration down.

The first rounds fell close to it, but before I could correct onto it, it retreated about a 100 yds and waited to see what would happen next. The answer was another group of 4.5 inch shells, which were too close for his comfort. He set off at full speed, disappeared into the village of Esquay, and did not return. (When the village was eventually captured, a Tiger tank was found abandoned, with one track off.[7] I like to think it was the one I had seen off earlier).

[Editor: A German Tiger tank commander, Ernst Streng, was in the same battle. He kept a diary, which for that day reads:

That damned English crow is hanging in the sky again. Doesn't he know there's a war on? He's got a nerve, flying in curves and circles over the front like that!

A machine-gun could easily bring him down. But nothing stirs in our front line. The infantryman there knows that the slightest sign of life will bring down the shells from the enemy batteries – and they will be bang on target.

Throughout the intense heat of the July afternoon our infantry lie motionless in their holes in the ground, following with their eyes every movement in the sky above.][8]

Later the same day I put a heavy concentration on what was reported to be an infantry HQ, and Freddie destroyed a group of vehicles in Maltot. In the afternoon several FW 190s passed low over the ALG and did some bombing on the road north of Baron-sur-Odon. It rained heavily next morning and we could do nothing, but the afternoon was clear and Geoff did several shoots on Point 112 with medium guns, shooting up tanks and infantry localities. We learned later that Operation 'Goodwood' had come to a halt, partly on account of bogging down in mud and partly due to meeting stiff German defences. However, it had captured Caen, cleared the high ground to the

Water colour. Auster MT169 and Tiger tank on the hilltop by Lyell Munro.

south of it and tied up the German armour, although at the cost of heavy casualties once again. Operation 'Jupiter' had not yet achieved is objectives, and the battle for Point 112 continued unchecked. We had noticed one or two graves in the paddock adjoining the Field Dressing Station beside us; in the last few days they had increased steadily until it was filled with rows of white crosses. As usual in Normandy it was the infantry who bore the brunt of the casualties and to a lesser extent the tank-crews. We had some consolation in knowing that the artillery support they received was proving a battle-winning factor, but it was always the poor bloody infantryman who had to occupy the ground.

The life of the infantryman in Normandy, in fact, was 'nasty, brutish and short' when in the line. The bocage, with its small fields, steep banks and hedges was ideal for a defensive battle; even the soil was hard and stony, so that digging-in was slow and difficult. The German soldier was both capable and courageous; many of the units opposing us were SS: battle-hardened and totally ruthless. His tanks were much superior in most respects (although, despite being able to see any Allied tank off, the Tiger was so big and heavy that it tended to get bogged down). He used mortars, usually dug deep down in narrow pits, often sited behind banks and hedgerows and always skilfully camouflaged. These positions were extremely hard to detect: the propellant that discharged the mortar bomb itself was virtually smokeless and flashless. The Germans were masters of this form of bombardment and our infantry suffered accordingly. We spent much time observing the accuracy of our own replies to these bombardments: large numbers of field guns would simultaneously shell the suspected mortar sites. Although I never detected a mortar-position, shoots on known mortar-areas were one of our frequent tasks. These must have been effective, because it was found that if an Auster was in the air, mortar-fire in that part of the battle stopped. One particular shoot was a concentration of fire brought down on the village of Maltot on 22 July, which had been identified as a key mortar-area. Known as barrage 'Express', it involved every available gun, including the Navy, in 2nd Army. I suppose some 700 guns of all calibres were brought to bear on the village area. We were to observe on the effectiveness of this attack, and report. Few rounds fell outside the target-area, which simply seethed with bursts and dust. How long it went on I don't remember – it just went on and on pulverising that unfortunate village. We were not concerned about the German troops in it – they should not have been there, quite simply. The French inhabitants had long since left. The German forces appeared to have little artillery support other than the dual-role 88 mm gun, and thanks to the RAF, the Luftwaffe provided precious little air support.

It was clear that the battle was nearing its climax, with Point 112 its focus. A series of attacks and counterattacks broke over the hill until its lower slopes were littered with burnt-out hulls of British tanks, some with their turrets lying yards away, quite unable to withstand the fire of German static and mobile 88 mm guns. We could do little to help our tanks once the battle was joined – they were hopelessly out-classed in armour and firepower. Freddie had to watch three Churchills knocked out by a single Tiger, picked off one after another as they breasted a ridge; he was quite unable to warn them as he was not on their radio frequency. The Sherman deserved its German nickname of 'Tommy cooker' (after the infantryman's little methylated spirit stove), as one of our pilots discovered the first and last time he looked inside one that had 'brewed up' after being hit.

On the same day as we observed 'Express', I also shot the guns of the whole Corps on targets in St Martin[9] and Avenay. The sheer volume of shell-fire, by day and by night was reaching a crescendo; Bill Heath, our much-loved Commander Royal Artillery in the Division had by now been on the wireless-set at his command-post for twenty-four hours continuously directing artillery fire in support of the infantry assaults on Hill 112, until he could hardly speak. Everyone on the Flight did their best to respond; in particular our unpaid, untrained, rear observers, still doing their normal duties when not on a sortie, did us proud. And proud of them we were; I still look back with respect and affection on these people of my own generation who gave us their confidence and also gave us something to live up to within the Flight.

Back on a more humdrum level, we replaced our Sergeant Q (who had been a pain in the neck for some time) with a more congenial person, Sergeant Maughan, who was better suited to the special RA/RAF mix of an Air OP flight. In addition he had an agreeable light tenor voice, and his rendering of *When Irish Eyes Are Smiling* was popular with all ranks. I also had a bit of luck when three new aircraft were required to replace losses,

Hill 112 in 1944.

MT169 over Hill 112, as painted by the author.

and needed three pilots to fly them over. We drew lots, and I joined Dickie Thrush (from 'A' Flight) and Jock Scott (SHQ) the next day (23 July) on an Anson bound for Northolt via Bognor. (Butch Pritchard was already bringing another aircraft back, due on the same day as we left.)

By the time the navigator had wound the Anson's wheels up, slowly, inch by inch, it was nearly time to start lowering them again. As we left Normandy, the beachhead looked clearer and calmer than it did when we had first flown in after the big gale. Bognor looked quite good too. We landed at Northolt and then went straight off to our respective homes, where we would wait for a call to pick the new aircraft up. I went to Paddington to get a train to Slough, and must admit I felt a stranger in a strange place. For years, France had been as unattainable as the moon to all of us and now we were firmly established there – none of us doubted that for one moment – we were just a few hours away from London, with a regular air service between Northolt and Normandy. London, however, was under bombardment again, this time from steadily increasing numbers of V1 flying bombs. A second Battle of Britain was now being fought, with heavy damage and casualties already being inflicted on the southern suburbs of the city. Attacks on the launching-sites in the Pas-de-Calais were absorbing much RAF effort, but it was already apparent that the real answer lay in the outright capture of the sites themselves. This was yet another incentive to mount the breakout from the beachhead and drive the German Army out of France and Belgium.

I was glad to get back to my family and give them assurance that things were going well, and that I was in good heart. (My brother had been killed while flying in 1941; since when his young son was being looked after by my parents. I kept him supplied with oranges and tins of juice from my aircrew rations).[10] All the same, I was impatient to return to Normandy and get on with the job.

[After the memorial service held at Findhorn to honour the author, a letter was received from his former comrade-in-arms Captain John Turnbull concerning 653 Squadron's badge and motto. In it, Captain Turnbull told us that the Squadron Leader had given Captain Munro the task of *'visiting the Herald's Office* [College of Arms] *in London to arrange its creation. A task, I think, dear to his heart and done most expeditiously'.* Later, Lyell wrote *'..the 653 Squadron crest, whose design I had chosen from several which Mr Henniker-Heaton, then Chester Herald in charge of these matters, had offered as possible contenders. I had been told to visit him at the Royal College and make the choice. I avoided*

653 Squadron Crest.

all heraldic puns and went for the motto "Ubique speculabundus" *("The eyes of the guns are everywhere"), as stressing the RA connection and the main function of the squadron, reconnoitring everywhere. The crest showed crossed artillery-pieces and an eagle's head.'*]

Jock, Dickie and I picked up the new aircraft at Selsey as planned, and then had to hang on in Bognor (staying, if my memory serves me, at the King George V Hotel) waiting for better weather for our trip back to B14 airstrip near Bayeux. We got away in good order on the twenty-eighth and had an uneventful crossing. This time there was no feeling of excitement as there had been on our first crossing. I just wanted to get it over and pick up where I had left off. We took one hour fifteen minutes for the trip – thirty minutes less than our first crossing, mainly because we were now lightly loaded, and there was less of a head wind to slow our progress.

When I landed at Secqueville I found the Flight enjoying a rest, along with 43rd Division, who had pulled out of action on the 26th. Operation 'Jupiter' was over; the Division had achieved its objective, the recapture of

Going back to the Front: at Bognor Regis, Captains Dickie Thrush, Jock Scott and Lyell Munro wait to return to Normandy.

Hill 112. After I had gone back to England on the 23rd, tank hunting had become the sport of the day. Later we let the RAF in on it, and put red smoke target-indicators down for the Typhoons to get some practice in with their rockets. These aircraft each had the firepower of a naval destroyer and their effect on German armour was crippling.[11] Even Tiger tanks could offer no protection to their crews, and Point 112 was thoroughly pasted by Typhoons for two days running. Nevertheless, Freddie was fired on by a tank which he was harassing the day before the Flight pulled out; it was, however, no more than a gesture of defiance – Point 112 was at last firmly in our hands,[12] although it had been a bloodbath for both sides. Both 15th Scottish and 43rd Wessex Divisions had lost many of their finest infantrymen in this battle for a piece of high ground known to posterity only by its height in metres above sea-level.

Forty years afterwards, I returned to visit Point 112. While little of the beachhead area is now recognisable after that lapse of time, there was no mistaking that curiously isolated piece of high ground rising out of the coastal levels. Even those hedgerows I knew so well, which I had watched so intently and at which I had directed so much high explosive, have grown up again; but in one there is still a gap, and it is where I blew up the half-tracked ammunition-carrier on 13 July, 1944. The fields are now cultivated again but among the ploughed furrows can still be found shell-fragments, bullets, shards of steel, glass and plastic and fragments of human bones.

The hilltop was quiet and deserted and before going on our way south we brewed a couple of mugs of tea and drank them in silence. There is now a large square monument to the dead of 43rd Division on the main road nearby and at the foot lay a wreath from German servicemen in memory of their opponents who died in those terrible days of battle. It could be termed a platitude to say that 'they did not die in vain'; but when we remember the state of brutal repression in which the whole of Western Europe lay at that time under the Nazis and compare it with the condition of those same countries – including Germany – today, those many young men could have no better or truer epitaph. The average age of those buried in the sixteen British war cemeteries in Normandy is just 23 years.

During my absence from the Flight on ferrying duties, it had been business as usual; our contribution to Operation 'Jupiter' had exceeded our expectations and what was pleasing was that our masters saw fit to thank us for it. First of all the CRA (Bill Heath to us all) had a few words with Freddie which caused some blushes. Then a few days later when the battle was over, the Flight was ordered to attend an address to be given to 43rd Division Artillery by the Divisional Commander, General Thomas (known as 'Butch' to the troops). He had a reputation as a hard taskmaster and had created a division that, by any standard, knew its job as well as any in 2nd Army and had just proved it in battle.

Freddie had characteristically got the Flight down to some basic soldiering as soon as it pulled out of action. Vehicles and aircraft were serviced and cleaned up and as Freddie put it in the Flight diary, were 'looking smart, up to peace-time standard'! That was followed next day by a kit inspection ('very few deficiencies were found', Freddie noted). That afternoon we got news that the Divisional Commander wished to address all ranks and so the rest of the day was spent blancoing belts and gaiters, polishing boots and brass and putting creases in best battle-dresses, ready for the big event the next day.

After the Divisional Commander's address, which congratulated the Division on its showing in its first battle and the artillery regiments supporting it in particular, Bill Heath had a few words to say to his gunner officers, including us. The Flight diary records: 'Between the two of them, bouquets slumped to two-a-penny and cheerfulness and goodwill toward men prevailed'. Another bonus was when the Flight moved out of the Squadron HQ landing ground at Secqueville back to our original home (or field) at Rucqueville. It was not that we were not made very welcome at Squadron HQ – we just preferred to be on our own. (It was also true to say that Squadron HQs landing-ground was very dusty and scruffy (having been bulldozed), whereas we were an all grass field. Also, the Germans had acquired a habit of lobbing 88 mm rounds at Secqueville).

I got back just in time to take part in a round of pleasure which took up the last two days of July, as far as 'C' Flight was concerned. There were liberty-trucks to Bayeux; Tom Place and I took a ride in one to try and find some wine – several thousand thirsty British servicemen had got there first. But we did meet a lot of people we had known in earlier days, in some previous state of existence or another: on a course somewhere, on an exercise in Sussex, or just in a pub in Eastbourne. Bayeux at that time, and for a few more weeks, was the rendezvous for a whole generation of wartime conscript soldiers, or rather, for those whom four years of war had so far spared and were now gathered together in Normandy to undergo a final ordeal by fire.

Freddie laid on a programme of basic duties (such as vehicle and aircraft maintenance) every morning, followed by football, softball and bathing on the beaches which had been the scene of conflict and heroic endeavour only a few weeks before.

We also had time to look around and take stock of our situation. We were quite confident that we would hold our own; whatever the German Army could throw against us, the bridgehead would hold. Our forces, and of course those of the American Army, were being reinforced as quickly as the new arrivals could be absorbed and there was no effective interference by the German Air Force or the German Navy. We understood and accepted what Monty had told us from the very beginning – that the role of 2nd Army, and the Canadian and Polish forces, was to hold the eastern flank of the beachhead and, by a series of limited attacks, draw in the armoured divisions available to the German command piecemeal. The intention was to allow the Americans to capture the Cotentin peninsular, the port of Cherbourg and as much ground as necessary to enable the mounting of a massive breakout by General Bradley into the heart of France. Caen, and the high ground to the south of it across the Orne and Odon rivers, was the hinge on which the American breakout would swing unhindered and unopposed by the armoured forces of the German Army.

As far as the British soldier was concerned, that was the role of 2nd Army, a role that it carried out faithfully and well, but at enormous cost in infantry casualties. As a consequence of those losses, 50th (Tyne and Tees) which had fought since el Alamein, and 59th (Staffordshire) Divisions, were soon to be disbanded and posted within 2nd Army, as were many junior officers from A/A regiments and similar units.

Morale in 'C' Flight itself was high. We had been tried in battle and not found wanting. We had been lucky enough to go into action for the first time with the Division we had trained with and whom we knew. We had reason to feel pleased with the way everything had gone within the Flight and the fact that we had been congratulated by our divisional commander and our CRA gave everyone great satisfaction.

During our operations in July we had in fact flown a total of 151 sorties in the face of the enemy and carried out forty shoots, including observation of Barrage 'Express', the greatest concentration of artillery fire on a single target throughout the whole campaign, as it proved. My personal tally was thirty-seven sorties and nineteen shoots. The figures for our observers, however, put those totals into the shade. Lance Bombardier Windle flew no less than forty-three sorties; AC Lewis thirty-seven, LAC Graham twenty-four and LAC Sellicks twenty-three. These involved the following times in the air; Windle twenty hours thirty minutes; Lewis fourteen hours fifty-five minutes; Graham eleven hours thirty-five minutes, and Sellicks ten hours fifty minutes. These young men were all volunteers, had no formal training, received no flying pay and had no expectation of promotion. Their time in the air was in addition to their normal duties. They were well aware that their chance of survival if anything went wrong was slender; a fact made clear when Captain Watkinson and his airman observer were killed in mid-air by one of our own shells just before we went into action. We did not carry parachutes and the observer's chance of getting out of a crashed aircraft on the ground was much less than the pilot's, because he sat in the rear of the aircraft looking aft. As a commissioned officer, I was paid considerably more than they were, partly because I was expected to set an example; in fact, they set us the example in Normandy and were paid nothing for doing it.

The first weeks of August were relatively quiet. With the capture of Caen and the long-awaited start of 'Cobra' (the breakout of US 1st Army from the Cherbourg peninsular towards the Seine) there was at first sight not much for 2nd Army to do but mark time while the whole Allied front wheeled round to the east. What emerged was the chance to encircle the German forces locked up south of Caen and now being outflanked by the US breakout. This was to create the Falaise pocket and lead to the elimination of German ground forces west of the Maas. XII Corps played little part in this encirclement, but by 20 August hopes had risen of a dash by 15th Scottish Division for the Seine and beyond, supported by 'C' Flight (as the phrase has it).

Hopes, however, were deferred from day to day, but we were cheered up by the arrival of our full complement of 3-tonners, in place of the miserable 15 cwt. trucks we had been allowed for our landing on the beaches. We also got a UK leave vacancy, for which, after lots were drawn, I was lucky enough to be put forward. In fact, no sooner had I left on the twenty-third, the move began towards the Seine, the Flight moving to a landing-ground at Trun, on the edge of the 'killing-ground', as Eisenhower called it, of the Falaise pocket, in which some 10,000 German soldiers died and 50,000 prisoners were taken.

It was noticed, in the Flight diary, that the attitude of the French villagers in the area that we were now entering was friendly and welcoming. In Normandy we hardly saw a native; where they had fled to we did not know. Their farms and houses were ruined, their animals mostly dead and in advanced stages of decay – an offence to sight and smell. They were, of course, completely shocked by the onset of the invading armies. The bombardments from the air, on land and from the sea had not ceased for weeks on end, resulting in countless casualties – their friends and their families – and the total destruction of all their property. They had undoubtedly suffered from our arrival.

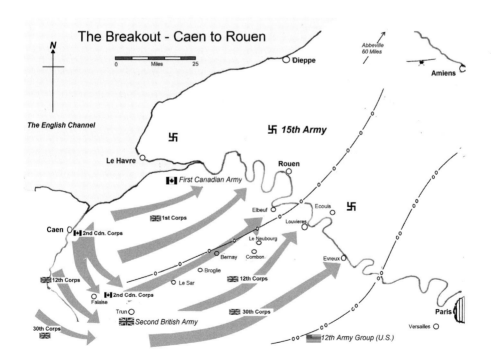

The very word 'Liberated' had already become a sour joke among us – it came to mean 'looted' or 'destroyed'. Not long after we landed in Normandy, at Rucqueville, we did try to find some crockery for our humble tented mess in the ruin of a house near the landing-ground; all we could find intact in the rubble were two cheap plates, souvenirs of French songs popular in 1914. One had a tawdry picture of a young man and his girl, with the inscription 'Embrasse moi, Ninette'; the other, the arch of a bridge over a river, with courting couple, centre, and the title 'Sous les ponts de Paris'.

In that heap of broken bricks the other surviving amenity of any use was an enamel bath. After I had emptied it of bits of house, I dragged it out and organised two or three dixies of hot water from the cookhouse. I was just getting nicely soaped when all hell broke loose overhead; all sorts of A/A started firing and streams of tracer appeared, passing straight over my head – so did two Me 109s, only just above the trees. I never felt so conspicuous before or since, nor so helpless, sitting in a white enamel bath in the middle of a ruined courtyard, in bright sunshine and total nudity, clutching a piece of soap and a face-flannel as my only defence against the Luftwaffe. It completely spoiled my bath time.

By the twenty-fifth the Division, plus an Armoured Brigade, had begun to pick up speed, passing through Broglie and on to Bernay, where M. le Maire generously provided flowers and wine, and where Tom Place was warmly embraced, then on to Combon. One Lieutenant Eastgate had flown in at crack of dawn with a camera aircraft, in spite of ground mist – the shape of things to come. But the next evening, when the ALG was at Combon, Geoff Burgess, having being on a sortie, did not turn up. The next day, Harry Eastgate came back with his camera, still hopeful of taking some shots to show the course of the River Seine. The Flight moved to La Vacherie near Louviers and Harry managed to do two runs along the Seine, but there was still no news of Geoff.

The pace was now very hot – 'just like Point 112 days', said the diary, with pilots and their observers getting down to some shooting with something more lethal than cameras. Sadly, there was no news of Geoff, in spite of every effort by SHQ and 'A' Flight.

On the twenty eighth Harry Eastgate (freshly promoted to Captain), came in as his replacement, and Dick Thrush brought his section in to beef up the Flight and help it to cope with the six field regiments that it was supporting.

It was not until the morning of the thirtieth that the news came that Geoff had been killed near Le Neubourg, south of Rouen, where he had been flying in support of an Armoured Brigade. Freddie and Tom Place set off at once to the scene of the crash to do what they could, while Butch Pritchard, with Joe Hargreaves, who had now joined the flight from 'B' Flight, went off to 53rd Welsh Division whom we were to support for a new operation across the Seine.

Geoff was buried in the parish church at Le Neubourg, with a simple wooden cross and the broken propellor of his aircraft beside it on the grave. The Flight diary for 30 August also records 'the end of the day saw the Flight established across the Seine at an ALG at Ecouis. It poured with rain in the evening'. The 2nd British Army had made it at last; Geoff, with thousands

Geoff Burgess's grave, Le Neubourg, near Rouen 1945.

of others, was left behind in Normandy. Not just one among the ordered ranks of the dead in some vast cemetery, but in a small village churchyard amongst the graves of country people like himself.

When I got back from leave on 1 September, Bobby Brown, our adjutant, met me off the aircraft and told me the news. Geoff and I had been close friends all our time together in 'C' Flight. Many had been the evenings in Kent that we had 'tired the sun with talking, and sent him down the sky' in some village pub. He came from Hexham, was married with two young bairns, and was proud of his Border ancestry. There are many degrees of friendship, affection and love; comradeship in arms must rank amongst the most rewarding and enduring of relationships throughout the ages. But by the same token there is no place in war for sentimentality, and there was a job to be done. Geoff's death made us more determined than ever to get on with it, and finish it.

Notes

1. This was the American harbour, partly because it was more exposed and partly because the British harbour was "more carefully assembled and 'planted'." Chester Wilmot.
2. The most likely culprits were RAF ground crew from either 660 or 661 AOP squadrons attached to 1st Canadian Army artillery Corps.
3. 653 Squadron Diary claims the date was the 29th, however Lyell's Flight Log endorsed by Major Pollitt shows the date as the 28th.
4. The slip of paper with a list of compass courses. The proxy is unknown but may refer to a box camera given to record the experience.
5. Although 'C' Flight diary mentions St Martin, it is really the village of Vieux and not St Martin. Major Howe's maps in 'Hill 112' also place St Martin where Vieux stands. D-Day maps (GSGS 4249, Sheet 7F 1st Edn) were the first to contain the error, although the Ordnance Survey map of 1943 is correct. For consistency, this account uses 'St Martin' also.
6. This would refer to the 25 pounder howitzer; the medium gun firing 4.5 inch shells would have been the BL 4.5 inch medium gun.
7. The Tiger was just possibly No 214, belonging to Heavy SS Panzer Abteilung 102 supporting III Battalion of SS Panzer Grenadier Regiment 21 – According to the account, 'a lucky shot was enough to break its track'. Hence its withdrawal, in reverse gear, to Esquay. (See *Panzers in Normandy Then and Now*, a detailed account by Eric Lefevre). Freddie Riding had a similar duel with a Tiger at

Point 112 before the German infantry withdrew, leaving the feature as a fire-swept 'no man's land' when they finally yielded it to 43 Wessex Division.

8. 'Hill 112' Major JJ Howe MC.

9. Almost certainly Vieux not St Martin – see earlier footnote.

10. Alan Munro recalls: 'It is probably my first memory, sitting up in a Victorian high chair waiting to see my unknown uncle "coming back from the war". My father had been killed in a flying accident in 1941 and in some ways Lyell was a replacement. I still clearly remember seeing him walking through the gate in brown No.1 uniform, wearing his conspicuous Royal Artillery red and blue fore-and-aft cap and carrying his raincoat, gas mask and small army suitcase. My grand-parents were relieved and excited, of course.'

11. RP-3 rockets fired by Typhoons were capable of destroying a Tiger tank but their accuracy under battle conditions was questionable. It is claimed to be more likely that a rocket attack would devastate the morale of tank crews leading them to abandon their vehicles!

12. In fact, the hilltop was not recaptured but became a no-man's land between the opposing forces. In early August when Caen had fallen the Germans decided the hill was no longer important and left their positions. 43rd Wessex suffered 7,000 casualties from a strength of 16,000.

Chapter 6

Break-out to the Netherlands

23 August–31 December 1944

The battle for North-west Europe completely changed in character once the Allies had broken out of Normandy and crossed the River Seine. On 26 August, Monty issued his last orders as commander in the field of the combined British, Canadian, Polish and US forces in Northern France and handed command to the Supreme Commander, General Eisenhower. He was given a field marshal's baton in exchange. Eisenhower's operational headquarters moved across the Channel and opened up on the Continent a few days later. However strong the political reasons for the resulting change in command-structure, the military effects were far-reaching and probably prolonged the war.

The fact was that the casualties sustained by the British divisions in Normandy (in particular the infantry) while drawing in and destroying the German armoured divisions, left the 2nd Army numerically weaker than it was on D-Day. The luckless 59th Division had been disbanded and its manpower posted to make good shortages in the other divisions and 50th (Tyne and Tees) would soon to be disbanded to serve the same purpose. The Canadian 1st Army had also taken severe losses, which could not easily be made good. This was the logical and foreseeable outcome of the bloodletting around Caen.

United States forces, on the other hand, enjoyed a continual flow of reinforcements, both to make good casualties and to increase the number of divisions and logistic support available to their two Army Group commanders – General Bradley (6th) and General Devers (12th Army Group). To have allowed Monty to remain as tactical commander of these forces might have been militarily sound – but it was simply politically unacceptable to American public opinion. (The fact that Eisenhower was compelled to reinstate Monty during the dark days of the Battle of the Ardennes is just part of the irony of history). The growing preponderance of American military strength meant that US political considerations began to outweigh military strategy in the conduct of the attack on Germany, whilst the influence of the British Government on events either in the field or in the conference room was weakening.

In Normandy the Allies had now eliminated the German 7th Army (under the late but not lamented General Dollman who had died of a heart attack on 29 June) and now faced 15th Army. This enemy force had already had some of its strength destroyed in the Normandy cauldron when it was belatedly drawn west across the Seine. Apart from such remnants as had managed to get away from Falaise, the 15th Army now had six divisions under command (about 100,000 men) with their equipment. As we now know, the German High Command had prudently decided to withdraw from northern France and Belgium and retire to an area north of the River Scheldt and the line of the Albert Canal from Antwerp to Maastricht. This move would have the bonus of denying the Allies the use of Antwerp as their major port in support of whatever attacks might be launched into Germany.

Monty, with his usual clarity, had set the tasks that lay ahead of the Allied armies. On the right, or southern flank, the US 1st Army (as part of 12th US Army Group) was to go for the area south of Brussels and west of the Meuse (or Maas). General Patton, commanding the US 3rd Army, was already 80 miles beyond Paris, which had been taken by the Free French 2nd Armoured Division on 24 August. He was still going strong, in spite of a shortage of petrol which was being sold on the black market in Paris off the back of US Army trucks.

[Editor's note. A member of US Army recalls:-

The earliest and simplest way [to obtain gasoline for the black market] *was to drive your truck to a dump and tell the GI attendant:-'My CO sent me here to get gas'. Back in the fall of 1944 so many outfits were moving forward, and the emphasis was so much on speed that gas dumps serviced any and every GI truck. There was no time to check whether a driver was telling the truth, and no adequate system of requisitioning had been set up … The gangs succeeded because … it was easy to acquire and dispose of the gasoline. As one convicted racketeer put it: 'Any damned fool could make a*

fortune without even trying'. Sergeant Allan B. Ecker, *Yank Magazine,*
4 May 1945.]

The British 2nd Army was to make for Amiens on the River Somme and drive
forward through industrial northeast France into Belgium. The Canadian
1st Army (with 51st Highland Division and the Polish Armoured Division)
was to clear up the Channel coast, going first for Dieppe (of tragic memory
for all Canadians), then clearing Le Havre and then on to the Channel
ports. Within the 2nd Army, XXX Corps was to go hard for Brussels and
Antwerp. It comprised Guards Armoured, 11th Armoured, 50th and 43rd
Divisions. On their left flank, XII Corps, with 7th Armoured, 15th Scottish
and 53rd Welsh Divisions, were to deal with islands of enemy resistance left
behind by the armoured divisions.

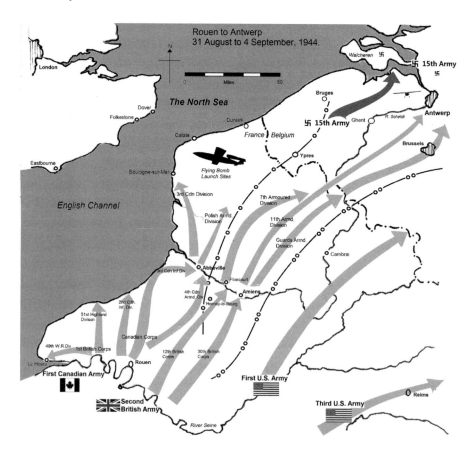

We were operating in support of 53rd Division whose advance beyond the Seine was now beginning to pick up speed. (The division were part of the rapid advance through Northern France into Belgium where an important bridgehead was secured, after heavy fighting, by crossing the Junction Canal near Lommel.) Freddie split the Flight up into advance and rear parties, with new landing-grounds being located by air as fast as they could be occupied. Freddie travelled in his Jeep, with the signals truck, so that he was in constant touch with the aircraft. On 1 September, the Flight left Louviers on the banks of the Seine and covered the fifty miles to Hornoy-le-Bourg, twelve miles west of Amiens, by dusk, with a pause northeast of Rouen at Forges-les-Eaux and at Pierrement [sic]. The Flight diary recorded that 'welcomes were up to standard, and Captains Pritchard and Hargreaves came into Captain Place's class by being heartily embraced by an over-zealous(?) French female'. (When I rejoined the Flight that evening I was too late for these manifestations of gratitude.)

The next day we drew breath at Hornoy and I went off on a long-distance reconnaissance across the Somme to look for a landing-ground east of Abbeville; we needed it to be near where the Division wanted to locate its next HQ. Vehicles were now crossing the River Somme by a bridge at Picquigny, which had been taken by 11th Armoured before the Germans could blow it. As usual I flew along the column of vehicles, turning left as I crossed the Somme and heading for the blue-grey roofs of Abbeville, which I could see shining in the sun.

When I passed over Flixecourt, halfway to Abbeville, I noticed everyone out in the main street, with tricolours flying from the houses and a small group of trucks making their way through the crowd. This looked to me like a liberation welcome and I assumed, judging by the enthusiasm, that these were the first British troops who had so far come this way, so I climbed to 2,000 ft, to be on the safe side and proceeded with caution. There were no vehicles on the road ahead as far as I could see.

I saw a likely area for a landing-ground and began to come down for a closer look. As I did so I heard some popping sounds, which at first I thought was from the engine as a result of throttling-back too far. Then I realised it must be rifle fire aimed at the aircraft, so I turned back towards Flixecourt. When I got there, it still seemed to be en fête.

The leading vehicles were now clear of the town and passing through a small valley beyond and I decided I should warn them that there were active German troops ahead. After writing out a message saying where the firing had come from, I flew in low and dropped the message-bag with its coloured streamers in a field just beside them. At once heavy small arms fire broke out. A lot of it was coming up at the aircraft, like a swarm of yellow bees, so I banged the throttle open, kicked hard on the rudder and stuffed the nose down feeling considerably alarmed. I got away without further trouble, but the vehicles had obviously been ambushed and were coming under fire. I flew back towards Amiens until I found somewhere to land beside the road and then stopped the first vehicle that came along with a radio tuned to the right frequency. I told them what had happened and that they were to send a message back to 53rd Division. I then returned to Hornoy and confirmed my message on our own radio-link.

Next morning Butch Pritchard and I flew back to Flixecourt. We had learnt that the recce party had been captured, with one motorcyclist killed, but that an attack had gone in that evening and recaptured them. We decided it was all right to use a landing-ground there and found a nice big field on a ridge to the east of the town where we both put down to have a look. Some inhabitants were coming out to greet us, but they turned back as soon as firing broke out on the far side of the field. We took cover, drew our .38 revolvers and prepared to sell our lives dearly, should any German be so foolish as to come within range and give us the chance. However, it turned out that the French resistance (the FFI) had, like the US cavalry, arrived in the nick of time and were having a private battle with the Germans.

French Resistance forces greatly aided the pursuit to the Seine in August … by interfering with enemy railroad and highway movements and enemy telecommunications, by developing open resistance on as wide a scale as possible, by providing tactical intelligence, by preserving installations of value to the Allied forces, and by mopping up bypassed enemy positions.

Pogue, Forrest C., *The Supreme Command. Washington DC:* Government Printing Office, 1996.

Before long it all became quiet again, but I decided then and there that in future I would carry at least a .303 rifle in the aircraft to defend myself until I could get hold of something better, preferably a semi-automatic weapon. The Flight moved into the landing-ground that afternoon and was welcomed by the town authorities without any more disturbances. In the evening, after being assured by the FFI that there were no live Germans in the area, Butch and I took a stroll over to the local chateau that was said to have been the local German HQ. It seemed deserted and had an air of shabby grandeur that so many big houses acquired during wartime occupation.

We walked warily up to the gate in the big walled garden and looked in at the gravel paths and weed-covered flowerbeds, but we did not care to enter for fear of booby-traps. As we returned up the lane we met an elderly French man and woman who were both dressed in black. As they passed by they asked us if we had seen any graves in the garden. We replied that we had not gone into the garden and so we had seen nothing; we asked them what was the matter? 'Oh', they said, 'the day before the British arrived the Germans had taken two young men from the town, brought them back to their HQ in the chateau where they had shot them'. One of the young men, they told us, was their son and they wanted to find his grave. It was the first of many such experiences that were to teach us that Nazi-occupied Europe was nothing better than a vast prison camp run by criminals.

French records reveal who these men probably were:

Ernest Armand Daussy: born April 20 1914. Arrested on the night of 31 August 1944 during an observation mission and intelligence along with **Roland Binet**, *Section Head and* **Georges Outrebon** *by members of an artillery convoy. After interrogation and torture he was murdered in Kommandatur Flixecourt, 31 August 1944, under the command of Lieutenant Luppe or Lugge. Chevalier Légion d'Honneur awarded posthumously 1961, Croix de Guerre Étoile d'Argent Citation No. 1319 of 11 October 1945 'Excellent intelligence officer in occupied territory. Was shot down while on a particularly dangerous mission through the enemy lines.' Rests in the cemetery of Flixecourt.*

Georges Outrebon: born December 13 1914. Questioned at the Kommandantur Flixecourt by the Viennese Lieutenant Luppe or Lugge felpost No 28444, hits the officer in the face, escapes and is hit by a burst of machine gun fire, 31 August 1944. Rests in the cemetery of Flixecourt. fr.geneawiki.com/index.php/80318-Flixecourt-Mortsauxguerres#M ortsdelaguerre1939-1945.

The 2nd Army was now moving rapidly north east through the old battlefields of 1914–1918 in which the fathers of some of us had fought thirty years earlier [the Somme]. It took us less than a week, however, to pass through the area where the Allied and German armies had been locked in battle for four years of the bitterest fighting. We were through and out the other side without even realising it.

The French Resistance fighters names on the memorial at Flixecourt.

For the Canadians and 51st Highland Division (who were under Canadian command) there were more recent memories. At Dieppe, the bitter Canadian losses, some 800 dead during Mountbatten's abortive raid in 1942, required atonement. At St. Valery-en-Caux there were also scores to settle, for it was here that in 1940 the 51st had been effectively abandoned so that the remainder of the British Expeditionary Force could be rescued from Dunkirk. Over 10,000 of their number were to spend five years in captivity. (On a lower moral plane the Highlanders beat the odds when they found the safe at one of the better-known casinos, opened it and distributed its contents).

Apart from the obvious strategic value of re-opening the Channel ports, it was both militarily and politically vital to capture the V1 flying-bomb sites in the Pas-de-Calais and north Belgium. Also known as 'buzz bombs' due to their distinctive and alarming engine-noise (hearing the engine stop was the most alarming part as it meant the bomb had started to fall) they were making life increasingly hard to bear in London and the south east of England. All the efforts of the RAF were unable to put a stop to the bombardment – it required the physical occupation of the ground by British and Canadian troops to achieve that. It was only just in time – the growing menace of the more powerful V2 rockets was the next part of the story.

While XXX Corps, with Guards Armoured at its head, was blazing the trail along 'Club Route' [marked by the playing card symbol] – the sign of the Corps axis which was to reach from Normandy to Lüneburg in Germany – and racing to Brussels, XII Corps was to have a less glamorous objective: the port of Antwerp, via the mining and industrial areas round Lille, past Ghent and south of the Scheldt estuary. XXX Corps' route lay through pleasant rural scenes at first, with small villages every few miles. Wherever we landed there was always something to remember [It is not clear either from the Squadron or Flight Diaries to whom 'C' Flight was attached]. At one village we noticed three young men taking a keen interest in the aircraft and with them three attractive young women who drew our attention. They eventually came up and introduced themselves as members of an RAF aircrew, who had evaded capture after bailing-out of a bomber. After giving them news of the war we asked if they needed anything. Obviously they were not doing badly, but would they like to give us their names, so we could put

Crowds of people inspect MT169 as C Flight reaches Belgium.

83rd Group in touch with them? They thanked us for the offer, declined all help and faded into the background. We did not see them again; obviously they knew where they were well off.

It was quite different with two American airmen whom we picked up west of Arras. They had been taken prisoner, and had been turned loose when the Germans fled. All they wanted was to get back home – wherever that was – and quickly. So to get them started, Joe Hargreaves decently undertook to take them back to Corps HQ by jeep. They could hardly wait to get away, and when they arrived they clambered out and walked off without saying a word of thanks.

Near Fleurbaix we met a more sinister figure. By now it was accepted that we came under the protection of the local Resistance group as soon as we had set up a landing-ground. They usually had armbands, Mauser rifles and berets, sometimes with the cross of Lorraine. Others were clearly Communists – less forthcoming, contemptuous of the Gaullist Resistance and better organised. On this occasion our protector was a tall, heavily built gentleman with curly black hair and a blue jowl. He had on a pair of ex-German jack-boots, and carried a Luger at his belt. His second-in-command was a small wiry character, who kept in the background and said nothing. We were told, politely, that if there was anything we needed, we only had to ask for it, and that our vehicles and aircraft would be perfectly secure. An armed guard would be provided throughout the night. He then left.

One of the locals told us he was in charge of the local left-wing Resistance, that he was known as 'the Gorilla' [or Guerilla?], and that his outfit specialised in mugging German soldiers after dark and shooting them with their own weapons. Presumably that was the means by which the Luger and the jack-boots had been acquired. At any rate, he was as good as his word, and we were glad that he was on our side.

A lot less menacing were the local children who operated a trade in eggs, cigarettes being used as the currency. They were a pretty bright lot, and I have no doubt we paid an outrageous price – but then we would not be coming back that way.

Apart from 'keeping up with the Jones's' little was done in the way of tactical sorties. Tom Place and Harry Eastgate had done a useful job flying up supplies of maps to keep up with the advance, which were distributed to the leading formations. A few flights were made to spy out the land ahead, but there were simply no German formations still in being along our route. On the Channel coast, however, they put up a stout defence in the key ports of Calais and Dunkirk, which remained an embarrassment if not a serious military threat. As well as tying up elements of the Canadian and Polish divisions, German A/A guns took a steady toll of the Allied aircraft that strayed over these pockets of hostile air space, almost invariably because of careless navigation.

Late in the evening of the 8th, we crossed the border into Belgium. It had poured with rain all morning, and Freddie had set off by Jeep to find a landing-ground. It turned out to be a Luftwaffe airfield just outside Courtrai (or Kortrijk), and a pretty creepy place at that. The trouble was that the whole place, hangars and all, had been prepared for demolition by the Germans; large bombs were positioned everywhere, but Freddie was confident that there was no danger. I did draw the line, however, when our cook started up his petrol-cookers beside two 500lb bombs just inside a hangar. He agreed to set up shop elsewhere. (As a matter of history, it was from Courtrai that Mussolini had despatched Italian bombers against targets in London, during the Battle of Britain. Most of them were ignominiously shot down – the rest were withdrawn.)

[Editor: Lyell's nephew, Alan, tells of a mission to Coutrai he made seventy years later: Lyell had once told him a story of a house in Brussels where he said three sisters 'entertained' British officers in return for their divisional patch. Each trophy they won they stitched into a patchwork bedspread.

Intrigued, Alan contacted Belgian journalist, Jean-Paul Mulders, to see if by some remote chance the priceless quilt might be found in some Brussels attic. He flew his little aircraft, with a former RAF colleague, to Kortrijk airport to meet Jean-Paul for lunch. Remarkably, it turned out that they were sitting within just a few meters of the spot where, according to Lyell's account, 'C' Flight's nonchalant cook lit his petrol oven next to a large unexploded German bomb! Whilst the bomb may have been long gone, the German concrete command bunker was still there, underpinning the air traffic control tower. Alan and his companions decided that Lyell would have been amused by the survival and useful employment of the sinister remnant.

And the three sisters? In February 2014 an article was published in the Belgian Sunday newspaper Die Standaard entitled 'The Fiery Bedspread'. Despite causing a rush of interest in the matter, including deeper comment about the behaviour of populations towards occupying armies, the item never appeared and very likely it is just a soldier's tale from the front, possibly inspired by the classic Greek legend of the three fates or morai. However, Alan says that as a positive result of the publicity, a church in Ghent recovered a rare icon, looted from it during the war.]

After a quick meal, we decided a change of scenery would be good for our morale, and set off in two jeeps to have a look at the nightlife of Courtrai. It seemed to be closed so we had a look at the map for somewhere else and found Armentieres, over the border in France. The name rang a bell in our collective folk-memory, and off we went. It also looked shut, but we did find a cafe with a few customers propping up a bar at one end of a brightly lit brasserie, so we parked the Jeeps, immobilised them by removing the rotor-arms, and went in.

As we made our way to the bar the atmosphere was rather like one of those scenes from a western movie, when the good guy rides into town, hitches his horse outside the saloon and walks in, greeted with a deathly hush and a codfish stare from the barman. There were one or two civilians, dressed like stage Frenchmen in shabby berets, and three uniformed types looking like a cross between a gendarme and a World War I poilu *[French Infantryman]*.

I sucked the froth of the top of my glass and racked my brain for a conversational gambit. I didn't think an enquiry as to the health of 'Mademoiselle' would go down well, but I couldn't think of anything else. Eventually we must have bridged the gap created by four years of German occupation and the previous twenty of national misunderstandings. It turned out that the chaps in uniform were members of the Armentieres fire brigade, and that we were in their favourite cafe. They were, they said, very glad to see us. Things were quiet because the Germans had only recently left, and they had not yet quite got used to the idea.

It all got more friendly after that and the cafe began to fill up. Someone came up and whispered to one of the firemen, who put down his glass and said to us 'you are invited to dine with us. Everything is ready. Come with me.' We left the cafe, went round the corner and up a flight of stairs in a block of flats adjoining. He opened a door and showed us into a large room with a table laid for about a dozen people. Various other characters turned up and we all sat down.

It was one of those memorable evenings of which, in fact, one can usually remember very little next day. We ate, we drank, we even sang. And in French, too – *Alouette*, of course, and *J'ai perdu le do de ma clarinette* – the wine must have been good. It would have been long after midnight that an apologetic message came in from Madame le Commandant – she could not get to sleep, nor she feared could any of the neighbours. It was time to go. I did my best to express our thanks to Les Sapeurs-Pompiers d'Armentieres for the splendid hospitality, and we shook hands with everyone – sometimes more than once I suspect. We wandered off in search of the Jeeps. One refused to start, so we all piled into the other and returned to base. (When someone went to tow it in the next morning, the rotor-arm was found to be missing. It turned up in Harry Eastgate's pocket).

13 September

My Dearest Jean
Thank you so much for your letters: the post is rather better now but for a long time nothing could catch up. We had a very fast run up here with none of the conventional things happening. I got back near Bayeux [1 September] *by six: got a jeep at eight and we drove solemnly off to the Seine: we got there at 12.30 and I spent a chilly night with 3 blankets on a stretcher. I got up to the Flight next day and found my kit had departed into the blue.*

I ultimately got myself together and we moved off through France at speed. The further we went the better the hospitality until we ended up with the Captain of the Fire Brigade at one celebrated town [Armentiers] *with his Lieutenant named Maurice. They invited us to eat with them and I think we did in the end. It was the alcoholic preamble that made things remarkable. I feel that one could do much worse than become a fireman if that's how they live. If a fire had occurred things would have been amusing, at least for us.*

All this was more or less an introduction to what goes on now: I went to Brussels on a job and went into the town: more like a fair than anything else with enormous crowds surging down the streets full of geniality and hospitality.

It's very much the same here too, except of course the language is incomprehensible: everyone seems to speak some English however and there's nothing people won't do for you. All very nice. The only thing is that we cannot get any money of any sort, so we are all broke.

Things are very quiet here except for a very fine unexploded bomb which came down with a shriek and descended 20 feet into the ground. It was about 200 yards from the tent, about supper-time and we were all under the table with tea dripping onto us in no time. It's the good old Normandy training!

I trust there are no buzz-bombs: four fell in France for every one that came over the Channel. The bombing of the sites must have been extremely effective too. We came through an area of them, and they are very highly organised and de-centralised so that every village has a store or a headquarters for them.

So much for the past time: rather too much of a good thing and very tiring with no time for much except food and sleep.

You are not getting much fun at Winchester [HMS Flowerdown] *by the sound of it: come and join the BLA (now means Burma Looms Ahead). My boots, by the way, have just arrived: very fine things for idling in!*

The weather has improved here after some torrential rain and my things are drying nicely. No wasps, few mosquitoes and not too hot.

So much for the glorious present.

By this time, Guards Armoured had entered Brussels (3 September), to a tremendous welcome. 11th Armoured had captured Antwerp intact and the docks south of the Albert Canal. XII Corps was now to take over the northern flank of 2nd Army from XXX Corps, thus freeing them for the advance into Holland. The next day, 9 September, I flew off to find a landing-ground in Antwerp.

The ex-Luftwaffe airfield[1] seemed an ideal choice, if larger than we really needed, so I went back and reported. The Flight moved in that evening.

[Editor: In the Squadron Diary's entry for the ninth, Captain Scott (a friend of the author who later commanded 657 Squadron) flippantly records: '*5th* [sic] *September, Capt Munro selected Antwerp airport as A.L.G – Just about enough room. Capt Hargreaves and Capt Place have accidents due to very difficult ALG*' Such an incident would not have been possible: Captain Place was on leave in the UK and Captain Hargreaves did not join 'C' Flight until the following day, 10 Sept. The comment must indeed have been a light-hearted reminder of the much earlier episode described by Captain Burgess in the Flight Diary, 16 July: '*Capt Place tried to extinguish himself by hitting aircraft 960 violently against aircraft 958 during a take off. He was very annoyed. So was the flight commander. Capt Place showed his annoyance and flew away in 169. The flight commander concealed his annoyance magnificently. Maybe Capt Riding was feeling charitable having just evaded 3 FW190s which made a pass at him over Fontaine-Etoupefour*'. This episode had 'evaded' the spotlight of the Squadron Diary.]

It was pleasant to fly past Ghent at a leisurely 500 ft and look at its ancient buildings bright with flags. I felt we were really back in Europe again, with Paris, Brussels and the ancient towns of Flanders free and not seriously damaged. (After all the devastation of Normandy it was curiously exciting to see a steam-train puffing along the line; here was hope that civilisation had not come to an end.)

There were however some loose ends. Calais and Dunkirk were still in German hands; the enemy presence on the island of Walcheren and the north bank of the River Scheld likewise, denying us the use of the badly needed port of Antwerp. Worse still, the greater part of the German 15th Army had been allowed to cross over at Breskens into Walcheren and South Beveland without interference by XXX Corps or the RAF. We were to pay dearly for that oversight by General Horrocks in the months to come. As he wryly remarked years later – 'My name's Horrocks – not Napoleon.'. War, after all, is a series of loose ends, any one of which can trip up the most brilliant commander, and Horrocks was about as good as they come.[2]

We settled ourselves into the airfield. There was room for whole squadrons, let alone four little Austers and a dozen or so vehicles. Next morning I was up early, with work to be done, still with the Welsh Division. Shortly after breakfast a Jeep dashed up to the Flight office. The driver (who was also shouting into his wireless-set and reading a map all at once) uncoiled himself from the steering wheel and bounded through the door. This was Brigadier Friedberger, CRA 53rd Division, known as 'Mad Dick'. Before the war he had been a fearless steeplechase rider, with nerves of steel. He wanted a pilot to reconnoitre a big anti-tank ditch just north of the Albert Canal, and he wanted it done now. Freddie said I was just the chap and so I received instructions from the Brigadier exactly how, at what height and where I was to fly. (I got the impression that he would have been ready to leap into an aircraft and do the job himself, if he had not had more pressing commitments).

In fact we had some good aerial photographs of this ditch that could be quite easily plotted on the map without leaving the ground. It was also known that whole area was strongly defended with 88mm and 20mm flak originally sited against RAF night-fighters and bombers and I believed that if I followed the Brigadier's flying intructions I would probably not survive to tell the tale. So I just saluted, and went off to get my map, my pencil and my flying-helmet. Mad Dick shot off in his Jeep, leaving a cloud of dust, and sanity (as I understood it) returned. I did the job in my own way, flying well out of range of the opposition, to the complete satisfaction of the Brigadier.

If he liked to put it down to the care with which he had briefed me, who was I to complain?

[Editor: The Squadron diary reports that Captain Eastgate's aircraft was hit by tracer and small arms fire on 6 September after being poorly briefed and being *'sent too far over uncleared country… and being briefed for the second sortie whilst still airborne on the first sortie'*. *'10 Sept: Capt Munro spotted anti tank ditch N. of Albert Canal.'*]

Flying over Antwerp was a curious experience. The front-line was the Albert Canal in the dock-area of north of the city. Most of the time we were flying over Antwerp itself, and in the middle of it was the sheer-sided Boerentoren, said to be the highest inhabited building in Europe at that time. It made an ideal reference-point for lining up one's flight-pattern while observing – so long as one did not look down the side of the tower to

The Albert Canal – the front line in Antwerp.

the streets below. For some reason that brought on a feeling of giddiness, as if one was about to fall out of the aircraft.

There were advantages on the social side. Most evenings we would drive into the town after supper and try the various bars. By day, life in Antwerp seemed to go on normally, but in the evening certain cafes became meeting-places for small groups of civilians armed with rifles and pistols. After discussing plans over a glass or two of brandy they would infiltrate the German-held areas near the canal and do as much damage as they could to any Germans they met. Some of these 'White Army' men claimed to have been tortured by the Gestapo, and they showed injuries to prove it. They also told us something of the organised cruelty at the nearby Breendonck concentration camp,[3] where Belgians were held for offences against the German occupation-forces. They would not accept drinks on our account, so they were obviously not trying to cash in on our sympathy.

For a few days we flew sorties over Antwerp, looking north into the flat countryside with its villages and doing shoots on targets like the splendid star-shaped Fort de Merxem – a relic of the classic era of fortification. However, it was quite clear that the front had stabilised and that no progress was going to be made through the floods north of the River Scheldt into Dutch Zeeland, for the time being. It was the end of a phase and of XII Corps operations that had started less than a month ago in the break out from Normandy. Once again it was XXX Corps under Lieutenant General Horrocks who would be required to take a new initiative and that could only mean a move into the dreary flat landscapes of southeast Holland – the provinces of Brabant and Limburg.

We began to edge tentatively southeast along the Albert Canal, a waterway crossed by dozens of small Cantilever bridges; each of which had been demolished with German precision in exactly the same way. One bearer or buttress on the north side was blown up, causing the end of the span to drop bodily into the canal bank. To the layman, it seemed only necessary to jack up the span again and shore it in place with cribs. Not only were we moving into a spell of poor weather but also the fields available to us for landing-grounds were miserable strips, intersected with ditches. Everything, it seemed, squelched underfoot and even the firmest piece of grassland was soon cut up into muddy ruts under the pressure of wheels. We were now, in fact, in Holland.

On 21 September, we moved onto the Luftwaffe airfield at Eindhoven, not far from the big Philips factory to the west of the town. The runways and taxi-tracks were surfaced with millions of red bricks, all beautifully laid on sand. At first we had the place to ourselves, but when a wing of 83rd Group Typhoons moved in, we withdrew into a quiet corner, using the taxi-tracks as our runways. There was a light railway on one side of the airfield, in working order, and this attracted much interest although I never managed to get a ride on it. Less attractive was a big store-room, which we thought might be good for the cook-house, but it turned out to be full of 'butterfly-bombs', which could be dropped by air, with little parachutes and wings that opened out as they fell. These devices were anti-personnel weapons.

Between 17 and 25 September, while XII Corps was un-dramatically making its way northwards into Holland, the tragedy of Arnhem was being played out not many miles to the north. It was an operation called 'Market Garden'. The plan was for two airborne divisions – one American (the 82nd), one British (1st) – and the Polish Parachute Brigade – to be dropped in daylight to capture bridges over the rivers and canals on the road to Arnhem; they were expected to link up with the US 101st Airborne Division whose task was to capture Eindhoven. Meanwhile XXX Corps, in the shape of

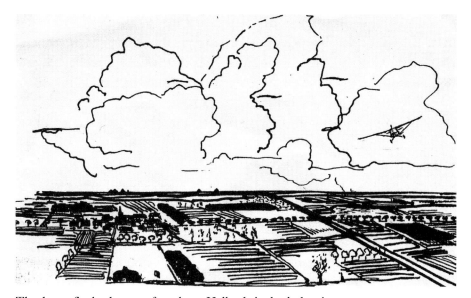

The dreary flat landscapes of southeast Holland. Author's drawing.

Guards Armoured Division, was to drive north from Bourg Leopold on the Belgian border and open up a road corridor using the captured bridges. They would thus open the way for 2nd Army into North Germany, across the River Maas and the two arms of the River Rhine, called the Waal and the Lower Rhine (or Neder Rijn) respectively.

Despite intense fighting, of which the towns of Nijmegen and Arnhem bore the brunt, together with brave efforts to supply the airborne forces by air, the operation failed. On either side of Nijmegen the enemy had repeatedly cut the road; the Guards Armoured were hampered by a shortage of supplies and the follow-up by 43rd Division lacked the determination for which its commander was renowned. By 25 September it was obvious that the Allies could no longer hold off the German forces and the 1st Airborne Division was ordered to withdraw from the northern side of the Rhine. Operation Market Garden's objective may or may not have been realistic, but the fact was that Monty's gamble had failed. The Allied armies would relapse into Eisenhower's strategy – if it deserves the name – of separate uncoordinated thrusts along the whole front. Whatever chance there might have been of ending the war in 1944 had disappeared into the autumn chill of Holland.[4]

The contribution we in 'C' Flight made to Operation Market Garden was minimal and no doubt the same was true of 53rd Division.[5] The weather had turned wet and misty, with visibility that made flying pointless. Due to the poor flying conditions, much of the flight's time was spent playing gin-rummy and the diary records that guests from 'B' Flight were 'robbed at Bridge' during what was said to have been a 'very pleasant social evening'. Visits were paid to sample the nightlife of Eindhoven, but it was thought to be much inferior to Antwerp – which was quite understandable in the circumstances. Whenever the weather did lift, we seized the opportunity to fly: sorties were flown to make photo runs, investigate bridges or even to do the occasional shoot. On 25 September I had the novel experience of firing a battery of 12inch Howitzers – a fairly elephantine performance. It seemed to need ten minutes to reload after every round fired, which destroyed any sense of urgency. The explosions on the ground were gratifying and impossible to overlook.

Tom Place came back from sick leave in the UK on 29 September, but was not to stay with us for long. He had begun to suffer from bouts of double vision, which was eventually diagnosed as the result of battle-exhaustion.

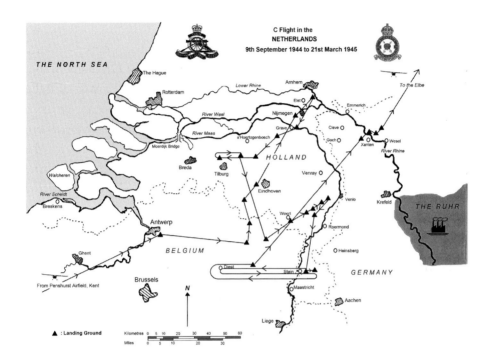

C Flight in the
NETHERLANDS
9th September 1944 to 21st March 1945

He had, in fact, kept going long beyond his elastic-limit and, on 5 October, he left us to return to the UK for a rest. He was a good deal older than the rest of us and probably should not have been posted to a flight in the first place, simply on grounds of age. But he was the last person to give up and we were to miss his steadying influence.[6] At least his replacement was Harry Eastgate who came into the Flight once more, this time to stay.

October had just begun and already it felt like late autumn with winter not far away. The general feeling of gloom was further increased since, as the Flight Diary records: 'the C.O. visited us later in the day and we were sorry – No, 'Cheesed' I think is the *mot juste* – to hear that we were going in for a spell as intercom flight' which meant transporting senior officers around as if we were flying taxi drivers. There were some reasons to be cheerful however – 6 October was a red-letter day; the sun came out and dried our washing and that evening we went to an ENSA concert in Eindhoven, which was an unqualified success.

October 8

My Darling Jean
We are still hanging around doing nothing much: we were at Eindhoven for
a while where we had a very decent hut on the edge of a wood complete with
doors and a roof: the doors rather full of holes and the windows missing, but
with shutters up and a stove, things were pretty cosy.

The only trouble was the usual Germans who kept getting captured in
the woods around. One imagined quite a number of things in the still of an
evening.

We got caught up in the usual crowd of Civil Affairs, Town Majors and
ENSA parties and gladly moved on. Once they get in, it's time to move. The
free and easy life departs too and most of the cafés shut!

At the moment we have a private orchard which is a cause for satisfaction
although the pears want to ripen a bit. The grapes are rather sour too but
are all right if kept.

The weather is not too bad: cold but fairly dry. The problem of housing
will no doubt solve itself in Germany but just now we keep fairly comfortable
in tents.

I don't know what the leave angle is because though it's nearly due to end
one cycle, we may wait a month before beginning again. I don't know why,
any time will suit me.

Just now we are in the Cigar Country: every man his weed [refers to
the variety of tobaccos] *and some of them are shocking. Prince Bernhardt*
(whom God preserve) gave 35 to every member of one corps, for which he
will have to answer one day. Goodness knows where they all come from.

I don't know what the form is re the war – I take it you have more news
than I. The odd newspaper comes through but what we want is some gen
from the big chiefs themselves. I don't think the Germans can take much
more.

This is the close season just now: no work before 7.30 or after 6 and anyway
the visibility is pretty poor. It ensures a maximum of sleep interrupted by
meals.

I hope to get a day off sometime and go to Brussels. Which is rather better
organised for relieving people of their spare cash than any other place I

*know. One can get a bath and a change of scenery which is a great deal. I
saw a hill the other day and it was quite an event. Canals and ditches are
the only feature usually, with the odd windmill.*

When, on the ninth, we were given the order to leave intercoms flying and
join 50th Division we were more cheerful. We moved up past Nijmegen to
The Island, a large area of low-lying country between the Waal at Nijmegen
and the Neder Rijn at Arnhem. The landing-ground we occupied was near
Elst where we dug ourselves in, if only as far as the water table let us.[7]
Between Arnhem and us, the Neder Rijn flowed beneath a shallow cliff on
which stood Oosterbeek, the site of the heaviest fighting during the airborne
attack. The woodlands on top were splashed with blobs of bright colour,
which were parachute canopies caught in the branches – the relics of the
supply-drops. As the days passed these parachutes vanished – pulled down
by the Germans or the Dutch. There was nothing left by the end of the week
to remind us of what had happened – still less of what might have been.

For a while we shared the landing ground with 'A' and 'B' Flights and
some genial Americans; I traded my useless .38 Webley pistol with an
American sergeant for a bottle of whisky and a .30 semi-automatic carbine
with a folding butt – an ideal weapon for carrying in the aircraft. Poor Harry
Eastgate was left behind at Squadron HQ to carry on with communications
and we got a camera aircraft instead. It was all go again: Butch did two shoots
in the Arnhem area with 90th Field and in the bright intervals between rain
and poor visibility; Freddie flew the camera aircraft, while I escorted him
to keep an eye out for German fighters. Divisional HQ warmly thanked
him for the photos he took – they were indeed very good. We were learning
how to use these fixed, sideways-looking cameras, which could be set for
individual shots, or more usually for long runs. At HQ we were lucky to have
a real enthusiast in John Harrison, who made a speciality of photographic
techniques. Being himself a pilot, he knew what was needed and was expert
enough to provide it. After that we only had to press the button and fly
straight and level – John and the camera would do the rest.

On 12 October I managed to do an interesting shoot, on a villa at the
top of the bluff. Taking advantage of the sunny morning, I had been flying
along the river when I saw a glint from one of the upstairs windows in

one of the villas. It looked like a reflection of the sunlight. I came back for another look and the same thing happened. I reckoned someone was looking at the aircraft through binoculars – it wasn't just a windowpane flashing. So I called up the guns and began to range on the house, with the usual method of shooting 'over and under' then banging away in the middle. With the benefit of my Normandy experiences, instead of putting down the whole regiment on it and wasting ammunition I decided to do the job with a single gun.

The target being on top of the bluff posed a problem: any rounds not falling short and instead passing over would land out of sight in the trees beyond. So it would be difficult to know at what point I had bracketed it correctly and would thus be able to engage it effectively. However I stuck to the book, completed my ranging and then went to fire for effect with a single gun. On seeing the result falling just short of the house, onto the bluff below, I gave a fine adjustment by raising the 'angle of sight' on the gun (this compensates for the difference in height between the gun-position and target). The very slight change worked and I got an effective hit on the house and followed it up with five more from the single gun. There were no more flashes from the window and I reckoned some German would be looking for a new OP.

Just a few days later on the seventeenth, despite the weather closing in again, we were encouraged to hear that 50th Division had successfully defended 'the Island' against the ferocious enemy attacks on their positions. They would be able to pull out and we would be re-deployed elsewhere. One reason we were glad to go was that the Germans were mucking about with the sluices that control the heights of most of the waterways in Holland and we were getting flooded out. There was water and mud everywhere and taking off in it splashed mud over the windows and windscreen. By the time we left it was touch and go whether we could get the aircraft off the ground at all.

I learned that one of the casualties of 43rd Division's vain attempt to break through to Arnhem was Lieutenant Colonel Bishell,[8] from 94th Field. A shell had landed just beside him while he was giving orders and killed him instantly. 'C' Flight lost a good friend and I felt it particularly since I worked with his regiment in England and in Normandy. The war was wearing away these links with the past and strange faces were everywhere.

We were, however, adapting ourselves quite well to operating in a part of the world that was simply not suited to provide landing-grounds for even the smallest of aircraft. The agricultural system seemed to be based on the more conservative practices of the Middle Ages – a multitude of narrow strips, intersected by ditches and farm-tracks. These were peppered with groups of modest dwellings that offered minimal shelter and comfort to the quite large families who lived in them. Even the names of these hamlets seemed odd to us – Erp, Donk, Oss, Eersel and also Olland, which must surely have been a misprint. We had even acquired a little Dutch. On the island of Elst we had found a man who offered to cut our hair, which was getting rather un-regimental, in exchange for cigarettes. The man himself had a style that would have gone down well at the Guards' depot, so we looked up the Dutch for 'not too short' and told him to get cracking. 'Niet te koort', I said firmly as he began work, but it didn't seem to register and we all ended up looking like prizefighters anyway.

Shopping expeditions in Nijmegen and Eindhoven produced very little, apart from one classic phrase that described the economy of occupied Europe in a nutshell. Whatever one sought to buy, in whatever kind of shop, there was nothing on display. The black market ruled supreme and '*nix in die winkel alles in die keller*' [sic] was the reply. 'Nothing in the window – it's all in the cellar'. Holland, in fact, had gone underground. You had to know your way around.

For most Europeans World War Two was experienced not as a war of movement and battle but as a daily degradation, in the course of which men and women were betrayed and humiliated, forced into daily acts of petty crime and self-abasement, in which everyone has lost something and many have lost everything.[9]

That apart, people were most helpful – usually in inverse ratio to their wealth. (There was nothing new in that). Frequently, people who were obviously hard up offered us the very small silver Queen Wilhelmina coins – five cents, I think – which they said they had kept as tokens of loyalty to their queen. (All the other bronze and silver coins having been taken by the Germans, melted down and replaced by grubby looking, cheap discs of zinc). Much as we would have liked to take the coins as souvenirs we did not feel able to accept them even as gifts. They represented a symbol of Dutch loyalty and the people of the villages were in any case, short of almost everything, especially food. The Germans had looted the whole country before our arrival.

And so, on 18 October, we pulled back to Grave and the Flight diary records that we got ourselves very comfortably installed in billets. Autumn was indeed upon us, with winter following close behind. We took the chance to clean everything up (including ourselves) after the mud of Elst, and Butch Pritchard and Joe Hargreaves made a reconnaissance into Brussels. Their report was most encouraging. We soon got our marching orders. There was an operation afoot to clear the area south of the River Maas (or Meuse) from Nijmegen westward to 's-Hertogenbosch and Tilburg, where elements of the German 15th Army under the indefatigable von Rundstedt were holding out. (He had done his best to make our lives uncomfortable by blowing locks, sluices and dykes, as he said in an order of 7 September, 'to put North Belgium under water'. It certainly gave us good practice in making landing-grounds out of sodden meadowland).

From the north of Antwerp, lst Canadian Army under General Simonds (including 1st British Corps, again under his command) was to launch attacks to clear the Germans from south of the Lower Maas, thus linking up with XII Corps in the Breda-Tilburg area. Few of us, if any, had any idea of the topography of this singularly dreary part of the Low Countries. Even the mighty Rhine seems to lose all sense of direction or purpose in these parts, although the Maas, just south of it, makes quite a good attempt at getting to the North Sea in one piece. (Or at least did, until the Dutch started messing it about with their new delta scheme).

Capt. R.L. Munro
C Flight
653 AOP Sqdn
RAF BLA
22nd [October 1944]

My darling Jean,
Thank you for the good map, which just about fits the area! I know roughly
what's where now. I call this learning geography the hard way and the
occasional map is a help.

I hope to get some leave soon: mid November at the height of the fog
period. It will be a change from this rather determined rain which has just
about sunk Holland. A little more and we shall have to be evacuated by the
Navy. Luckily we've had a fine day today. The last field I left was a mud
patch and we staggered out in a shower of spray.

Still, we've got a house now: bags of milk and a stove, which we expect
to leave any moment now! Tents are very unsatisfactory in continual rain,
so we shall just have to get another house. There is a roof shortage in our
expected area, so we will stay here until the last.

Nothing special has been on around here: we haven't seen any jet planes
yet but two bombs appeared from a clear sky so we reckon it must have been
from them. The worst thing is this Dutch: very hard to speak and we can
only guess what double-Dutch is. Not so good maybe. We get around though.

What's on in S. England? I suppose the general situation is quite good;
less blackout and so forth. It's the trains they want to get organised first,
then the licensed trade. Incidentally we wrote to Guinness about all this
"Beer for the forces" racket, since we haven't had a bottle since Falaise, but
no answer, so far. Rumour has it that the Germans have a secret weapon, a
mine that sinks all beer-carrying ships. The stock excuse is always "Oh the
ship bringing it over got sunk". I expect the RASC [Royal Army Service
Corps] *drink it all (perish the thought).*

No King seen: he didn't get far enough and anyhow we are too busy to
bother about visitors – playing cards usually. It's all very busy and so on.

We are being flooded by leaflets on how to be demobilised, but there is a
certain vagueness about the whole job which rather spoils it. This Burma
Looms Ahead business is also bad. Luckily we are used to a diet of rice and
Holland largely swamp as far as I can see.

We sustained a nasty blow in Brussels – no hot water just now due to miners on strike, so I haven't been over. Also the electricity is very short.

Nothing exciting doing: routine bashing of Germans continues unabated – till further notice, one presumes. Meanwhile we are conducting the war with caution and we hope, dignity.

We joined the medium gunners (3rd AGRA) for this operation, named 'Pheasant' for no known reason and we got down to marking up our maps and looking at air-photos [Editor: Operation 'Pheasant' was to liberate middle and eastern Brabant area of Holland and began 20 October. Operation 'Colin', part of 'Pheasant' was 23 October with the advance to Schijndel, and also liberated Vught on 26/27. The advance on Schijndel began from St Michielsgestel. 51st HD was fighting under command of 1st Canadian Army]. Our task was 'counter-spotting the positions of hostile artillery batteries' by looking for the effects of shelling, directly observing the flashes from guns, or by locating them by taking bearings on their sound. This was all new stuff to us, and entailed observing from 2,000 ft. It also meant providing continuous cover, with one pilot relieving another at half-hourly intervals. This again was not really our style.

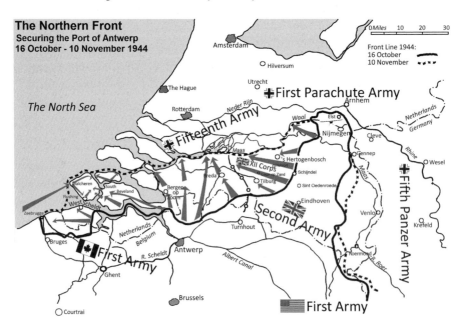

The Northern Front
Securing the Port of Antwerp
16 October - 10 November 1944

There were four divisions involved in 'Pheasant' – 15th Scottish, 51st Highland, 53rd Welsh and the 7th Armoured, the former 'Desert Rats', who were now looking somewhat bedraggled having had a thoroughly undistinguished campaign so far in Europe. They were to operate through country, which in its own way was as dangerous and frustrating as the Normandy *bocage* of evil memory. There was a network of dykes and minor waterways intersecting the whole area; woods, coppices and rows of poplars; the roads had no solid bottom to them and were necessarily steeply embanked; the water-table had risen so high that when you tried to dig a slit-trench it filled with water in a matter of minutes. Much of the time it was raining and when it was not raining, it was misty and dank. To cap it all, mines and minefields abounded.

Flooded Holland on a good (clear) day.

Butch Pritchard, our faithful diarist summed it all up, 'the battle progressed smoothly, but owing to poor visibility 'C' Flight did not do much to help it'. It got so bad that between 23 and 28 October we were virtually weather-bound. To avoid being left stranded in the rear, hobnobbing with such things as mobile bath-units and other camp-followers, we abandoned our better judgement on the twenty-fifth and tried to move forward to a new landing-ground at Vehgel, during a momentary clearance in the mist. As soon as we were airborne it closed in again. I managed to get down in a field which was being used by 'A' Flight; Joe landed beside some abandoned US gliders at St Oedenrode (relics of Arnhem) and Butch actually made it, with Freddie popping off Verey lights to help him in. (We all managed to get together again in time for tea, which was just as well since the next two days were even worse).

The upshot was that we lost touch with our gunners and were reduced to having a field day on maintenance, playing gin rummy and going to an ENSA show in Eindhoven. We could hardly believe our eyes on the twenty-eighth when the weather cleared and we could see the church of nearby St Oedenrode standing out clear against the sodden landscape. Freddie was off in a flash to find a new field for us near Helvort. We ended what was a frustrating month, just north of Tilburg at Loon op Zand.

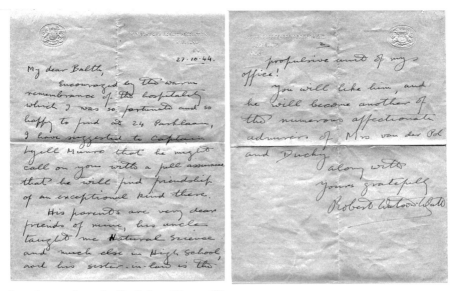

Introductory letter by Sir Robert Watson-Watt.

[Editor: Amongst the papers left by Captain Munro was a letter that he would have received when near Eindhoven in late October or early November. Dated 27 October and addressed to 'Balth' it was a introductory letter written and signed by Sir Robert Watson-Watt. The latter was a family friend whose personal assistant also happened to be Captain Munro's sister-in-law.

Internet research revealed 'Balth' as Balthasar van der Pol who, in 1922, had been appointed head physicist at Philips Physical Laboratory in Eindhoven. 'Van der Pol was one of the most interesting characters in the whole history of Philips Research, he was a gifted speaker, a man of great culture in its widest sense and he contributed greatly to fundamental radio theory and to the reputation of Philips. He left Philips in 1949 and died ten years later at the age of 70': Ronald Dekker, Philips, Eindhoven. In 1920, Van der Pol had been a correspondent with Edward Appleton (later Sir Edward Appleton) concerning the radio detection of thunderstorms. At the same time Watson-Watt was working separately on the subject but a year later Watson-Watt and Appleton were working together for the Radio Research Board.

In 1939 Philips were the sole supplier of the EF50 valve – a key component in early RADAR that was technically difficult to produce. It had been wrongly assumed that Mullard in Britain produced the valve. At effectively the last minute, in February or March of 1940, it was discovered that 'for the production of one of the key components of their precious Radar systems, they depended on tubes imported from Holland, which was itself under threat of invasion by Germany'. Almost certainly at the behest of Watson-Watt, the head of Philips valve production Theodoor Philibert Tromp, travelled to meet with him in the office of S.S. Eriks, the managing director of Mullard in Britain in Century House in Shaftsbury Avenue, London. This would not have been easy to arrange due to the restrictions on travel imposed after the declaration of war.

Although unaware why the valves are needed, Tromp arranges urgently to provide tooling for Mullard to produce the valves in Britain.

The technicians and tool shops at the Emmasingel work day and night to comply with Tromp's request, and finally in the evening of 9 May a truck was loaded with the machines which had been hurriedly put together … It was, for everybody, clear that the Germans could invade Holland any moment, but nobody loading that truck that evening could have guessed that hours later, around five o'clock the next morning, the Germans would actually cross the border with Holland. Having no idea of the events that lay ahead, the driver headed to Vlissingen where the precious cargo would be transported to Britain by one of the ships of Zeeland Steamer Company (ZSM). After the war in England had officially started the 1st of September 1939, service to Harwich had become difficult. From the 25th of November service was suspended altogether, and all ships were grounded. The shipment of the machines and components therefore must have been carefully planned. Most likely Tromp himself played an important role here. Besides his job with Philips, Tromp also happened to be a government commissioner (regerings commissaris) with the ZSM. By the time the Germans crossed the border, the machines and components in all probability had already been loaded into one of the ships, and when news reached the coast of the events at the Dutch-German border, all three ships of the ZSM were hurriedly prepared to leave for England. On sea, all three ships were attacked by German airplane bombers and the Princes Juliana was damaged so badly that it had to return to Hoek van Holland. The brand new sister ships Koningin Emma and Princes Beatrix were also attacked, but safely reached Downs. Which one of these two ships carried the tubes is unfortunately unknown. The ships reached London on the 15th of May 1940, where they were converted for military service. The head office of the ZSM in Vlissingen was damaged so badly during German attacks that after the war the service was resumed from Hoek van Holland.

Having returned to Eindhoven:

… from 1942 Tromp became more and more involved in the Dutch Resistance and espionage for the Allie[s]. He financed the resistance, helped other colleagues involved in espionage leaving the country, and was involved in the building and setting up of a backup radio transmitter network which should come into action in case the Germans would destroy the Dutch broadcast transmitters in an invasion of the Allied Forces. He gathered crucial information regarding the production for the Germans of Philips and other companies in occupied Holland. [Theodoor Tromp by Ronald Dekker].
    [I] had the possibility of making microfilms and sending them over to England though various routes, I have sent over to London all the

manufacturing specifications of these German Tubes. Later during the war, when a radio transmitter and radio telegraphist was dropped from England, I obtained the possibility of sending secret coded telegrams to England.' Tromp in a letter of 1979.

There was a pleasing symmetry in the way Watson-Watt was keen to meet his old friend Van der Pol, having met with Tromp at the start of hostilities.

In the uncertainties of the post-capitulation weeks and months it was, however, desirable that we should explore, more conveniently and completely, those technical devices of the enemy which, though happily less successful in the aggregate than our own, still had lessons for the future defence of a civilization already under the shadow of new threats ... we explored the uses to which the enemy had put the great Philips Gloelampenfabriek installations at Eindhoven. Our talks with pre-war friends and colleagues there were occasionally interspersed with the crackle of rifle and machine-gun fire as the Moffe were gradually (a little too gradually for our complete comfort) winkled out from their woodland cover. Bean soup can seldom have tasted more delicious than when it came from a big pot in the garden of my old friends the van der Pols, whom I had not seen since I gave a talk at the Philips Laboratories in 1937. [Watson-Watt: Three Steps to Victory].

What part Captain Munro was able to play in bringing about the reunion may never be known. In the 1950s one of his most treasured possessions was an expensive, state-of-the-art transistor radio, made by Philips].

November opened on a more cheerful note – the sun shone and I did a couple of shoots to celebrate. It was too good a chance to be missed. [Flight Diary *(Butch Pritchard) 1 November: Although visibility was very good there was little in the way of Bosche activity to be seen – however Capt Munro's keen eyes found a couple of guns which he duly engaged. Later he again shot 72 Med. Regt at an orchard that had a suspicious look*]. The next day I had another go at a pontoon bridge over the Maas which was reported to be put across at night and moored along the bank by day; no bridge was found but boats fastened along the bank were targeted with a 72 Medium Regiment and when their number increased they were given more of the same treatment –

it certainly improved my morale and I hope it depressed the Germans. Soon after that it was obvious that we were running out of Germans – or they were running out on us. We had a final fling with a small operation to expel them from north of Tilburg and 's-Hertogenbosch, which had by now been liberated (in the best sense). It would clear the whole of the south bank of the Maas from Nijmegen to its estuary north of Breda. This involved another continuous-cover job, looking for hostile guns. I was up at 2,000 ft, feeling as usual rather over-exposed, when I noticed a large lattice-girder bridge well over to the west. It spanned the river (passing over the Hollandsche Diep channel, south of Dordrecht) as it widens out at its estuary.

As I looked at it through binoculars I noticed little puffs of smoke spring out of its structure and then the surface of the river began to ruffle. The whole thing seemed to be breaking up as I watched it and then great sections of steel started to fall into the river, until the whole bridge had collapsed. This was the Moerdijk road and rail bridge and its destruction by demolition meant that the German 15th Army had retreated into North Holland.

(Many years later I had to go to a meeting at the German Ministry of Defence in Bonn, with a friend of mine in the Ministry of Defence. We decided to go by rail, being fed up with British European Airways. As our luxury 'Rheingold' express rushed south of Rotterdam heading for the German border at Venlo, it shot across a huge steel bridge over the Maas – at Moerdijk. Ironically, we were going to discuss with the Germans a joint project to develop a mobile self-propelled pontoon bridge (called the 'M2'). I wondered if some of our German colleagues at our meetings had perhaps been among the dispirited troops who had retreated across the Moerdijk Bridge in 1944).

Having cleared the Germans out of that sector, it was decreed that XII Corps should be rewarded for its success by giving an encore along the west bank of the Maas between Roermond and Venlo. The upshot was that 'C' Flight moved to a new landing-ground at Peer, in Belgium, which turned out to be some three miles from Bourg Leopold where we had set up shop on 17 September – the fateful day on which the airborne divisions had set out for Arnhem with such high hopes of 'victory by Christmas'. It hardly looked like that. We were a lot wiser now and a little sadder as well.

However, we were young and youth being what it is, there is no trace of despondency in the Flight diary. Three of us went off to Brussels where 'a good time was had by all'. (Which, being interpreted, would probably mean a few drinks in the officers' club and then dinner at the Belgian Aero Club, which had opened its membership to such as ourselves for the duration. After that, a stroll along the Rue des Arts and down the side street where the bars seemed to be occupied almost exclusively by young (and not so young) women wearing dresses with plunging necklines and skirts designed to reveal rather than conceal. We bought two of the girls a drink (fizzy lemonade at champagne prices) and passed on. As one of us said later, rather wistfully, 'Ah can get it for nowt in Yorksheer').

What we really appreciated on our Brussels visits was the outward signs of civilisation; being waited on in a restaurant with a clean tablecloth, choosing food from a menu, a long hot bath and laundered sheets on the bed. And not having to turn out for a dawn sortie, only to find one couldn't see the length of the field for mist and rain. Looking back, how well the British soldiery behaved – of all ranks. Of course we all drank too much an occasions, but there was no rowdy-ism; I don't remember seeing or hearing of anyone breaking up a bar and those who had a drop too much were either happy or somnolent. How different, it must be said, from the behaviour of the US soldiers who soon began to find Brussels a convenient centre for 'recreation'. We soon became the poor relations and went there less and less.

Back at the landing-ground it was business as usual: rain, mist, mud and increasing cold. The cast was the same: 15th Scottish, 53rd Welsh and 7th Armoured. The landscape was, if anything, even more depressing. We were now moving up the west bank of the Maas towards Blerick, a suburb of Venlo just across the Xaas and on the edge of the 'Peel' country. Now 'peel' in Banffshire means a pool, as I suspect it does in Low German dialects elsewhere and what with the flooding of the Maas itself and the rise in the water-table the area round the little town of Weert could not have been better named. It was wringing wet, overhead and underfoot. 'Rain all day – no flying'; 'a very high wind and rain – no flying today'; 'move to new ALG postponed due to bad weather'; 'two three-tonners stuck in the mud – got out with aid of a Scammel from the 59th Heavy Regiment'; 'ALG waterlogged – made a new one'. We would have been better off with flying boats.

To cap it all, we were woken up on the night of the twenty-sixth by the sound of German aircraft nearby. They dropped flares and followed that up with a carpet of anti-personnel bombs that stopped unrolling about three fields away. We had failed to put camouflage nets over the aircraft and felt very exposed. Oh how we wished we had! And if only we had dug some slit trenches, too. ('A rain-sodden ridge tent is not bomb-proof' – write it out ten times). Joe Hargreaves, however, had dug a trench, in the low embankment of a farm road alongside our field. He jumped in, clad only in shirt and underpants, to find it had quietly filled up with icy rainwater. Luckily the Ju 88s decided they had frightened us sufficiently (which indeed they had) and caused no more trouble that night.

Human nature being what it is, we spent the next day digging the slit trenches we should have dug the day before. They also filled up with water. I relieved my feelings by doing a shoot on a large grey gas-holder in Venlo, which was being used as an enemy OP; I had hopes of causing a major explosion, but nothing happened. The next day I had another go, using only one medium gun, with the same result. (As I went past in the train, on my way to Bonn many years later, I noticed that the gas-holder had been removed. I doubt if it would have been much use to the community after we had finished with it).

Venlo's indomitable gas-holder.

The month ended typically: 'the strip had become somewhat muddy and the aircraft were moved to another field in the afternoon'. But we had tried; we had flown 114 sorties and flown fifty-nine hours, with just five shoots. We had occupied nine landing-grounds, mostly made usable with our own hands – laying strips of grass together, removing wire fences and posts, filling in ditches and chopping down poplar trees (we tried explosive charges but it did not always work – and anyway it looked untidy).

December began (typically) with another move that brought us to within a few miles of Blerick, the last German position west of the Xaas. It was due for the chop. It was however, protected by a 600-yard belt of barbed wire, mines,

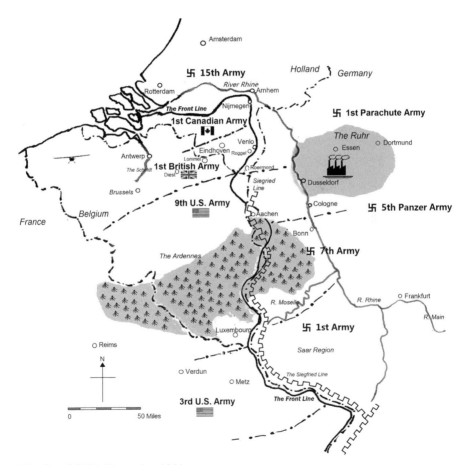

The Stand Off in December 1944.

an anti-tank ditch and another deep minefield, then a network of trenches. There was, therefore, to be a set-piece attack, by the indefatigable 15th Scottish, preceded by the specialised fortress-busting tackle and vehicles operated by 79th Armoured Division. (This was Operation. 'Guildford'). Our job, once more, was spotting enemy batteries, or anything else that could be troublesome. The combination of the armoured 'funnies' and the Scots proved overwhelming, and Blerick was almost painlessly eliminated by nightfall on 3 December.

This seemed to enrage the Germans, now relegated to the east bank around Venlo. Next day, as Harry was pottering about looking for something at which to shoot, they took a poke at him with some 88mm flak guns. (Their shells burst with an oily black cloud of smoke and a thump on the aircraft as if you were inside a drum). We had never heard of an Auster being hit by a 88mm, but then there could always be a first time. After that they attacked Freddie during his engagement of a hostile battery he had spotted. Some sixty rounds were fired at him, while he calmly got on with his shoot and he rounded it off, literally, by doing a couple of loops before going in to land. As the diary entry for 8 December said, there was 'much serious thought in the flight'.

That being the end of Blerick, we were pulled back a few miles along the way we had come and installed ourselves near Roggel beside a small farmhouse and a steeply embanked road that ran between Roermond on the Maas and Helmond in the north. The weather promptly reverted to normal – unfit for flying. We passed the time as best we could, devising new schemes for sharpening up our flash-spotting and getting a rapid reaction to our reports from the infantry. Gin rummy filled in the gaps when we were not poring over air-photos or studying maps. Freddie and Harry even attended a Squadron dance (of all things) at Weert one night.

December 5th

My Darling Jean,

Large prospects of a watery grave have gone by the board: mud, yes, but total immersion in one's sleep seems remote. We got to drier ground having used up 3 landing strips in as many days. We have room in a house which owns eggs as well as four walls and a roof, so that's a good thing.

A major internal crisis has just passed by – slightly worrying for us, but we have got our way. It's awful when you have to do your superior's job as well as ones own, but that's what's got to be done I suppose when all else fails. Things may go better now the situation is clear. We are too close to Germany to be fussy about personalities, but it's not pleasant.[10]

I hope you haven't quite despaired of my letter-writing capabilities. There is almost nothing to say about the local news except that we have temporarily run out of Germans, but what a topic!

We got some Christmas cards from TAF (Tactical Air Force) which are quite jolly. Parts of it are still to be explored, as you will see. My only hope is we will get round the circuit before my next leave!

How do you find the heights of Winchester these cold winters days? There's nothing to beat fresh air but you must be rather weary of a perpetual passage of it past you.

I hope my last letter was not as mournful as it seems in retrospect! Things were a little much there at the time. Even though they pass, how different they leave one. I realize what a long time has been spent at this racket and how far one drifts from the past. I think I'll cash in on the job, grow a ginger moustache and forget I ever existed otherwise. Perhaps it wouldn't work: the prospect is not too encouraging.

So on it goes – talk about too much leisure. I must take to cross-word puzzles and stop thinking about anything except next leave.

Things were livened up over the next few days by the arrival of the first jet aircraft. These were German Me.262s and they were quite prepared to stick around. Having watched our A/A trying to hit them, there was no reason why they should not. One of them came down the road at 50 ft over a column of bren-carriers and trucks belonging to 15th Scottish. It was being desperately pursued by two Spitfires, which were banging away at it with their cannons, without the slightest effect. There was more serious thought in 'C' Flight. We were doing long sorties at 2,000 ft plus and were easy meat for a low–flying jet.[11]

Letter of 23 December: *Not less unsettling but very funny have been the jet planes. They look very harmless but make a noise just like a bomb, so you never know if one has been dropped or if the plane is passing over harmlessly. We got chased into a ditch by one which came straight for us at no height at all, chased by a fighter or so.*

At this rather trying point, on 21 December, SHQ decided to move Freddie over to 'B' Flight and I was told to take over the Flight. This meant that I would be required to spend less time in the air and a lot more in a Jeep reconnoitering new strips by road and liaising with our masters. I did not complain, however, since Geoff Pollitt our CO had only a week or so previously asked me if I would like to go back to the UK and train as a flying instructor. (Apparently they wanted one or two pilots with operational experience). He was kind to ask me, but I said no; I felt I must see it through with the Flight to the end, having come so far.

[Squadron Diary 20 December: *Capt. Thompson took over command of 'C' Flight from Capt. Riding. Capt Riding took over Capt. Bandy's section in 'B' Flight. Lt Turnbull promoted to A/Capt. and posted to 'C' Flight. Captains Scott and Bandy leave for an instructors course in the UK.* (There is no other record that Captain Thompson took command of, or even flew in 'C' Flight).

Flight diary (Butch Pritchard): *21 No flying – thick fog. Capt Riding relinquishes command of Flight to Capt Munro and leaves for 'B' flight in the morning.* Captain Riding was mentioned frequently in the Squadron Diary afterwards and it was clear that he was a very active 'B' Flight section leader.]

By now the Hawker Tempests were putting in an appearance. These powerful new propeller aircraft *[developed from the Hawker Typhoon]* had a sporting chance of bouncing a jet if they were around at the right moment. However, we decided to do our own thing, and whenever we had a plane up on a sortie we kept an officer on watch, who would be in wireless touch with the pilot. We took the parachutes over to Eindhoven and had them repacked;

after being thrown about in the back of a three-tonner since D-Day they probably needed it. We also got some US flak jackets, or rather waistcoats, which were not too heavy and were generally worn by the Liberator and Fortress crews. Armour plate was still out, because of its weight – and it had a higher priority on the floor of the new flight-commander's Jeep and under his bottom, in case of land mines.

The weather was now doing its worst, with fog rising out of the sodden ground night and morning. It began on 19 December, and persisted for several days. On the twenty-third we were bidden to take ourselves along the Maas southwards to Stein, where Squadron HQ had set up a landing-ground. Because there was some lifting of the mist and our presence seemed to be urgently required, we took off one after another and set forth. As we persevered, so the mist turned to fog. Having taken the decision to fly and being in the leading aircraft, I felt I had a certain obligation to arrive, rather than travel hopefully until we either ran out of fuel or landed in Germany. It says a lot for careful pre-flight planning that I arrived over the Squadron landing-ground with the rest of the Flight behind. As far as SHQ was concerned we did not even rate the courtesy of a Verey light to help us in – we might have been arriving from outer space. I landed, in fairly thick fog, and fired off all my own Verey cartridges until the rest of us got down safely, but it was a close run thing. To add insult to injury, we were then left to find our own billets.

R.A.F. 2nd Tactical Air Force 1944 Christmas Card.

Flight Diary (Captain Eastgate): *23rd Flight flew off to Stein (8 km east of Gouda) Sqdn ALG. Light fog at start of journey but very bad fog encountered towards destination. SHQ had made no effort to assist incoming aircraft by Verey lights, etc. Capt Munro fortunately found strip and assisted remainder of aircraft by firing much appreciated Verey lights. State of chaos in billeting situation.*

Next day we set off for Diest, due west and back again in Belgium, but further south than we had so far penetrated. Here again, but with good reason, we were not expected, but there was an RAF airfield here with 125 Wing offering us much appreciated hospitality. As for billets, after we had got the aircraft tied down on the airfield, we made do with a large unoccupied and dilapidated house in the middle of the little town. We all piled in; the paper was peeling off the walls, some of the doors were missing and there was no electric light. But there was glass in the windows and slates on the roof, so we lit our hurricane and pressure lights and made the best of it. It was Christmas Eve, 1944.

[Flight diary: *December 24 Flight moved off to Diest. Very much appreciated hospitality from 125 Wing RAF. Flight settles in. Now under command 30 Corps, Capts Munro and Hargreaves contacted 30 Corps HQ but were unable to find 3 AGRA.*]

The cause of all this upheaval was a certain Gerd von Rundstedt – a survivor if ever there was one. At half past five in the morning of 16 December, von Rundstedt launched the Ardennes counter-offensive, whose aim was to strike northwest from an assembly area in the Eiffel Hills on the Luxembourg border on a narrow front. The 6th SS Panzer Army under Sepp Dietrich was to cross the Maas near Liege and drive for Antwerp (the main supply-base for the British Army), while the 5th Panzer Army under von Manteuffel was to cross the Meuse near Namur and capture Brussels. The fogs which had so plagued us recently had prevented air reconnaissance which might have revealed these plans and it also prevented any air attacks on the German troop concentrations – had these been discovered. [Editor's note: For a considerable part of the war the Allies had been able to rely on the 'Ultra' decrypts to reveal much about the enemies intentions. The intelligence came from German coded radio messages intercepted routinely by British listening stations and decoded at Bletchley Park. It is said that the enemy unexpectedly switched to using meetings and telephone calls to organise the Ardennes offensive, leaving the Allies unaware of their intentions.]

The concept was the Führer's and it did not have the support of his generals. Von Rundstedt, for example, regarded it as a gambler's last throw (which it was) – 'es geht um ganzel' – 'we're going for broke'. But he lacked the moral courage to refuse to put it into effect. The shock and surprise of what was, after all, a 1940-style blitzkreig had a devastating effect nevertheless on the American 1st Army, which bore the initial brunt. Two things saved the day: first, the fighting qualities of certain divisions of the US Army – the 2nd Division at Monschau, the 7th US Armoured at St Vith and the 101st Airborne at Bastogne; the other was the irrepressible Monty, whose clinical professionalism restored some semblance of command and control in the vital early days while the American commanders (including General Eisenhower) were floundering and at a loss.

[At 10:30 am on 20 December, Eisenhower, having lost contact with General Bradley, had telephoned Montgomery and ordered him to assume

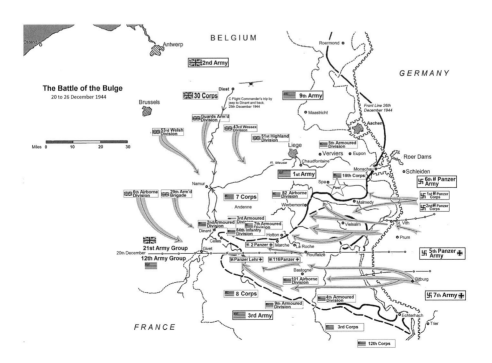

command of the American First (Hodges) and Ninth Army (Simpson) – which, until then, were under Bradley's overall command.]

That was the explanation for our presence in an abandoned house in Diest on Christmas Eve; we were just a small element in the considerable British force that Monty, now the de facto Allied commander by default, had switched south from Holland. He wanted to form a stop-line on the Maas (or Meuse, in this area) between Dinant and Liege, in case the Americans failed to halt the German advance. We were part of the XXX Corps with Guards Armoured, 43rd, 51st and 53rd Divisions. But within the salient created by the Germans, Monty left it to the US VII Corps to fight the battle. He was in fact 'maintaining his objective' which was not to respond to German pressure by committing British troops in support of the Americans, but to hold them in reserve and in readiness for the clearance of the area between the Maas and the Rhine, to the north, ready for the decisive assault crossing of the Rhine and the final advance into North Germany.

Monty set about imposing his own type of order on what had been in the first few days a shambles. First of all, he set up his own communications by sending out wireless trucks to key positions; next he sent out his personal liaison officers to gather hard information about the state of the battle. He was thus able to connect a series of individual actions into a coherent battle fought in accordance with a clear plan. [When Montgomery ordered US forces to retreat from St Vith to west of the Meuse. CO Brigadier General Bruce Cooper Clarke agreed, remarking 'This terrain is not worth a nickel an acre to me.']

While the US forces were finally slowing up the German advance, Monty had already moved XXX British Corps into place to hold the line of the Meuse, he then began to withdraw US units from the less critical areas of the battle and regroup them to form a reserve which could launch a counter-offensive at the appropriate moment.

23 xii 44
Capt Munro
C Flight
653 Sqdn RAF
BLA

My dearest Jean,
Thank you very much for the cheering present that arrived at a somewhat gloomy period and made things brighter!

We've just had a pretty tense time; getting rid of the Flight Commander which is a tricky job. Interviews with the CO and what an atmosphere of intrigue. I might make a good Borgia. Thank goodness he's gone and good riddance to him. It's been getting us down![12]

Not less unsettling but very funny have been the jet planes. They look very harmless but make a noise just like a bomb, so you never know if one has been dropped or if the plane is passing over harmlessly. We got chased into a ditch by one which came straight for us at no height at all, chased by a fighter or so.

We did a demonstration flight after that, first to cheer the Germans up & let them know we were still around.

We've got a room in a house now: eggs, milk (sometimes) & better weather. Also Christmas supplies: the first beer since Falaise: brandy & whisky, so it looks as if they expect us to make up for lost opportunity.

The Americans are having a time: glad I'm not there. Still so long as it doesn't stop leave, it may be one way of polishing off all the Germans.

Don't talk about inspections. We got all ready for one and it failed to materialise! Just as well.

There's a lovely fog here: it comes and goes day after day & never leaves us. That's what one hoped for, for Christmas, but it's a little premature.

'C' Flight, meanwhile, were getting down to the more urgent task of creating Christmas out of chaos. The largest room in the house was set up as a kitchen, with Aircraftman Sutch in charge of two roaring petrol cookers and more volunteer *sous-chefs* than most five-star restaurants could boast. By the time Christmas dinner was cooked – and a very fine dinner it was – the whole house was warm, partly from the blast from the petrol cookers and partly from one or two fires that were drawing nicely in long-cold fireplaces fed with broken floorboards and doors. Everyone was in good spirits – especially the head chef, whose professional enthusiasm had been kept going by frequent tots of rum. These celebrations at Diest (and the one the year before at Penshurst) are among the most cheerful Christmas parties I can remember. I don't think anyone in the Flight was capable of going anywhere after our Christmas lunch. The diary recorded: 'A very good Xmas day plus an excellent lunch … slept off the Xmas dinner… ' All that is, except the new flight-commander, who had to go off in a jeep and try to find our gunner HQ near Dinant some fifty or sixty miles away.

The mission was an experience that proved to be 'interesting'. That the roads were covered with icy snow was one thing; the other was that I was moving into a US Army area. First of all, the unit signs were all different from the British. A British Corps on moving into an area took with it a complete matrix of unit sign boards and route-signs, which were put up by the individual unit or by military police. Every vehicle had its own unit and sub-unit sign painted on it and unit number. Wherever the Corps moved, its signs went with it. Both within a Corps, or moving into another corps area, you knew exactly what sign to look for in order to find any particular unit; the further forward you went, the simpler the range of signs. Back in the rear areas it became more complex and less familiar. Now I was moving into the rear area of the US 1st Army, into which had arrived fighting units thrown back by the German attack. It was pretty chaotic, even if I had known what some of the signs meant, which I didn't.

Added to that, the US troops were very jumpy about German special units whom they imagined to be operating as saboteurs, dressed in US uniforms and speaking American. These units, they seemed to think, were everywhere.[13] I was stopped at various roadblocks along my way, while they tried to work out who the hell I was and what I was doing. Most of them had never seen a British uniform before and I even got a carbine stuck into my ribs at one point while they looked at my identity card – which of course might just as well have been Greek to them. I refrained from saying that I was just trying to help them in their hour of need. It was not a pleasant experience and I was happy to learn from the gunners that our operation was winding down and that we might not be needed much longer. I was also very glad to get back to Diest, as an attack of the jitters is very infectious. Christmas Day finished with the whole Flight, less a couple who remained on guard at the house, going off to the Ralph Reeder Gang Show at 125th Group.

The flap did indeed peter out; Butch and Harry took a night out in Brussels; 'a respectable time was had', the Diary noted rather ambiguously. We moved back to Stein in fog and snow without a repetition of our previous dicey arrival. This time SHQ gave us a good reception and we were cheered up by hearing that we were now back in XII Corps and best of all due for an operation with 43rd Division early in the new year – possibly into Germany, near Aachen.

[Flight diary: *29th Capt Munro to 653 Sqn following message to revert to 12 Corps.*]

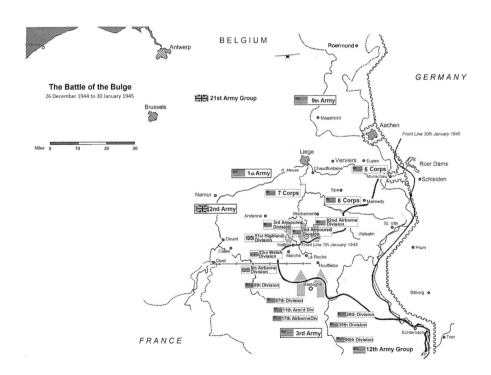

Notes

1. Antwerp-Deurne was used by bombers and for aircraft storage from Aug 40 to Jun 41 and then turned into a major repair facility for fighters in the old Stampe et Vertongen Works on the North West side. 1 Jagdgeschwader 4 commanded by Hptm Wilhelm Steinmann (26.8.44 – 3.45) was the last German operational unit to use it between 29 August and 4 September 1944; they then moved to Lachen-Speyerdorf, Germany. 'Luftwaffe Airfields 1935–45, Henry L. deZeng IV'.
2. Horrocks' choice may have been limited by fuel supplies. Among other issues, stretched supply lines (and possible misappropriation by black marketers, see above) meant that XXX corps may not have had enough fuel to reach the 15th Army in time to stop them. Some say he was a scapegoat on this occasion.
3. Fort Breendonck is preserved as a memorial to those who were its inmates during the Nazi occupation.
4. After the war, General Blumentritt, who had been Chief of Staff under Model and von Runstedt stated that had General Bernard Montgomery been unleashed earlier for a concentrated armoured assault (as he had wished) rather than fighting on a broad front, 'Such a breakthrough … would have torn the weak German front to pieces and ended the war in the winter of 1944.' Wilmot, Chester (1952) *The Struggle for Europe* p.539.
5. Military historian Robin Neillands points mainly to a failure to prioritise objectives on the day. Some US commentators have made every effort to pin the blame solely, and in his view unjustifiably, on Montgomery and British forces. *The Battle for the Rhine 1944* (2005).
6. 'C' Flight Diary credits Captain Place with twenty-eight sorties in July, twenty-four sorties in August and fourteen sorties in September; the Squadron Diary has no entries for sorties other than moves to landing grounds and no records of individual sorties during June or July. After July, it is likely he performed as a liaison pilot until he became unfit to fly an aircraft.
7. The Island was the scene of intense fighting during the first half of October as the Germans attempted to destroy the Allied bridgehead north of the Waal.
8. Lieutenant Colonel Bishell was posthumously awarded the DSO on October 19, 1944: 'Throughout the operations carried out from the ODON bridgehead between 1 and 15 July he has displayed the highest qualities of leadership, meeting all emergencies with calm and resolute action and setting an example of devotion to duty and contempt for danger which has been an inspiration to all those in contact with him. The efficiency and morale of his Regt under the most exacting conditions have been of the highest order.'
9. *Tony Judt, 'Post War' 2005.*

10. See later reference to his taking over the Flight in the text and in his letter dated 23 December 1944.

11. The jets were so fast it is unlikely the Spitfires got close, only the Tempest posed a threat. Once the German pilots became used to the concept, the Me.262 was a very successful fighter. Luckily the development was slowed by Goering's preference for piston engines.

12. Lyell says little of the change in his account. It appears Captain Riding was transferred to 'B' flight after a period where morale in 'C' flight and its effectiveness as a unit had declined. Captain Riding probably needed a break from the extra demands of commanding a flight in tough conditions. He and Lyell later became and remained close friends until Captain Riding's death many years later.

13. During the 'Battle of the Bulge', a German 'false colours' operation called 'Greif' [Griffin] was led by Waffen-SS commando Otto Skorzeny. Germans troops, able to speak American English, used captured Allied uniforms and equipment to infiltrate the American positions. One of their objectives was to capture the bridges over the Meuse but although that attempt failed, the exercise was very effective in causing 'alarm and despondency'. Some captured Germans were executed as spies by US forces but later it was decided not to execute such soldiers unless they actually fought wearing a false uniform.

Chapter 7

Beyond the Maas – Over the Rhine

1 January–31 March 1945

New Year's Day, 1945, and it was a sunny morning with a light covering of snow that was crisp and bright. 'C' Flight were still to be found with Squadron HQ, on their landing-ground at Stein, just east of the Maas, in a Dutch coal-mining area. We were waiting for orders from 43rd Division, our new masters, for an unspecified operation. What we got was a sky full of low-flying German fighters over the strip, gallantly pursued westwards by a solitary US Thunderbolt.[1] Luckily they

MT 169 across the Seigfreid line near Heinsburg, January 1945. Preparing for Operation Blackcock.

were not interested in the dozen or so Austers parked in the snow; they swept on to better targets, like the Field Marshal's personal aircraft at Evere airfield, Brussels, where much damage was done. (We knew something unusual, and perhaps unpleasant was going to happen. To begin with, while maps were being spread out after breakfast, an unopened bottle of whisky was knocked off the table on to the stone floor).

We were quite glad, therefore, to move off that afternoon to our own landing-ground at Jenstraat, near the small town of Brunssum just short of the German border. Once more we were in a mining area and we had good billets and the use of the miners' baths. (Harry Cookson, who had experience of the coalmines in Staffordshire, was amazed at the amenities provided for Dutch miners). Everyone was in billets and treated very kindly by the locals. We were also close to Divisional HQ, which saved travelling. The weather remained cold and bright and we did a number of recces for possible landing-grounds to suit all contingencies.

3.1.45

My darling Jean

I like this European travel, I don't know how many miles I've done in a Jeep lately, but it adds up! Ice-bound roads: got back on Christmas day with my eyelashes stuck up with ice. I sympathise therefore with your cold.

I passed through Aachen recently: it's somewhat ruined: worse than Caen. The odd German is around, looking a bit browned off and rightly so since there is scarcely a habitable building left. The Dutch on the border nearby, however, are extremely jovial. In spite of have a rather riotous morning with assorted enemy aircraft rushing around without much idea of what to do, life is pretty quiet. We've got a room in a farm and a little coal so things are looking up. So long as no-one decides to send us off to some place in the middle of a Dutch bog we feel we'll get along nicely. It's pleasant to see hills again. Eggs also abound!

Things are in fact as good as could be expected. At least we are not stooging around in Brussels doing the social round – if there is any life we usually see a bit of it. The only boredom is that there are such periods of bad weather and standstill.

That is all the news that's fit to print – not that the censorable stuff is interesting! In my wanderings, by the way, I heard a buzz-bomb: the engine cut out – started again – cut out and all the windows shook. It was a solemn moment. Memories of Dover or Penshurst, where they flew down the ridge-poles of our tent, or so it seemed.

Suddenly got several letters from you – most – pleasing! The old Dakotas suddenly get in with a rush when the weather clears – of course it's snowing now again but thawing at the same time. Mud again, we guess in a knowing way.

Leave for the ground people has started, you'll see. Very tense lotteries are held and the whole thing is watched with hawk-like care by one and all. I'm taking odds on mid-Feb for mine – anyone putting it to the ballot will be firmly discouraged.

You must have had a pretty quiet Christmas: we had the odd meal (the cook, in spite of consuming most of the rum ration did very well), and the odd bottle, but we should have been in Brussels to do any good. We couldn't wangle it unfortunately.

Well, time moves by and the war gets nearer the end. The Germans must feel very reluctant to play the last few moves but they have no alternative. Only a little more and they will be about ready to receive the final push – whichever side it comes from. The Russians are not standing still.

I wish I'd managed to get into my skating boots – too small. I'll try to get some in Belgium: it would be a pity to waste the ice. Still, no time for unmilitary diversions nowadays – what a life.

It soon emerged that XII Corps was to take part in an operation known as 'Blackcock' the purpose of which was to clear the German salient south of Roermond, between the rivers Roer, Maas and Wurm – the Roer triangle – through which ran the southern end of the Siegfried Line. Those involved were 7th Armoured Division on the left, 52nd Division in the centre and good old 43rd on the right, on the boundary with the 9th US Army in the Aachen sector. We were to have help from the 'funnies' from 79th Armoured flail-tanks to clear mines, bridge-layers, armoured troop carriers and flame-throwing tanks. There was also a Canadian battery of 'Mattress' multiple rocket-launchers – a novelty for us.

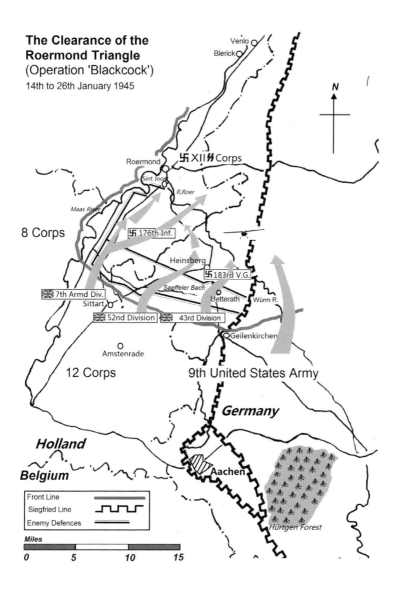

The Clearance of the Roermond Triangle (Operation 'Blackcock')
14th to 26th January 1945

The landscape was snow-covered, with small well-defined villages in open countryside, from which for centuries past the villagers would have set out at dawn to cultivate their fields and return home at dusk. Each village had now been turned into a strong point from which the enemy was to be systematically dislodged by a series of outflanking attacks. The final objective was the now ruined town of Heinsberg in the north – before being comprehensively bombed, it was a cotton spinning and manufacturing centre. The terrain included several small streams and boggy places and with the minefields as well as the prepared defences, the two German infantry divisions in the sector could cause a great deal of trouble. But this was essentially no more than a large-scale mopping up operation – carried out in the most difficult conditions, not least of which was the wet, freezing cold weather.

On 14 January, 7th Armoured opened the ball on the western flank with 52nd Lowland[2] (or Mountain) joining in next, with 43rd coming in on the east flank to roll the whole thing up. Massive artillery support was made

Midwinter on the Roer.

available, plus Canadian rocket-launchers and a new idea called a 'pepper-pot'. This was simply a method of bringing down fire on enemy positions from every gun which could be brought to bear – tanks, Bofors A/A and heavy machine-guns – at the start of an attack.

All this firepower must have been reassuring for the infantry and although we did not begrudge them it, we nevertheless had cause for concern. The reason being that with the high volume of shellfire passing through, the limited airspace available to us did not provide much room for an Auster. Each salvo from the Canadians was capable of launching 350 rockets at once into an area 200 yards square. The effect on anyone straying into the path of that lot on its way to the target would be dramatic and lethal. When I had worked out the flight-paths or trajectories of most of the heavy weapons that would be firing during the battle, from gun-site to target area it became clear that there was no safe zone or height in which we could operate without risk of being hit by our own shellfire. Quite illogically, we felt better for having come to that conclusion once and for all and got on with the job. As Napoleon, or someone, said 'la guerre, c'est une chose aléatoire', or as we would have said, if we had thought of it, 'war is a dicey business'. Later, during the Rhine crossing on 24 March, four Austers were to be destroyed by mid-air shell-strikes while observing. It was by then a well-known problem for which we could find no practical solution.

Operation 'Blackcock' had been set up as one of a series of phased, deliberate operations intended to blast the opposition off the face of the earth, bit by bit, at intervals dictated partly by the weather (which was foul) and partly by the time needed to concentrate the armour and artillery for each phase. It snowed and it froze and day after day a veil of mist or fog lay on the face of the earth. Flying would have been pointless, even if we had been able to get the aircraft off our snow-choked strip; 43rd Division was likewise obliged to wait until the weather improved, while planning went ahead.

As soon as we could get a runway cleared we intended to move the Flight to Amstenrade, where the other two flights were sitting. We towed a farm roller up and down behind a 3-ton truck until we had made the snow really hard and took off about midday on the twelfth. The next week we spent doing whatever we could to help in the planning. We flew in a camera aircraft from SHQ, fitted with infra-red film and did several runs of air-photos, which were then widely distributed to the infantry. Whenever the visibility allowed, we also took up the infantry battalion commanders on sorties, to reconnoitre their objectives.

On taking infantry officers on familiarisation flights, we often had the time to offer them a mug of tea, either before or after. It came as a surprise to me how many of them took the opportunity during such occasions to assure us how much rather they would keep both feet on the ground and not risk their necks in one of those funny little aircraft. We, of course, took exactly the opposite view; our admiration for the courage of the infantry was unbounded and completely sincere and we would do anything we could to make their task less dangerous. Our casualty-rates were far less than theirs; our living conditions were much superior. At the same time, some of them were ready to admit that the odds against their survival until the end of the war were against them; we knew that their casualty-rates were appalling and could say little to reassure them. What could we say? At least this made us try harder.

General Montgomery issued a special order of the day to all gunners:

I would like to pay a compliment to all gunners and I would like this passed on to every gunner. The gunners have risen to great heights in this war; they have been well commanded and well handled. In my experience, the artillery has never been so proficient as it is today; it is at the top of its form. For all this I offer you my warmest congratulations. The contribution of the artillery to the final victory in the German war has been immense. This will always be so. The harder the fighting and the longer the war, the more the infantry, and in fact all the arms, lean on the gunners. The proper use of the artillery is a great battle winning factor. I think all the other arms have done well too, but the artillery have been terrific and I want to give due weight to its contribution to the victory in this campaign.

Our part of the battle began on the twentieth, with several useful sorties flown. It began to be quite lively. We had in support a squadron of Typhoons, which circled the battle in their customary cab-rank at about 3,000 ft, waiting to be called in by the usual signal of red smoke-shells fired into the target area. They would then peel off one after another in a steep dive and fire their rockets onto the target. It was highly effective, as this unsolicited German testimonial illustrates:

> *We cursed the little dark-green high-wing aeroplanes. We knew that one of them in the area would precede a barrage and we tried our hardest to shoot then down. If we gave them too hard a time they were impudent enough to fire off a few flares and call up the Typhoons to rocket us. We dreaded those little observation aeroplanes – they were the angels of death to us.*[3]

One morning I was watching the village of Uetterath when I saw a glint of light from a haystack just outside the village, possibly reflected from binoculars. So I put down red smoke from the guns to call in the Typhoons. They dived down and fired their rockets; in so doing they ran into heavy flak that brought one Typhoon down. I had noticed that as soon as the red smoke came down, troops had run out of the village and taken up positions near the haystack. I went back and landed and arranged for red smoke to be put down again an hour later, just to give things time to settle in the village.

As soon as the smoke came down I was ready to see what would happen. The Typhoons were circling round, duly briefed and the German troops ran out again and took up their positions ready for the Typhoons to come in. This time however, a divisional artillery concentration came down on top of them. The Typhoons then came in and rocketed them for good measure, without a shot being fired in reply. These RAF Typhoon pilots in 83 Group were much respected, as they made a contribution to the ground battle, out of all proportion to their numbers. By contrast, the well-meant efforts by Bomber Command to soften up German positions were almost always counter-productive, causing massive obstacles to both tanks and infantry with the huge bomb craters that they delighted to create, instead of using smaller antipersonnel bombs.

Another weapon, of horrifying effectiveness, was the 'Crocodile' flame-throwing tank. This was basically a Churchill tank with a flame-projecting jet, towing a trailer of viscous inflammable liquid under pressure (an early version of napalm, or a latter-day brand of Greek fire). The jet could be aimed and the liquid ignited as soon as it left the nozzle, leaping out in a huge, sustained gout of yellow flame towards its target – usually a strong-

Flame throwing tanks in action in the Roermond Triangle. *IWM*

point or heavily defended position. When the flame hit its target it enveloped it completely, penetrating every crevice and invading every space within. The target would then burn with black smoke pouring from it for several minutes. One could only imagine the ghastly effect on human flesh. The moral argument about the use of weapons like this has not been resolved, after centuries of debate. The wounds inflicted by shell-fragments or bullets, or suffered by men trapped in burning vehicles or aircraft are equally horrible. Those with strong stomachs can study the effects of warfare in earlier days shown with appalling realism in Goya's 'Disasters of War'. But the idea of setting out with deliberation to burn your enemy to death is still in a special category of inhumanity. But where can you draw the line – how can war ever be made humane?

Censored letter card 26.1.45

My dearest,
Nothing new – no revelations for posterity. Everything is well: even the
weather has given us a chance to get going on the old Normandy scale. It's
snowing again now but still very pleasant.

 No sign of the millennium* yet – what can be wrong? I reckon if my leave
looms up on time things will be well enough. I undertake to fly back through
hell and high water but don't think we shall meet such extremes. In any case,
I shall start in good time to get the best weather going. Meanwhile the world
rotates in its usual way. What strange things occur on its crust: I don't know
how people stand for it but there it is. One sees things that are really very
odd sometimes!

As the battle continued with clinical deliberation to its planned conclusion, Harry Eastgate began to find the cold and damp too much for even his dogged determination. He suffered from asthma and probably was marginally fit on that account for flying duties. However, being the sort of person he was, he kept going until one day he had to land while returning from a sortie, completely overcome by breathlessness. We sped him off to the nearest field hospital, where they prescribed a week in a warm dry atmosphere in one of their wards. After he had been assured that he would not be sent back to Brussels or even to the UK, he agreed to take a rest.

 When we got him back, a couple of days earlier than predicted, he was much better. He explained that he simply had to get out, since the ward sister had put him onto sitting beside the beds of casualties after they had limbs amputated or been operated on in some other way in order to keep an eye on them when they came out of the anaesthetic. This had proved just too much for Harry and it was doing his morale no good at all. We were just as glad to have him back as he was to return, although the battle was by then drawing to a successful close.

---

* Destruction as described in the Book of Revelations.

Before it ended I was to find myself in another bit of trouble involving bad visibility. We were doing some anti-mortar patrols near Heinsberg and I was just on the point of packing it in during the murk of a damp winter's afternoon when I saw a Typhoon slide past me rather too close for comfort. As it went by I saw it was on fire under one wing and the cockpit canopy was missing. I could see no sign of the pilot. It disappeared into the mist in a shallow dive. I took a quick look over my shoulder and there was a FW 190 somewhat further away following the Typhoon down. Luckily he had not seen me, but I stuffed my nose down and made for the ground in case there were any more where he had come from. Just to be on the safe side, I made for a large cliff above a bend in the river that I had noticed earlier as suitable cover in time of need. When I got close I saw one other Auster and a US Piper who had had the same idea, flying around in the circuit, like a couple of sparrows frightened by a hawk. It was time to go home, which I did at very low altitude, wondering what had become of the pilot of that Typhoon.

Harry Eastgate on the Siegfried Line, January 1945.

By 26 January, the Roer Triangle was clear of German troops, if not of Germans, for we had been fighting on German soil for the first time as far as we were concerned. We had managed to cross the Siegfried Line almost without noticing it and had established our first landing-ground in Germany. South of us was Aachen, in the US sector, which had been captured by the 1st US Army in October. It stood out desolate in the snow, crumbled into ruin through weeks of heavy fighting. Any further advance was blocked by stout German defence based on parts of the Siegfried Line and also by skilful manipulation of the floodgates of the River Roer. This had brought Bradley's 9th Army to a halt after a painstaking and expensive advance into Germany of seven or eight miles.

The scene was at last set for two major offensives. These were needed in order to release the Allied armies from the strategic deadlock that had resulted from Eisenhower's policy of piece-meal attacks on a broad front. The objective was to clear up the area between the Maas and the Rhine from Dusseldorf in the south to Nijmegen in the north and to establish a bridgehead north of the Ruhr across the Rhine. For this plan (which dated back to a conference at Brussels in October), General Bradley's 9th US Army was once more put under Monty's command. And the way in which the battle was to develop was to bear more than a passing resemblance to the grand design in Normandy.

Once more there were to be two converging attacks from the north across the German border from Nijmegen (one of the solitary fruits of the Arnhem attack) and from the Julich-Linnich area in the US 9th Division's Roer sector. The point of convergence was to be the intended bridgehead over the Rhine at Wesel. It was, yet again, to prove a bitter struggle against a determined enemy fighting to defend his own country and the abominable regime that still directed and inspired the German armies.

However this was not a XII Corps battle, and 653 Air OP Squadron was withdrawn to Diest for rest and refit, the first since the Squadron had been effectively brought together in June 1944. 'C' Flight joined the Squadron on 6 February, leaving behind a landing-ground which had already become, for all reasonable purposes, unserviceable due to flooding. The whole of February was spent refitting, maintaining and making our equipment up to scale. Parachutes were repacked, as a matter of form – we were not going to carry them again. As many people as possible were sent on leave; Joe Hargreaves and John Turnbull set off for Chamonix on what was ostensibly a skiing trip, which turned out to be more apres-ski than ski, by all accounts. I went back to the UK for a week's leave, hitch hiking over in a Mitchell bomber which landed at Blackbush. This was my first experience of an aircraft with the modern standard tricycle undercarriage. It seemed to need an awful lot of runway to take off and the angle of descent for the run-in to landing was spectacular. It was most enjoyable.

Towards the end of February, Alan Newton replaced our CO, Geoff Pollitt. Geoff had steered the Squadron through some difficult times and I felt we could not have asked for a more helpful and understanding guiding hand. To a great extent Flights were virtually independent units working directly to Divisions; but we did depend on an efficient superior formation for all our administration, logistic support (especially as regards aircraft) and in later days for vital photographic know-how. The fact that we had got as far as we had, in as good shape and spirits as we were, was something Geoff and the RAF administration staff had played a major part in achieving. We were also lucky to have in Alan Newton someone who knew the score and was content to follow the same policy.

[653 Squadron Diary 15 February: *Maj. A.H. Newton arrived from 660 Sqdn to assume command of the sqdn and spoke with Capt. Eldridge who was commanding in Maj. Pollitt's absence on leave.* On 22 February Squadron Command passed from Major G.P. Pollitt to Major A.H. Newton. Maj. Pollitt left to assume new role as GI at the Air Ministry. On 23 February, Maj. Newton laid down proposed training syllabus.

Major Newton is mentioned in *Unarmed Into Battle*. He was a pilot in 651 Squadron during their Tunisian Campaign, late 1942. On 28 November, Capt Newton was shot down and escaped his burning aircraft. Capt Billingham went to his aid in spite of machine gun fire and was later awarded the MC for that and his work at that time.]

25.ii.45

My dearest,
This is the life! 48 hours in Brussels coming up, breakfast 08.30, nice weather, nice billet.

The only snag is everyone would rather be doing something more active: the usual contrary set up. Nothing ever satisfies us.

Of course it is frightfully dangerous here. The wireless was blown off the window sill this morning by a buzz bomb and a bottle of whisky was only spared by a miracle.

The wireless set being Dutch still carries on with true national stolidity, after we put the valves back in their sockets again. We are a bit short of windows but luckily all the holes are filled in. Another lucky thing was that the thing landed just before it was time to get up so we lost no sleep. But oh for the peace and quiet of the forward areas!

The new CO is a very genial soul – almost hearty, but I think he knows his stuff. It's still rather early to tell – time alone will show. So long as I am left alone!

Is your spring-cleaning (unofficial) complete? Your idea is good but the execution seems rather circular, requiring careful organising so that the chimney is swept before distempering. Or am I wrong?

What do you think of the way the war goes? We must get a really good bash at Germany before it's too late. Otherwise I shall feel that the weary years I've spent being herded from one end of Britain to the next are wasted.

I will endeavour to find a Belgian photographer willing to risk his apparatus and send you the answer. There's a very fine picture of me at Aachen standing in the Siegfried Line but unfortunately it was so cold that only the tip of my nose shows – a sort of let's get this over air pervades the job.

It was not until the middle of March that we were to be called on to get back into action, with 15th (Scottish) Division for the next phase of operations – the crossing of the Rhine. While we had been putting our feet up in Diest, XXX Corps and II Canadian Corps had been fighting their way south between the Maas and the Rhine from a start-line east of Nijmegen.

Operation 'Veritable' was put under command of Canadian 1st Army, General Crerar, with the whole of the operational strength of 1st Canadian and 2nd British Armies, amounting to thirteen divisions. XXX Corps was in control of the initial assault, with the 2nd Canadian, 15th Scottish, 53rd Welsh and 51st Highland and massive artillery support. The Reichswald area was the first objective; the forest itself had become the northern extension of the Siegfried Line, with isolated bunkers and trench systems organised in great depth.

Apart from the formal fortifications, the battle had to be fought in country where armour was virtually useless, because of the forests and the bogs, craters, roadblocks and mines that abounded. The whole area was waterlogged and progressively became more and more flooded. Every yard had to be fought for, under a volume of enemy fire that was the heaviest of the whole campaign. Here the German troops were among the best and the last still available, including four parachute divisions, Panzer and Panzergrenadier divisions and Panzer Lehr (training) Division. The towns of Goch, Cleve and Emmerich were reduced by air attack to rubble and craters – which then had to be fought through. The pillboxes and bunkers were dealt with by the flamethrowers and petards of 79th Armoured Division.

It was to take a month of some of the bitterest fighting yet seen to clear the Germans out of the northern Rhineland and gain control of the west bank of the Rhine from Nijmegen to Wesel. It had been a second 'battle of the hinge', with 21st Army taking on the bulk of the German reserves held in the Cologne plain, consisting of ten infantry and armoured divisions. When the US 8th Army struck, two weeks after the start of 'Veritable', it was faced only by weak German divisions.

General Bradley had once more been held up – as in the Normandy battles – while British and Canadian troops drew in more and more of the German reserves. This time the enemy caused the delay by blowing up the floodgates of the Roer dams, sending the Roer River itself down in a huge torrent of icy, muddy floodwater. The water could neither be bridged nor crossed by boats as it rushed along at over six miles an hour. It was not until 23 February, that the 9th Army's attack could begin the crossing of the Roer with seven infantry and three armoured divisions. The corps on the left flank of this advance made rapid progress from the ruins of Julich, and on

3 March, made contact with 53rd Welsh at Geldern and swung east to the Rhine at Wesel, just in time to see the huge railway bridge demolished by the retreating Germans. At the same time, the US 1st Army to the south had entered the western part of Cologne. The total US casualties over the North Rhineland front amounted to fewer than half of those suffered by the British and Canadian forces in operation 'Veritable'.

The west bank of the Rhine was now clear of German troops from Dusseldorf to Nijmegen and the scene was set for a set-piece crossing of the Rhine north of the Ruhr. For a month XII Corps staff had been busy planning what was to be revealed as Operation 'Plunder'. (The whole operation had been upstaged by the brilliant capture by US 9th Armoured Division of the Rhine bridge at Remagen, just south of Bonn and the creation within a fortnight of a bridgehead ten miles deep and twenty miles wide). It remained an essential part of Allied strategy, however, that Schleswig-Holstein should be firmly in Allied hands before the Soviet armies could get there, regardless of any successes south of the Ruhr. That was the task of 2nd Army and the Field Marshal approached it with ruthless professionalism. Meantime the Canadians resumed their epic march up the long left flank, to drive the Germans out of North Holland, whose inhabitants were in desperate straits from a winter of food-shortage that had now reached the stage of mass starvation.

Our time at rest in Diest was now drawing to an end. It had been a welcome break during the unkindest month of the year; in winter there is a special kind of dreariness in that part of the world that makes even the sodden midlands of England preferable. The local chemist had risen to the challenge, in a slightly unprofessional way, by retailing at the back door a potent cocktail for restoring the tissues of those in need; since the main ingredient was wood alcohol, which in any quantity would drive you blind, he soon fell foul of the law and it was tough on his customers who might have indulged unwisely. There was a good deal of rough hooch in circulation; the Polish agricultural workers, or serfs, had taken to making potato spirit, which was often strained through a cloth smeared with raspberry jam. It looked like red wine when held up to the light, but there the resemblance ceased. It was said that some truck-loads of hydrogen peroxide (used as V1 propellant) had been found stranded on a railway siding and used by other displaced workers as the basis of an even deadlier cocktail. Poor devils.

Whether it was the winter gloom, or too much time to think, I do not know, but one of our quietest and steadiest 3-tonner drivers picked up his sten gun in the billet one morning and tried to blow his brains out. Luckily he missed and only damaged the ceiling (it was probably a desperate effort to get someone to do something about his personal difficulties rather than a serious attempt at suicide). It turned out he was an only son whose father had died years before, leaving him to look after his mother, to whom he was devoted. She lived in the East End of London, had survived the Blitz, but was now exposed to the V2 rockets. It had all become too much for him.

We got him off to see the MO, who passed him on to a psychiatrist, and in no time at all he was on his way back to England on a home posting near London. I hope it turned out well for him in the end. (It is interesting to think what might have happened to him in the 1914–18 War, when harsh punishment of other ranks for conduct like his seems to have been almost inevitable. As it was, everyone in the Flight felt sympathetic towards him and pleased that things had ended up as they had, without any disciplinary action being taken).

In the intervals between inspections and liberty-trips I tried to work out a way of doing reconnaissance flights deep into enemy positions using cloud cover. With the poor visibility and low cloud that plagued us so often during the winter I thought I could use these conditions to our own advantage. The idea was to work out the bearing and distance of a target area in enemy territory from the landing-ground and then take off, climb up into (or just above) low cloud cover and fly at steady height and speed on a course which after a given time in minutes and seconds would bring you almost up to the target-area. After the estimated time you would descend and hope to break cloud directly over the target, which could then be observed or even photographed with a vertical camera. Having taken the photographs you would again climb into the cloud and fly back on the reciprocal course until your estimated time of arrival over the landing ground.

I did a few experiments round Diest, which worked out well, particularly in near-windless conditions. What I did not manage to test was the ability or otherwise of German flak (especially the horribly effective 20mm. flak vierling (four-barrelled) weapon) to engage unseen slow flying aircraft.

I suspect it was quite fortunate that the sort of warfare that we indulged in from then on made this technique unnecessary; fortunate, because the quantity and effectiveness of German flak got greater and greater the further we pushed into Germany. But it was a nice idea all the same.

Early in March we were delighted to hear that we were to come under command of 15th Scottish Division later that month, for their assault crossing of the Rhine – to be known as Operation 'Plunder'. It was a XII Corps operation and with General Neil Ritchie in command and 51st (Highland) Division on the left flank. The Scots, as so often in the past, were to carry out the assault. When Churchill learned that Montgomery was relying on the two Scottish divisions (15th and 51st) to make the assault crossing of the Rhine, he asked if Monty had considered the consequences for Scotland, should it miscarry with heavy casualties (like Arnhem). Montgomery replied that the operation would succeed with few casualties among the ground forces. That proved to be the case.

In support of these operations and those of the US armies opposite the Ruhr heartland, the RAF and USAF began a furious assault on the vital communication centres, oil installations and factories still left intact. It was launched on 22 February, by over 8,000 aircraft operating from bases in England, France, Holland, Belgium and Italy, with fighter support; its objective to achieve the final disruption of the German State and its productive capacity. With what skill and ingenuity it had been maintained and indeed developed, in spite of years of strategic bombing, only became apparent as the Allied armies forced their way into the Reich. For that, Hitler had to thank the evil genius of Albert Speer, his minister of production, the loyal support of the German industrial establishment and the army of conscripted workers and slave labour from all over occupied Europe that kept the German armed forces in the field. Whatever spark of opposition to Hitler there had been was snuffed out by the failure of the Generals' bomb to do its business on 20 July [1944], and the subsequent summary execution of some 2,000 German suspected dissidents.[4]

7.iii.45

My darling,

Life is at a low ebb- nothing to do and all day to do it. I am sending the whole flight to Brussels tomorrow in a 3 tonner. They will return less a week's pay, plus a few souvenirs. I wish they'd give me a week's leave or let me do something: sitting in idleness is no darned good to any one. Even the weather has gone bad on us – low cloud and rain so I can't even stagger into the air.

I've just got our stove to go. It takes about two hours nursing, and produces a phenomenal (local) heat just as one is ready to go to bed, sick of prodding it. The best way to manage it is to sit on it which ensures maximum heat absorption.

Well the Germans are now reaping a reward. I hope they are satisfied. There are horrors to come. The mad idealism of the Nazis is leading to a Wagnerian end: Normandy is a garden suburb to what every German town will be. It's all horrible, but there seems to be no alternative.

Meanwhile I wonder if the new danger is not already revealed over the Polish question. Justice is not expected nowadays – as in 1938. Expediency is the aim. I hope I am wrong. One war at a time!

Just had a look at an instructor type out from England on a sight-seeing trip. What a life – Gawd elp us. Going back in two days. If I hadn't got to have something more or less interesting to amuse me I would join the ranks of the well-paid men and get a nice job doing circuits and landings at Andover. I would then not allow three months to elapse between glimpses of you. I haven't the face to pack it in. But I do envy the people in England when I think I might be seeing you on Monday instead of having a day off and nothing to do on it. It's no use binding, they say, so we'll just trickle along quietly until April.

The British Army, you may be glad to hear is still around and my newspaper tells me that more will be heard in the near future. The sooner, the better, anyway. Otherwise my lips are ceremoniously sealed.

Best wishes for the new place.

As plans and preparations were made for our final assault across the Rhine, we could watch the vapour-trails from USAF bombers reaching out into Germany; sometimes two or three trails would spring up into the sky as if to meet them, only to shake out into a zig-zag pattern and decay. These were the trails made by V2 rockets, launched on the approach of the bombers, either in defiance or perhaps just to get them off the ground before they could be bombed. And at night the RAF bomber streams took over. Sometimes the flash of exploding bombs could be seen in the sky over the eastern horizon and the drone of engines could be heard. One night as we watched the sky we saw a bright flash some way above the horizon. It grew brighter and redder and began a slow downward curve that grew faster and steeper until it met the earth, and burst into a huge ball of red light. As the darkness shut in again, we heard a faint hum which grew louder and higher in pitch, ending in a massive explosion which could almost be felt. Then silence. Some luckless Lancaster had bought it over Germany.

There was less dramatic evidence of the intensity of fighter effort by 83 and 84 Groups RAF. Since we had first flown into Diest in December, the piles of broken Spitfires, Typhoons and Tempests beside the airfield had grown bigger by the week. As the intensity of operations increased, so there was a disproportionate increase in the number of accidents on landing and take-off. Casualties, too, seemed to be overtaking the ability of Training Command to provide adequate replacements. And to make matters worse, the German Air Force was now putting into service a new generation of jet bombers and fighters that could outperform even the best of the Allied piston-engined aircraft. The Gloster Meteor Jet showed no sign of coming to the rescue.[5] And to cap it all, the Germans anti-aircraft defences east of the Rhine remained well equipped, well-trained and extremely formidable – years of practice against live targets by day and night had seen to that.

In his methodical preparations for the Rhine crossing, Montgomery had to balance the need for speed with the need to conserve British manpower. Although it was essential to reach the Baltic coast near Lübeck before the Russians could get there, and before the remains of the German armies could be withdrawn into Denmark there was the risk of suffering heavy casualties in crossing what is one of the greatest water obstacles in Western Europe, no less than 500 yds wide and flowing swiftly after winter rains.

The flood plain through which the Rhine runs in this area offers little cover for an attacking force, while by the same token providing good observation and uninterrupted fields of fire for the defenders. Operation 'Veritable' had shown that German troops were prepared to fight hard and skilfully for every centimetre of German ground.

'The good general must not only win his battles; he must win them with a minimum of casualties and loss of life'. The Field Marshal himself had summed it up, and there would have been few soldiers in 21st Army Group who would have disagreed with him at this late stage in the war. Having amassed what he considered a command of a size appropriate to the task – fifteen divisions in 21st Army Group, twelve divisions of the US 9th Army and the British 6th and US 17th Airborne Divisions, he brought up a quarter of a million tons of assorted stores in support, including, of course, a massive stock of bridging equipment and a flotilla of small craft, by courtesy of the Royal Navy. Nor were we to be short of firepower in 2nd Army – the 1,300 guns at General Ritchie's disposal were supplied with 60,000 tons of ammunition.

Although General Blumentritt, now commanding the German 25th Army on the eastern bank, could have been in little doubt where the blow was to fall, a strict limit was put on the number of reconnaissances made in the area, including Air OP flights. To obscure our intentions still further, smoke generators were laid out to provide a continuous bank of acrid fog along some twenty miles of the riverbank. It proved more than some of the troops could stand, and there were many temporary casualties from bronchitis among those who had to work in this area for long periods.

Business began to pick up after we moved out of Diest to a new strip near Zonhoven. While we had a steady job flying senior officers on Rhine recces, we still had to find an acceptable landing-ground within reasonable distance of the river. We needed something east of the high ground of the Hochwald Xanten, to cut down flying-time during the operation, but the small fields and deep ditches needed sapper help, which was fully committed elsewhere. (We were not allowed to bring our own working party forward). Recces by jeep to look for possible sites entailed eight hours travelling with only two hours available in the area for the serious business of finding a strip.

On 17 March I got permission for an air recce after all else had failed and succeeded in finding a reasonable prospect just west of Xanten at Labbeck.

Unfortunately it took so long that on the way back I ran out of fuel, at 100 feet above a big poplar plantation. I gained enough height with a dying engine to clear it and got down in a small meadow just beyond. When the full weight of the aircraft came down on the wheels as we lost flying-speed and lift from the wing, they dug into soft grass and I turned over gently but firmly. That was the premature and undignified end of the sortie.

I lowered myself carefully down on to the roof, got my map and helmet and wriggled out of the door. There were some helpful troops nearby and I got a message off to the Flight to send a jeep over. Meanwhile some equally helpful Belgians turned up, one of who was a local colliery official. He took me home for tea and whilst his wife was preparing this, his young daughter produced a linen tablecloth, covered with the names of British soldiers embroidered in bright silks. I duly added my name in pencil. Then, being asked 'would I like a record on the radiogram', I opted for Beethoven's Pastoral, so we all sat down to tea and cake while the last movement unrolled. I can't think of a better ending to a forced landing, or of kinder people. I never saw them again; the jeep turned up all too soon to take me back to the Flight and I stupidly forgot to ask their name. I was also worried about what Joe Hargreaves would say when I had to tell him I had bent his aircraft. What made it worse was that Harry Eastgate had turned his aircraft over the week before while landing, and I had rather teased him about it.

21.iii.45

My dearest,
Most unusually we are working! It is a shocking thing that someone high up has nothing better to do than give us work. I don't know how many miles I've done this week by jeep & aircraft, but we are now surveying the result for a day or two.

We have a nice house of our own with a roof and most of the windows intact. We also have three oil paintings, a table with cloth and several rugs and chairs. There are a few assorted ornaments and a hat-rack.

The Germans are somewhat browned off and seem to have something on their minds. Someone did a lot of digging round here – I have never seen so many trenches and holes of various sizes. There is also the odd pill-box.

The villages are all rather flat; such houses as stand are full of decrepit Teutons. There are the usual cartloads of refugees; no Nazis seem to exist in Germany – strange how the rumour ever arose!

The Rhine seems in good form – not too wide but looks a bit cold. Once the other side is reached, who is going to stop us and where?

Holland is still flooded, I notice – what a spot. I'd like the Dutch to admit that it's no good digging ditches when the whole country is awash – it just doesn't deceive anyone!

Your leave is over now, I suppose – too short as ever. It is difficult to please everyone who thinks you ought to be around. A dual personality is the answer, one would say. I hope my precocious nephew is standing up to the strain of modern life. He is losing some of his corpulence and assuming a more definite outline I am glad to say. I hope to get some toys for him in Germany.

Well, you probably know where you are by now – or does the security black-out forbid you knowing even when you're there – I wouldn't be surprised.

I hear the meat ration has gone for a burton – you can have the horrible pork and veg that has reappeared here. Luckily the odd egg still appears – why has no-one erected a monument to the noble bird? No glamour.

How slow things are – it's spring here already but nothing seems to grow here except grass – and not much of that. It's stopped raining though, that's the main thing these days. You'll probably guess that that's because the jeep has got side-curtains, & we are so warm we'd like to have the hood down.

That's all the news, I feel – not very informative, is it? The big stuff is to come I suppose, for further details see your local newspaper!

So it goes, the first five years are the worst.

My consolation was that I had found a landing-ground and quite a good one at that, after we had done a bit of work opening it up. We moved in a couple of days later, on 22 March. Harry took the road party up and as the diary appreciatively recorded 'enabled the camp to be laid out quickly and comfortably'. It was just in time. On the night of the twenty-third, the sky was bright with gunfire as heavy concentrations were put down on German positions across the Rhine. Then the sky-markers began to drift down over the town of Wesel, quickly followed by a rain of bombs from 200 Lancasters – 1,000 tons in all.[6] Monty's massive set piece now began to unfold with exemplary precision. As soon as the bombing was over, the 1st Commando Brigade moved in to capture what was left of the town – they had already crossed the river west of the town and moved in close to await the completion of the bombing. Wesel was the principal initial objective, so that a new railway bridge could be constructed by the Americans to supply future operations. 51st Highland had already begun their crossing at nine o'clock that night near Rees, some distance down river. At 2 am the next morning (the twenty-fourth), 15th Scottish launched their assault and at the same time the two US divisions set out just upstream of Wesel. It was a fine, still moonlit night with the first promise of spring in the air. All these operations were successful and mercifully light in British or American casualties. As the infantry dug in or prepared to push forward, the sappers began to launch their pontoon bridges ready for the follow-up and the amphibious tanks of 79th Armoured Division began to climb the far bank, looking rather like hippopotami.

When dawn broke the next day we began to fly sorties to see what could be seen; to identify in particular our own forward positions, and detect any enemy movement. Mike Chavasse marked it all up on a big map in what we grandly called our 'Ops. Room': a ridge-tent that also did duty as our mess. During the course of the battle we were able to bring together here a mass of up-to-date and accurate information about its progress that was simply not available elsewhere. It turned out a fine morning, with weak sunshine from a hazy blue sky. Visibility across the Rhine was poor with little or no wind to disperse the smoke and dust from the preliminary bombardments, so that observation became more difficult as the sun rose.

At 10 o'clock all gunfire ceased and 'Varsity' – the airborne landing which aimed to seize the bridges over the River Issel and then link up with the ground-forces – was about to begin. Bang on time the first wave of aircraft flew in at 500 feet, directly over our landing-ground. It was a mix of Dakotas and Curtiss Commandos and gliders towed by Halifax and Stirling tugs. They streamed over like a huge air-display, until the sweet-sour smell of cellulose paint, so characteristic of military aircraft, filled the air below. Suddenly things began to happen all around us; a Horsa glider slipped its

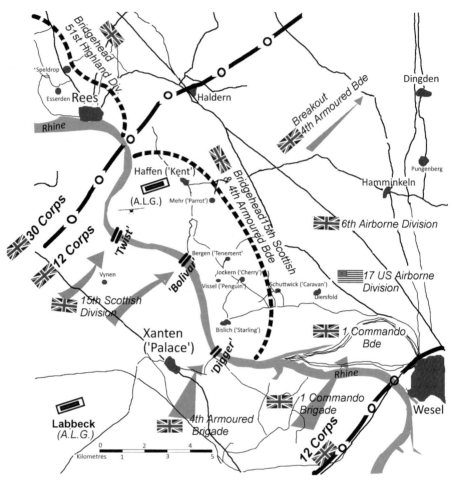

Crossing the Rhine: Operations Varsity and Plunder.

tow just short of the Rhine and came down near our strip. No doubt its crew, with more caution than courage, had decided to make the crossing on foot when things had calmed down.

A Dakota spilled its load of parachutists into the middle of a formation; they all landed safely. Meanwhile the German flak was beginning to take effect. Damaged aircraft began to straggle back, on fire or with engines stopped. Three Dakotas in succession crash-landed not far from the strip. I tried a sortie to see if I could see anything through the fog of battle. Visibility was now very poor beyond the river with the sun shining on the dust and

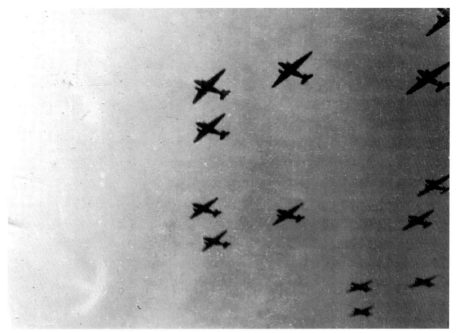

Operation Varsity. Dakotas cross the Rhine near Wesel.

smoke below the temperature-inversion, which was not much above 1,000 feet. This made it extremely difficult for the gliders as they came in to land and many of them crashed or made heavy landings. When I found myself being circled by a Dakota with one engine out, and had trouble getting out of his way, I decided to pack it in. As I turned home I saw him hit the ground near an orchard and begin to burn. I didn't see anyone get out and I hoped they had managed to bale out earlier. The final message got through when I was chased into our landing-ground by a flight of Liberators in formation at about 50 ft. We stopped flying till we could have the sky to ourselves again.

By now there were burning aircraft all round, but chiefly on the Hochwald ridge behind us. At one point I counted twenty-eight aircraft burning on the ground on our side of the Rhine. As we watched a Flying Fortress deliberately circling the dropping zone on the other side we wondered how he could possibly survive the flak that must be coming up at him. We worked it out that he must be the 'dropmaster' controlling the operation for the 17th US Airborne. When he could keep going no longer he limped back across the river

Gliders across the Rhine - operation Varsity.

with two engines out, and the crew began to bale out over a wood just north of us. The first man out went straight into the trees with his parachute fluttering behind him; the rest floated down safely. They were brave men.

That afternoon I flew over to the other side to look for an advanced strip, which I found in a nice meadow at Haffen. By this time the two pontoon bridges were across, and carrying endless lines of traffic, without any interference from the enemy. Nearby was the RHQ of 4th RHA, the gunner regiment supporting 4th Armoured Brigade, which would be handy for us. Early next morning John Turnbull flew over to Haffen (near Rees) with an airman, thus occupying what we hoped was the first landing-ground across the Rhine.

He flew a number of sorties, did one shoot with the regiment and ended up with a new propellor. He had chipped the tip of one blade while taxiing in after landing, which made the whole engine vibrate. So he radioed back for a spare, which was flown over, replaced and tested within the hour. (When our RAF engineer at SHQ got to hear of this, he told me the aircraft should have been grounded until they could test it for 'shock-loading'. I thought it

Rhine crossing point 'Digger', taken over Germany. *IWM*

best to bite my tongue lest he take offence and hold it against me on some future occasion).

Next day, the twenty-sixth, we moved the whole Flight across the River Rhine and set up a new landing-ground not far from the riverside. Nearby was a large barbed-wire compound that was rapidly filling up with German prisoners. Harry Eastgate did three good shoots. Mike Chavasse made his first operational sortie; he was also doing excellent work keeping the map up-to-date and briefing senior officers in search of information about the battle. In the afternoon General Ritchie, XII Corps Commander, turned up for one of Mike's updates and I then flew him down to Xanten.

The Flight was settled in comfortably after a busy day; Bud Abbott, one of the drivers, had done his own reconnaissance of a nearby farmhouse and returned with a goose under his arm. Being a real country lad from Suffolk he had immobilised the poor bird by stroking its back and then locking its wings together. It seemed resigned to its fate and I never liked to ask what happened to it.

Later that evening we had just settled down to our supper when German fighter-bombers put in a sharp attack on the pontoon bridges – their first attempt to react. We had a wonderful display of A/A fire, with red tracer arching all over the sky. In the midst of it all, our medical orderly set fire to one end of his consulting-room – a tent – after filling his Primus stove with petrol instead of paraffin. (It was his custom of an evening to brew up tea and entertain a few friends before turning in). It was the worst possible moment; the flames looked enormous, and seemed bound to attract every bomber in the area. Encouraged by all this the POWs started singing. However, we soon got the fire out and the bombers departed without apparently doing any damage of significance.

[Flight Diary 27th: *12 rds of A.P. shot fell in or near the camp. No damage to anyone but one tent caught fire due to a lamp, hurricane being turned over when the Flight took cover after the first rounds fell. Little damage was done.*

During the night we had JU88s trying to bomb the bridges and a camp full of POWs singing to keep their spirits up. Very noisy.]

For a finale, about an hour later, we felt a heavy thump on the ground outside the tent, with a rattle of earth and clods on the canvas. Several more followed further off. It seemed as if someone was having a go at us. In the morning we found the grass on the landing-ground had been ploughed up in a dozen places where armour-piercing shells had landed. Later we heard that a German tank fitted with an infrared night-sight had been put out of action nearby. We slept well that night, in spite of all.

Early next morning I had to go over to Haminkeln, where the airborne troops had landed. There were still a few RAF glider-pilots waiting for transport back and they were looking rather unhappy. I was not surprised after I had seen what had happened to their gliders. With all the dust and smoke, and the sun shining on the zone – to say nothing of the flak – landing must have been a matter of stuffing the nose down and pulling back hard as the ground came up to hit you; that is, if a tree didn't hit you first. Of the 8,000 airborne troops who went in from the 6th Airborne, some 1,000 were casualties by nightfall. But in military terms the operation had been a success and all the objectives had been taken. Of the aircraft which had taken part – some 4,000 Dakotas, Stirlings, Commandos, Halifaxes and Liberators – forty-six were counted as missing or destroyed. Massive fighter cover provided by 1,200 RAF and USAF aircraft had kept the German Air Force away.

29.iii.45

It's about time I wrote you a respectable letter! Things have gone very well here but we have been a little busy. We left Diest for Hasselt and came to Venlo prior to the big show. On D-day we saw the airborne go over and crossed on D+1. It was a pretty good time with a lot of excitement – rather grim sometimes but also very encouraging. The Scottish Division we crossed with are just the people to be with – we feel quite honoured to have done the job with them.

The Germans are rolling in as prisoners; a curious mixture of decrepitude and insolent stupidity. We're not too keen on the civvies, either – the farm we are near had twelve geese – they've got three now and no sympathy.

I flew a General to Brussels yesterday and back today – had a nice bath and a haircut. I also had a short session with the photographers – a gruelling experience which will be amusing in retrospect. I had two dinners too, a quick look at the Plaza Commandos and such chairborne types & went to bed (not enough blankets) & did a quick twelve hours sleep, thereby missing breakfast. When one leaves the big show, one stops trying to keep going & just goes to sleep. What with flying, barrages, bombs and shelling the nights are not very restful during the early days.

Well that's that and we reckon it won't be long now. All the parachutes are picked up now (we did our share) & most of the lads have their scarves made out of them.

Your new home seems better – more congenial in spite of all? Don't bother about the big shots – just smile sweetly and refer them to the war. Everyone has to do without these days!

No more news from here – I hope there will not be more to give but something tells me we will have to get mobile again.

With the 'logistics tail' moving across the Rhine in preparation for a move into Germany, Bill Heath (now the Corps Commander RA, XII Corps) was able to return to England on compassionate leave. His wife had pneumonia, but he had reluctantly put off going back to see her until the battle was to all intents over. (In those days before the discovery of the new sulfa drugs and penicillin, pneumonia was an even more serious and often fatal illness). On the twenty-eighth I flew him to Brussels to catch his flight on from there. It was an uncomfortable trip as MT169 began to play up on a magneto just after take-off. I climbed a bit higher and pressed on; fortunately Bill Heath did not appear to notice, having other concerns to occupy him. We reached Brussels, though and I saw him onto his flight at Evers in good time. Next day an air test failed to detect any problem with the magneto so maybe I was over-anxious.

The battle was indeed over for the moment. The bridgehead was thirty-five miles wide and twenty miles deep, with little opposition remaining; the front line ran from Emmerich in the north, which the Canadians now held, through Haltern in the southwest to Duisburg. As the Field Marshal observed, we were in possession of a springboard from which to launch major operations into Germany – a situation that he described as offering 'boundless possibilities and uncertainties'. For our part, the Flight diary says it all: '30 March: The whole Flight rather weary but triumphant after a gratifying week's work'. And even the most pessimistic (or superstitious) now had to admit that the end was at long last in sight.

Notes

1. The U.S. P47 Thunderbolt was the fastest piston-engined aircraft of World War 2. In service its speed was over 450 mph enabling its pilots to successfully combat the German Me262 and AR234 jet aircraft.

2. 52nd Div was originally 52nd 'Lowland', a normal infantry division. It was then retrained for a 'Mountain Warfare' role in Norway and finally sent into action in October, 1944, at Walcheren in Holland – below sea-level, as an 'air portable' division.

3. Quoted unascribed on page 99 – 'The Killing Ground', by Lucas H Barker, Batsford.

4. On 20 July 1944, an attempt was made to assassinate Adolf Hitler, Führer of Nazi Germany, perpetrated by Claus von Stauffenberg and other conspirators, inside his Wolf's Lair field headquarters near Rastenburg, East Prussia.

5. The Gloster Meteor had entered service in July 1944 but was used domestically to combat the V1 and V2 flying bombs. Some experts suggest that the plane was withheld from active service in North west Europe for fear that it might be captured and reveal its secrets either to the Germans or the Russians. As with the German development of jets, it was also believed for a while by their counterparts at the British Air Ministry that piston engine aircraft were better for combat purposes. It was soon demonstrated otherwise.

6. Wesel was one of many towns between the Rhine and the Elbe that suffered from battles fought since the seventeenth century for religious and dynastic causes. On the night of 23/24 March 1944 a force of 195 Lancaster and 23 Mosquito bombers of 5 & 8 Groups RAF attacked it. The raid was intended to divert attention from the landing of a Commando force across the Rhine as the prelude to 15th Scottish Division's and 6th Airborne's crossings. This final air attack made Wesel the most intensively bombed German town for its size during the war. Ninety-seven per cent of the buildings in the main town had now been destroyed; the population which numbered almost 25,000 men, women and children on the outbreak of the 1939–45 war was reduced to 1,900. How many were killed outright in bombing raids and the final assault by ground troops, and how many had been evacuated wounded or to save them from further bombing raids is not known. No aircraft from 5 & 8 Groups RAF was lost in this final raid.

Chapter 8

The Last, Long Mile

1 April–5 May, 1945

GOING into Germany from France and Luxembourg was like entering a tunnel. The friendly flag-waving of children and grownups that enlivened the dusty, jolting ride through towns and countryside in the 'liberated' territories gave way abruptly to a black, empty feeling of being alone, moving toward one distant objective.

James Stewart Martin *All Honorable Men*, 1950

In the spring of 1945 the prospect before 21st Army Group was very like the one that it faced after Normandy. Once more, during Operation 'Veritable', in February and March, the British and Canadians had been called on to fight a 'hinge' action against strong German forces. This action enabled the US armies to the south to make rapid progress against comparatively weak opposition. Then, as soon as the Rhine had been crossed at Wesel, Montgomery was relieved of command of the US divisions allotted to him (just as he had been after Normandy) and strategic direction of the Allied armies passed back to General Eisenhower. United States forces assumed the major role of encircling the Ruhr heartland and pressing on into southern Germany, while Monty's vision of a bold thrust to Berlin, like his earlier dream of bouncing the Rhine and striking into the heart of Germany, was not to materialise.

The reason was the same, and it was unarguable: Britain no longer possessed the military strength to back its political claim to influence the conduct of the war. The military initiative in Europe had passed to the Americans and to the Soviets as they closed in on Berlin; the cold fact was that General Bradley's US 9th Army alone now outnumbered Montgomery's 21st Army Group by nearly four to one, in terms of divisions under command.

Roosevelt and Stalin having settled between them the future shape of Europe at the Allied conference in Teheran (of all places!), it only remained to finish the war in Germany so that the frontiers and areas of influence agreed at Yalta could be put into effect. 2nd Army's modest part in the scheme was to fan out from the Rhine bridgehead and to carry out mopping-up operations across the plains of northern Germany, over the River Elbe and up to the Baltic.

3.iii.45

Poor old Poland has been cut up – no one ever knows what the Russians really want except Stalin and his mind must work in pretty dark patterns sometimes. It must be difficult for a Pole to decide who are friends and who are enemies. Stalin has learnt from Hitler how to use minorities to further his own ends. I thought we had seen where power politics lead.[1]

Within that plan were three major objectives: first, to capture Hamburg and Bremen/Bremerhaven (the latter would give the US forces the major port they needed to supply their troops); second, to establish as quickly as possible a British presence on the Baltic coast; and third, to block the escape of German forces into Denmark and Norway. (There was also a fourth and equally important task – a humanitarian one. That was to relieve the starvation and general deprivation of the Dutch population in North Holland, who for no logical reason had become the victims of Nazi spite, even though neither they nor their country could have any further part to play in the war. This last task fell to the Canadian 1st Army).

XXX Corps was given the objectives of Bremen and Hamburg, Enschede on the Dutch border and Lingen on the Dortmund-Ems canal. XII Corps in the centre was to head for Rheine (home of the Me. 262 jets which were causing so much trouble for the RAF), Nienburg on the Weser and Lüneburg south of the Elbe. On the right (or east) flank, VIII Corps was set to go for Osnabrück, Celle (on the River Aller) and Wittenberge on the River Elbe, with Lübeck on the Baltic coast as their final objective. Within this broad plan, divisions were to be switched between corps as operations progressed and the tactical situation demanded from day to day. And indeed the stubbornly defended and difficult terrain demanded a continually evolving exercise of military dexterity.

As far as we in 'C' Flight were concerned these wide prospects and strategies were well beyond our ken. Our first objective was to make our way through a terrain of woodland, moorland, minor roads and innumerable small watercourses that make up the catchments of the River Weser and its tributaries. A glance at the map showed the difficulty of finding landing-grounds – as bad as anything in the lowlands of Holland and in parts just as waterlogged. As XII Corps began to fan out from the bridgehead it was obviously our first priority to keep pushing our landing-grounds forward with the leading infantry, so that we could respond to whatever demand was made of us. The main requirement was for route reconnaissance and communications flights.

2nd April 1945

Thank you so much for the various things you've sent me – all very welcome!

Things are moving fairly fast and we stooge along with them – rather a gipsy life without much idea of where we are. So long as there are tanks in front & vehicles a little behind one can reckon that another few miles of Germany have succumbed but no one bothers much about places – they are mostly flat anyway. There are some left intact with the usual run of browned off locals – never was a Nazi touch [Editor's note: as in touched by madness] the whole time. We met a French prisoner on a farm just off home with a rucksack and a wide smile.

It is interesting to see the well-stocked farms here, full of good cattle, geese and pigs. The buildings are modern and well kept. Some people at any rate did well out of the war – the Germans. We have relieved them of a goose or two; one before the eyes of a colonel who was investigating looting.

Otherwise we press on regardless.

The weather has been foul today & yesterday with rain and high winds, producing very bumpy effects – not nice for us. I hope it's more moderate soon or we shall be left behind – which is a bad thing on one of these shows.

So much for the rapidly collapsing war! Communications flight is the next job, from Berlin.

I'm so glad you've got a pleasant job within the confines of the service. Bournemouth sounds just the place for a quiet sojourn so here's hoping it stays that way.

After the wilderness of Winchester you do deserve some amenities – I never knew such a dim place, especially in winter. Spring however is I assume inevitable judging by the odd greenery, cowslips, etc. We have two snowdrops in the corner of the tent, who knows what tomorrow – its normally thistles.

So much for the nature study, too. If the Dakotas get weaving soon enough I hope to be back in England this time next month (May 3 approx.) but who knows, everyone may be celebrating by then, in which case I'll wait for the hubbub to die down! Maybe.

We were now one pilot over strength, which came in useful. John Turnbull (former Desert Rat, M.M.) and Mike Chavasse had joined Butch Pritchard, Joe Hargreaves and Harry Eastgate – the old guard from Penshurst days – both settled in quickly and made an excellent contribution in their own distinctive ways. I understood that my responsibility was to keep the Flight mobile, closely in touch with current operations and also able, as far as possible, to anticipate future moves. To achieve these aims I split the vehicles up into a small advance party consisting of a jeep, a 3-tonner and a 15cwt truck, with Lance Bombardier Naylor and wireless in the 15cwt. Each vehicle had its usual driver and there were two airmen to perform aircraft servicing. They were equipped to provide a small section that was able to move rapidly to a new landing-ground and to service aircraft for up to twenty-four hours without reinforcement. To this end they had a ridge-tent, cooking equipment and rations, fuel and bedding, picks, shovels and wire-cutters and of course, small arms and ammunition. (It is satisfying to record that our excellent RAF Corporal Carter commanded this party). For my part I intended to keep pushing forward by Jeep, with a wireless, and reconnoitre suitable sites for landing-grounds before they were actually needed.

We set forth on 1 April (All Fool's Day), and set up shop near Ahaus, on the main road to Rheine. Once everyone was in and settled, I decided to take a Bren gun and have a look round the local woodlands. I leaned over the first gate I came to and put the gun over the other side before climbing over. This produced a severe pain in my ribs, which I had broken in 1940 while doing gun-drill on Salisbury Plain. I spent an uncomfortable night and next day found I could just about get into an aircraft, but getting the harness done up or turning round to look over my shoulder was not feasible. For the time being flying was out of the question and of course my other role, travelling on the ground by Jeep, meant bouncing about along roads that really were only fit for farm carts.

The next two days brought me to a point where I wondered if I could carry on any further. Fortunately Bombardier Cookson came to the rescue; the lads had found a barn full of vehicles that had been requisitioned by the German Army, including several cars. Among them was a nice Opel Kadett convertible that they were able to start up. The soft upholstery and coil front suspension were real pneumatic bliss and with such a vehicle, I felt I could keep going to Berlin.

1938 Opel Kadett already adapted for military use by the enemy.

Letter April 22nd:

We soldier on, but hope to get a little peace sometime! Still we are seeing
a good deal of Germany – what you'd pay for this in the ordinary way!
There are still the usual streams of ex-prisoners going somewhere or other
and various labour camps. The number of foreigners is really amazing; they
appear to out-number the Germans by a good deal. A good few British have
been set free and a horde of Russians and Frenchmen.

   I have acquired a little car, an Opel coupe but haven't had time to drive
it yet being a bit busy. During the past fortnight we have bashed about a bit.

[Editor: In wartime Britain leaving a vehicle without immobilizing it (by
removing an essential part like the rotor arm) was illegal; perhaps the
same was true in Germany – unless it was a requisitioned vehicle! The
date difference between letter and event could be for fear of the mail being
captured, as the Opel would have been a target if known to the enemy.]

   At Rheine the 53rd (Welsh) Division had a stiff fight to get across the
River Ems and the Dortmund-Ems canal. There were several airfields in
this area, heavily protected by flak, supporting an active population of Me.
262 jets; the RAF would be delighted if these were to be eliminated (and
so would we, as the jets were causing us some anxiety). In addition, the Air
Staff were eager to get their hands on as many intact or repairable specimens
as they could, for evaluation and research purposes.

   By now German opposition was becoming disorganised and a new pattern
of warfare developed. Stiff resistance was met at river-crossings and other
natural defensive positions, with great use of well-sited roadblocks, mines
and demolitions. To cover these obstacles pockets of German troops were
left behind in the general withdrawal; they were not afraid to sell their lives
dearly and have a crack at any British unit that might bump into them. (In
the course of the 2nd Army's 200-mile advance between the Rhine and
the Elbe there were so many obstacles that the Sappers had to build 500
bridges.) In addition, ground attacks by jet fighter-bombers became more
frequent and determined.

   To help counter these attacks by jet aircraft the Corps Commander very
decently loaned us a troop of light anti-aircraft gunners. They had a couple

of 40mm Bofors guns, each on a 4 x 4 Bedford truck and two White half-
tracks carrying hydraulically powered turrets, as used on Flying Fortresses.
Each turret mounted a pair of Browning half-inch machine guns and their
anti-aircraft crews were skilful and very keen. We had a demonstration of
their abilities when a Me. 262 came right over the ALG at a height of only
about 100 feet and going fast. One of the Bofors got a round under the
jet's nose as he approached, swung through 180 degrees and put another
round right up its tail. The armed half-tracks also proved very useful for
clearing lurkers from woodland or other likely cover close to our ALG's. A
two-second burst from their guns would immediately flush out the enemy
from any hiding place. We were very lucky not to lose one of them during
this work when it crossed a double row of mines in a narrow lane without
touching, or indeed seeing, them. Butch Pritchard and I were strolling up
close behind them when we spotted the mines so it must have been our
lucky day as well. Less fortunate were our other two flights that same day; 'A'
Flight had its ALG shot up by a fighter and in a night raid by ground forces,
'B' Flight had three aircraft damaged by small-arms fire and bazookas.

With all this excitement and with stray Germans liable to have a go at any
aircraft they saw, 'flak jackets and weaving [were] the order of the day', as
the Flight diary records. On one occasion while on the ground, I managed
to get my own back when a low-flying FW 190 came over and dropped a
bomb as big as a cabin-trunk a mile or so up the road. With a Bren gun at
the ready, I awaited his return, and as he came over, let loose a full magazine
at him. I must have given him a fright, as he put the aircraft up steeply and
swerved away. It gave me some payback for the fright I was given by a 190
near Heinsberg. Although we had strict orders not to open fire at any aircraft
at this time, I found it was good for our morale to have a crack at them once
in a while.

By this time, in early April 1945, we were nearing the last days of the war
in Germany and contrary to what might have been expected there was a
spirit almost of recklessness. We were all inclined to take risks that may have
been avoided in earlier days, as if, having survived so far, we had become
almost invulnerable. Nothing, of course, could have been further from the
truth. Looked at statistically, the odds were stacking up against each one
of us from day to day; we knew that perfectly well and indeed had earnest

debates as to whether, if having been sent out to Burma later on, we would start off with a clean sheet, or whether the odds would just go on stacking up. It was strange that we failed to adjust our behaviour accordingly and so became rather less cautious in the way we set about our business. Such a change in attitude proved fortunate rather than otherwise since our next few days were spent in the dangerous occupation of bridge reconnaissance, vital work that would otherwise have to be done by infantry patrols on the ground.

On 4 April, Captains Turnbull, Pritchard, Chavasse and Hargreaves were required to make a reconnaissance near Rheine to assess the state of the many road bridges over the Dortmund-Ems canal northwest and southeast of the town. Joe Hargreaves found the only way he could get the information was to fly directly over the bridges in face of continuous sniping by small arms fire and flak. Again the following day Joe went off on the early sortie, returning with holes in the aileron, and the day after that his efforts were rewarded with something large and jagged through MT349's main spar.

This type of reconnaissance certainly came up with the goods, but on this occasion Joe's aircraft was put out of service (or as it was reported in the Squadron diary: 'excellent results and damaged aircraft') and I wondered how long it would be before someone got shot down. The next morning, the seventh, Corporal Carter took a 3-tonner and went in search of an Auster that was reported to have crashed not far away and came back with one its wings. After the flight had moved to Drieirwald (where much work was needed on the ALG) Corporal Carter got cracking and had the aircraft back flying by the evening. The same day we also had MT169 back with us after servicing.

Joe Hargreaves remained undaunted by his experiences and on the eleventh he carried out a further recce on the twelve bridges over the canal between Neuenkirchen and Bramsche. They happened to be 5,000 yards within enemy-held ground, the weather was very misty and it took him two hours flying to compile an accurate report. He was able to obtain information that saved much ground patrolling by the infantry and enabled the Division to move forward many hours before it could otherwise have done. He was awarded the DFC for this work.

After the war Joe wrote me an account of the exploit:

In the evening Lyell had received his orders for the following day and returned to the ALG, his first words were "Who is Duty Pilot tomorrow?" The Joe of 1945 and the Ben of 1994 said "I am", and his first reaction after hearing the sortie requirement was he wished he was not! For Div wanted a bridge state recce, and the bridges were well into enemy territory. No chance of flying at 1,000 feet and looking over one's left shoulder for such detailed information 5 miles away. It must have been of some importance to have this intelligence for they had supplied Lyell with maps rarely seen at our level of work and which showed individual woods, buildings, bridges and even fields. We looked forward to our evening meal but it was sombre affair that night. I took the maps, folded them into a sequence for easy reference and ringed the bridges, there were 22 in all. The best plan seemed to be to fly from SW to NE, as we were on the left of the divisional area and so follow the valley.

Having made a plan it was apparent that this was not going to be an easy task – my recce of the Dortmund-Ems canal bridges earlier in the month was carried out in the midst of a battle between the ground forces of both sides who were fully occupied with each other and who would not be unduly concerned with a lone Auster. On this one it would seem I was going to be the focus of attention and my chances of survival diminished. Wireless silence had been ordered so that if I came to grief somebody else would have to carry on and Division would not be any the wiser of progress made up to that point! The headlong rush to the Elbe to beat the Russians had been a rush of blood to the heads of Staff thought process!

The full realisation of my involvement brought on retrospective thoughts, which was perhaps excusable at such a time. I had never settled to a communal life either at Public School or with the army but like us all, tried to make the best of a bad job, but there was no doubt that mentally things were building up and I had reached a point where life had become a bit of a farce. Conscription in 1939 into an infantry battalion of second line territorials had been a bad experience of inadequate training, lack of leadership, inedible food; the debacle of France in 1940. The great opportunity of training at OCTU, joining a good regiment in anti–tank, training my own troop to a high standard, sadly to leave them at the beginning of 1943 to go into Air OP when I realised I had become too attached to them and that 2pdr and 6 pdr gun were no match against German tanks, and I did not want to see either myself or my troop killed to no purpose. The non-dedication of certain pilots in Normandy in another flight. A marriage in March 1944 which I felt was not well-founded. The prospect of the Far-East when our 'own' war was over. All these aspects and others influenced me to go into the following day with the intention that my life was on the line and not being too bothered about it. In short I had become 'bloody-minded'. Those were my problems and like all things in life when accepted, action takes over and surmounts the difficulties.

As I recall, Division wanted the information by 08:00 hrs so it was early rising before first light. I had slept well and intended to do what was required. The aircraft was ready and started first time (not always an Auster feature, the priming pump was never consistent engine to engine, the volume too high or too low) – it was always an adventure to get ready to take off, and away we went, the little aircraft, a beautiful morning and me! The time to the area took a few minutes at Zero feet and I found my reference point spot on, a wooded hill. The warm sun, still air, cold and the entire valley shrouded in mist about 300 feet below. This was a problem for I could not see the bridges nor could the defenders be able to see me! It reminded me of the Wharfe Valley at home, which my bedroom overlooked and I recalled how this river mist would lift above ground level when the sun was shining, so I decided to have a look at my first bridge. My plan was to have plenty of speed in a shallow dive, to break through the mist, observe and pull out with full revs to gain the shelter again. There was no room for error, and no second chance, and the flying and map-reading training came into play – my first bridge was in the bag; it was exhilarating and replaced all my thoughts about being fed up. My Adjutant informed me [of the recommendation for the DFC] *on the Sunday morning of my return – it made me feel very humble also grateful for being amongst such a 'fine lot' during the NW Europe campaign, for they had contributed to such character as I possessed.*

By this stage our advance-party technique was proving effective. During moves we were communicating using our own Air OP frequency, a method that gave us speed and flexibility. The flight commander was responsible for keeping in close contact with the leading troops and one landing-ground ahead of the game, usually travelling by Jeep (my ribs had more or less sprung back into shape by now and with much regret I had bid farewell to the little Opel). Lightweight transport such as Jeeps could be a problem when we supported armoured divisions. Their forward elements travelled in armoured vehicles of one sort or another whereas the unarmoured Jeep had only its quick manouevrability and its firepower. Unsurprisingly I felt very vulnerable and I have no doubt my driver did too.

Capt R.L. Munro, letter dated April 22 1945

We took some prisoners the other day – also got smartly mortared but nothing damaged. Still I'd prefer an armoured car for this racket – it could save a lot of grovelling in the ubiquitous dust. I am told that the war is over, however – bar the shooting. I haven't felt so frightened for a while.

We wonder vaguely where we'll end up – storming the Bavarian Alps no doubt. It is going to be a bleak job stoogeing among the uncouth Teutons. They are getting rather unpopular locally.

A kind of climax was reached one day when we were moving up sandwiched in the column between various armoured cars and other vehicles. At a crossroads we came up to a group of picturesque thatched houses near which I saw a green field that looked like a good bet for a landing-ground. We turned off for a better look and whilst I was wandering about in the field, checking for mines and generally sizing it up, we heard the rushing noise of Nebelwerfer rockets. They landed in just the next field. As I got back into the Jeep an Auster shot overhead and over the radio came an urgent cry from Harry: 'You are being mortared', which helped to confirm our own view of what was going on. We drove rapidly back to the road as another salvo of rockets landed in the village, setting fire to the thatched roofs until the whole row was billowing smoke and flames as one house set fire to another. We drove flat out through the heat and the smoke to rejoin our recce group; one thing was established: it wasn't a good spot for a landing-ground. And if the German Army thought that was the best way to defend their country, at least it made a change for them to destroy the property of their own citizens.

With such diversions we pressed on through the watery, flat countryside. The road through ruined villages was sometimes wet with the sap from

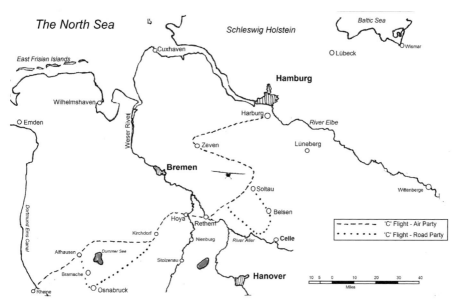

The Road to the Elbe. River Rhine to Hamburg.

shattered lime trees; spring was on the way but we did not feel much gladness. One of our problems was with prisoners. At first we rounded them up and sent them back in a 3-tonner. Then there were so many of them that we just took their weapons away (if they had not already ditched them) and sped them on their way to the rear on foot. During the process I learnt that the best way to smash a Mauser rifle was to pick it up by the butt and hit the muzzle on the ground; if you did it the other way round, which appeared to be the logical way, it just bounced back.

A rather more deadly risk than a surfeit of prisoners were the ex-Hitler Jugend would-be heroes, armed with machine guns, waiting round some corner and prepared to have a go, as John Poston, one of Monty's most trusted liaison officers found to his cost.[*]

---

[*] Major, POSTON, John William, MC and Bar, 87368; Liaison Officer to General Sir Bernard Montgomery Killed in action on 21 April 1945 aged twenty-five as the result of an ambush while returning to General Montgomery's TAC HQ on the Lüneburg Heath in Germany.

Every village had its wall with the final Nazi exhortation 'Sieg oder Siberien' ('Victory or Siberia'). It was a good example of a guilty conscience at work, after what the Germans had done in the Soviet Union. The SS, who were now the backbone of German resistance, knew very well what their fate would be if they got into the hands of the Red Army, but with typical stupidity they continued to oppose the British and US advance in the west while the Red Army occupied more and more of their country in the east.[2]

Whatever human sympathy we had with the plight of the ordinary German at that time was entirely changed by the discovery of the state of affairs at Belsen concentration camp between Rethem and Celle. The advance of 15th Scottish Division was suddenly checked a few miles south of the camp (which we did not know existed at that stage). There were rumours of high-level Red Cross negotiations about a risk of typhus and then the advance continued the next day. I was travelling along the Corps route with the ground-party when we came to a crossroads outside a small village. There was obviously something unusual going on, with small groups of people standing beside the road. One or two wore blue and white striped clothing, like pyjamas. As we came up to them we saw that they were desperately thin, their skin a dull grey-green stretched tightly over the forehead, cheekbones and lower jaw, with the neck-muscles standing out. Their heads were shaved and they were scarcely able to shuffle. Others were sitting or lying by the roadside, with a group of German civilians some way off just staring at them or looking the other way as if they did not exist.

That was Belsen. We had been held up to allow the Swedish (or Swiss) Government to organise an orderly handover of the camp between the departing German guards and our forward troops (true to the great German maxim of 'alles in ordnung', with no doubt an exchange of receipts for the live and dead stock within the camp). The fear was that typhus might break out and be spread far and wide by the escaping inmates, if the camp was left unguarded. In fact there were few indeed with the strength to struggle beyond the gates when the German guards withdrew.

As well as the civilian camp, there was also a Russian POW camp where 50,000 prisoners had died in captivity and not far away an SS tank-range. The people in the nearby town of Bergen preferred to ignore the whole matter, as they had done for several years past.

14th April 1945

We've just had a day off – first since we left the west bank of the Rhine, so we were quite glad of it. Since I did 100 miles by road the day before, I felt fairly ready for it. Still it's better to get on: my bed is well below ground (against the JU88s) & we're not due to fly until late tomorrow.

We lost the mail the other day but I don't think any of yours went adrift. Luckily we recaptured the driver and one passenger intact but the mail was gone. Such are the hazards of war!

[Squadron Diary 8 April: "Captain Munro reported an abandoned 15 cwt carrying mails had been found in a ditch in his area and that a body was lying alongside it. The truck was identified as one of SHQ and the missing men from the truck were BQMS Davidson and L/Bdr Peabody. Later the body was identified as that of Gnr Searle who was returning from workshops."]

I look forward to seeing the link up with the Russians – not long after that! I'm rather sick of the Germans – a horrible race of lunatics: there's no tendency to fraternise with such a misguided lot of throw-backs.

During the next few days we had to fly up or down the Corps axis over the camp. As the camp was cleared the dead were taken out of the huts and their bodies stacked like sacks in long heaps which grew bigger daily and could be seen from the air like big potato-clamps. The smell of putrefaction was so strong that it could be smelt a hundred feet above. As we had come through France, Belgium and Holland we had been taught what our fellow Europeans just across the Channel had had to endure under the Nazis. Belsen was the climax. I wonder if the shared suffering of ordinary people in those years of German occupation was not an underlying motive in the movement for a united Europe in which these things could never happen again; perhaps the reason we in Britain have been slow to take part in it is because mercifully we did not share that experience.

In front of the Corps there lay the great area of moorland and bog which surrounds the Dümmer See, a shallow lake surrounded by reeds which is no doubt of great interest to birdwatchers and wildfowlers. As far as we were concerned it was just an obstacle to progress. However, it gave us

658. AL. 642. 20. APR. 45. F. 20

Bergen Belsen. Burial party and the dead.

an opportunity to show how an Air OP Flight could be a highly flexible and mobile unit. The objective was to skirt the Dümmer See marshes by going south towards Osnabrück and get in position to cross the next river, the Weser, at Nienburg or further north at Hoya. Squadron HQ had set up a landing-ground at Barenburg, between the Dümmer See and the Steinhuder Meer. On 12 April, the aircraft flew directly to SHQ, while I took the ground-party south to Osnabrück and then up to Barenburg. I left Lance Bombardier Naylor at Divisional HQ with the wireless truck. He was to keep in touch and then follow on that night.

The aircraft continued to fly road recces from SHQ, while the ground-party covered the hundred-odd miles in five hours between Alfhausen and

SHQ (653) in Germany with Equipment Officer, Flying Officer Ellis, and Armoured Vehicle.

SHQ. Next morning, having got everyone together again, we moved off to a new landing ground, at Bruchhausen-Vilsen, just west of Hoya on the Weser, from where a series of bridge recces were flown along the Weser right up to Bremen. (The area west of the Weser is a maze of small rivers and large drains, crossed by a network of minor roads). These recces, not surprisingly, continued the next day. No doubt as a relief from this rather trying work, Joe shelled a railway bridge and Butch set fire to a large fuel dump, which raised a splendid cloud of black smoke capped with a little cloud of white cumulus, created by the heat. At this point we joined Guards Armoured and started to head north. They were making their way towards the small town of Zeven, in the middle of nowhere, midway between the Elbe and the Weser.

En route we passed the POW camp [*Stalag XIB/357*] at Fallingbostel, already taken over by its British inhabitants and established ourselves on a forward landing-ground west of Soltau. At nightfall we withdrew – there were too many stray Germans about for our liking after dark and 'A' Flight did in fact get shot up not far from here. (As a matter of curiosity, we got a landing-ground near the village of Neuenkirchen northwest of Soltau. A completely unremarkable place, except that it was the fourth – and last – village of that name we had passed since crossing the Rhine. If it means what I suppose it does, there must have been a boom in church building in this area at one time).

We were now flying many recces in support of the Division and doing shoots as a bonus. In preparation for the attack on Zeven we flew all the infantry commanders for a look at the ground and did more shoots and bridge and road recces. During the attack the next day, the twenty-fourth,

About to be attacked: Front line reconnaissance of Zeven (on the left).

we flew close cover and Harry did some shoots. At that time the German
2nd Naval Infantry Division [*2. Marine-Infanterie-Division*] were occupying
Zeven. This defensive unit was made up of surplus naval personnel and
was in retreat. As soon as they had been successfully evicted, we occupied
a landing-ground on their barrack square at Selsingen. Incidentally, the
Guards rather disgraced themselves here; they captured the German
Divisional Commander and entertained him to dinner – perhaps rather too
well, since he got away during the ensuing jollifications.

Letter: 24 May 45

*You're horribly right about the war – what a long time ago. I shall have to have
a week off when it ends and wonder what to do. In many ways it might be easy
to do something quickly but just now it doesn't seem to be near enough to require
any very urgent decisions! I must see what offers in the gold-brick business.*

*Everyone is volunteering to liberate Denmark just now as an alternative
to sitting in Germany. And of course there's Norway too. I get a kind of
dizzy feeling when I think of getting any more landing grounds to occupy.
God forbid that we ever have to start landing on frozen lakes at this stage.*

*The liberated prisoners are still as numerous as ever and still as keen to get
home. Meanwhile the old guns are pooping off at Bremen miles away: the
sky is free of Germans (who rushed ineffectually round the sky at dawn the
other day) and barring the telephone, things should be quiet. One looks for
SS men under the bed as a matter of course, however.*

*I have now got to get reluctant airmen to say on paper what they want
to be after the war. My advice is so bitter that I am thinking of letting some
keen type do it instead. I wish they'd tell the Germans the war was over –
everyone else thinks so apparently. Postwar this, V day that – it is rather
difficult to sympathise when aircraft come back full of holes.*

Still only? more days till my leave – we mustn't grumble!

XII Corps was running out of military objectives – not many months before
the Guards had been the toast of Brussels and now they had to content
themselves with the capture of a one-horse market town in the wilds of
Lower Saxony. Further east, however, there were still honours to be won.

VIII Corps was now lined up on the River Elbe at Lauenburg and 15th Scottish would add the Elbe to its record of major river crossings in northwest Europe, along with the Seine and the Rhine.

As always with the 15th Scottish Division, it went according to a meticulous plan; the assault was launched in the early hours of 29 April, preceded by the customary artillery bombardment (the last of the campaign) of the opposing troops. They established a bridgehead fifteen miles wide and eight miles deep into which moved 11th Armoured Division, 5th Division (from the Italian front) and 6th Airborne, on their way to Lübeck and the Baltic coast. The 15th Scottish swung left along the north bank of the Elbe and headed for Hamburg and, by 1 May, were within sixteen miles of it. The next day, the thirtieth, 7th Armoured Division crossed the Elbe and entered the ruins of Hamburg.

12th May 1945

Hamburg is a terrible mess. It is absolutely devastated for miles: walls but nothing inside them. There are rusty U-boat hulls lying on the slipways, sunk U-boats, sunk barges, oil tanks in all states of collapse. The whole city is glittering with broken glass: the river is covered with oil. There are two enormous square erections in the middle of one district − solid masonry the size of a block of flats, with flak guns mounted on top. A few bombs have just bounced off. Whole acres are deserted and abandoned.

General Blumentritt contacted General Barber to discuss the preliminaries of the German surrender; 11th Armoured Division entered Lübeck, while 6th Airborne, having advanced forty miles that day, entered Schwerin and made first contact with the Russian Army. That afternoon the lst Canadian Parachute Battalion (operating as part of the British 6th Airborne) occupied Wismar, on the Baltic coast; The 21st Army had thus achieved its final objective, 600 miles and eleven months after landing on the beaches of Normandy.

Hitler was dead and his hastily cremated remains were now lying outside a bunker in Berlin. Admiral Doenitz, as his successor for lack of a better*,

---

* On the 28 April Hitler expelled his preferred successors, Goering and Himmler, from the Nazi party on suspicion of trying to negotiate a surrender. That night, in his testament, he nominated Doenitz in their place.

Hamburg docks, 1945.

now began overtures for a general surrender of the German forces. After a good deal of shilly-shallying by various German generals, admirals, and chiefs of staff, probably to buy time for refugees fleeing the Red Army in the east, Admiral von Friedeburg led a delegation to Montgomery's headquarters in Lüneburg Heath to offer the surrender of all German forces in North Germany including those still facing the Russians. He was told that surrender of German forces facing the Russians would have to be negotiated with the Russians; Montgomery was only prepared to discuss surrender of those forces remaining in Holland, west of the Elbe and west of the Baltic. Having been shown the reality of the German military situation on Monty's maps, the Admiral burst into tears and went back to his headquarters to recommend submission. [Admiral von Friedeburg later committed suicide.]

By six o'clock the next evening Montgomery again received the Admiral who conveyed acceptance of the terms. They were for unconditional surrender as defined in a short typewritten memorandum that was at once put before the full German delegation for their signatures. Last of all, the

Field Marshal signed on behalf of General Eisenhower – and initially put the wrong date, 3 May, at the foot. It was half-past six on the evening of 4 May, in fact, and all hostilities by German forces were to cease at eight o'clock the next morning – 5 May.

The news was heard in the Flight without any great surprise or emotion. We had known for several days that German resistance was effectively at an end. There had been rumours of an arrangement for a cease-fire; by the time the formal announcement came, the feeling of expectation had changed into one almost of anti-climax.

12th May 1945

The trouble is that now the war is over here, I have no mainspring. When everything is going forward to a definite end it is quite easy to keep going, but it's rather hard to get much enthusiasm now.

C Flight pilots, Altona, May 1945: John Turnbull M.M.; Frank Pritchard; Lyell Munro M.B.E.; Mike Chavasse; Harry Eastgate M.i.D.; Ben Hargeaves D.F.C.

Flight Commander in
Germany, May 1945.

It was the end of a long hard road but we had got there, in good spirits
and good order, with more than our fair share of good luck. And we had
ended the campaign on a high note; during April we had flown a total of 345
sorties, of which 251 were in the face of the enemy, and had observed thirty-
four shoots. For their part, the ground-party had travelled some 1,220 miles
and created on the way fifteen landing-grounds where no aircraft had ever
landed before – and where no pilot has probably been rash enough to try to
land again. As Butch Pritchard used to tell us, with all the authority of the
Royal Military Academy behind him, 'You've got to get properly organised'.
I think that in the end, like so many other units in 2nd Army, 'C' Flight
probably was.

C Flight at Hoya 1945.
Back row: Gunners Abbott, Smith, Stevens, Steede, Bottcher, Gamble
2nd Row: LAC Graham, LAC Cook, Gunner "Taffy" Hathaway, AC Oxenbury, LAC Sellicks, Gunner Williams, Bdr Cookson.
Third Row: Gunner Clark, Cpl Hargreaves, L/Bdr Naylor, L/Bdr Windle, Gunner Blackmore, AC Baverstock, Cpl Carter, Sgt Maughan
Front Row: Capt Hargreaves, Captn Eastgate, Captn Munro, Captn Pritchard, Capt Turnbull. (Capt Chavasse absent on leave)

[Editor: The diary of 'C' Flight ends on the 30 April 1945 without ceremony: *30th: Flt reverted to SHQ at Lubberstedt.*

The Squadron Diary records that, with hostilities over, 653 Squadron pilots were engaged in 'intercomms and ferrying' until on 12 September it was announced that after operating for three years and three months the Squadron would disband three days later.]

The Aftermath

This is where the personal account by Lyell Munro finishes. However, there was a great deal to be done once the guns had (mostly) become silent in

Europe. The job of defeating the Japanese was still underway; during the summer of 1945 the Burma theatre was a matter of huge concern for all. And close to home, Europe was now a shattered continent whose fate was largely in the hands of the victorious Allies. Defeated Germany was a sullen and hostile country; its cities were in ruins, and the coming winter would be harsh with shortages of food, accommodation and resources. The population, many in denial of the immediate past, had to adjust to occupation either by the much-feared Red Army, seeking retribution, or the more humane British, Commonwealth and US forces.

Britain, war-weary, exhausted and bomb-damaged had to cope with its own returning army, and the fact that many would never return. A whole generation had grown to maturity fighting a war and doing little else; and there was at last to be a General Election, as democracy had been suspended during the war years. So much rebuilding was needed in a world that had become a dramatically different place in just half a decade.

Lyell Munro remained in Germany until the end of 1945 and his letters of the time reflect the reality of life as an occupier. There was also the future to look forward to with all the uncertainty left in the wake of such destruction and for a while the continuation of the Japanese war around Burma.

C Flight
653 Sqdn RAF
BLA
28.v.45

My darling Jean,

Rumours of war are the big feature of this weary life. We hope to hear our fate tomorrow: until then we just file every breath of gossip (quite a metaphor) and continue to play cards and speculate.

We put about twenty civvies in the jug during the lunch hour today for trespassing on the aerodrome. Unless we shoot a few they'll never realise that we aren't very keen on them! Brutality is a difficult art to learn.[3]

Himmler did the right thing at last: his two SS boys [his aides, captured with him] were thought to be attempting suicide in a similar way, and they didn't dare search them in case they did. So they asked them in for a chat and quietly knocked them over the head with something heavy and then examined them. It's a strange world, isn't it?

You can't imagine how nice it is to have a room to myself and not be parked in a room with four others – not to mention a tent. I've got a beautifully untidy desk where I can have everything handy at once, a wireless and an enormous green tile stove in one corner. I had a nice original water colour of "Russland – Summer 1942", by an unknown Nazi, but I tore it up. It was very amateurish.

How true it is that all the best billets are only temporary! Still, my dearest so long as you don't have to scrub, yourself, why worry? My chief delight is watching others work!

You want to get a really arty photo taken – look frightfully soulful and idealised. Do, and see what happens anyway.

I'm glad to say no one has yet asked me what I want to be when I grow up. It's a delicate question – they don't want to encourage much of the urge for Civvy Street in case we have to go via Tokyo. I think I'll be a realist and go in for a course in selling boot-laces. Quite honestly I am unable to give an opinion until I see some chance of getting out. Conducted aerial tours of the battlefields – I've only missed one [Arnhem] *– are the obvious answer…*

Goodbye for now, darling.

My love to you.

Lyell

Some optimists expected a return to 'business as usual':

Letter home 27 September:

A splendid example of the regular soldiers outlook came my way. One of the C in C's [Commander in Chief's] *liaison officers is a very pleasant chap called O'Brien who has a DSO, MC and Bar. The CO of the Defence Coy who is a long moustached regular, said of him 'Of course, O'Brien's such a civilian (scorn!), you'll never get any idea of the Army into his head!' Maybe I'm mad or is that remark the end of everything? 'Now the war's over, we regulars can get down to some real soldiering'.*

In fact 'real soldiering' probably simply meant policing the Empire and on that role the sun was well and truly setting after so many years. Nevertheless, for the time being it remained an option, preferably, as far as Captain Munro was concerned, from outside the confines of 'real soldiering'!

Notes

1. The Yalta Conference, held February 4–11, 1945, was the wartime meeting of Franklin Roosevelt, Winston Churchill, and Joseph Stalin to discuss Europe's post-war reorganization.
2. SS prisoners in British hands were later interned on one of the North Friesian islands, with the minimum of amenities; The Field Marshal took a personal interest in their welfare, possibly as a result of John Poston's death at their hands shortly before the German surrender.
3. Alan Munro recalls that when he was stationed at RAF Wildenrath in the Westphalian Rhineland long after the war, the local Stadtdirektor (Town Clerk) asked him why the RAF always held a cocktail party in September, as if he did not know. In return Alan asked him why he and the Mayor were so friendly towards the British; 'Easy. When I was sixteen I was put into a uniform too large for me with holes in it and blood. I was told to shoot the first British soldier that crossed the Roer. This I did. The British took my gun, smacked my bottom, sent me home and told me not to do it again. No other nation on Earth would have done that.' His gratitude lasted for a long time.

Chapter 9

When this Bloody War is Over...

Five years of conflict in Europe had ended with the signing of the German surrender on Lüneburg Heath but Britain was still at war in the Far East and troops from the European front were starting to be sent on to Burma.

Lyell's nephew Alan, remembers that in 1945, at the age of four, he was sitting on his grand-father's shoulders in Hyde Park watching a long column of khaki-clad troops with sloped arms marching 'to the war in the Far East'. The crowd was subdued and probably resentful as it must have been a painful sight after the tumultuous celebrations on VE night, 8 May, not long before. In his letters to Jean, Lyell had mentioned the uncertainty of being sent to fight under 'SEAC' (South East Asia Command):

19 May:
Apart from the daily crop of rumours about Burma, absolutely nothing happens and there is no work to do except to keep the Flight going.

22 May:
The main activity is gathering rumours: everyone is very Burma-conscious and everyone has a new rumour. No one knows what is going to happen, apparently.

23 May:
Everything is ominously quiet here – I feel it will only need a touch and we shall all disperse to the earth's ends in a wholesale dissolution. Rather a trying period! Aircrew leave has also stopped – instead we get 10 days every four months. Not that I'll be here for four months – no one can imagine where we'll be then. It's all so unsettling! There's scope for a crystal gazer in these parts at the moment.

By the end of May he wrote that the uncertainty was over. Sixteen members of the squadron had been selected or volunteered to 'go to Burma' and Lyell was not one of them. It appeared that aged twenty-six, he was too old. Then the war in the Far East started to come to an end, first in Burma, then Malaya and Singapore, and finally, after the USAAF B29 dropped the two atom bombs on Hiroshima and Nagasaki, the World War ended with the Japanese surrender on 14 August 1945.

Most of the 12 AOP squadrons involved in active service were quickly stood down, including all three Canadian units. On 15 September 653 Squadron was disbanded at Hoya, just outside Hamburg, in what was to become West Germany. Lyell was moved to 657 Squadron, by now a part of the British Army of the Rhine (BAOR), which then reverted to War Office control in the November of that year. In October 1945 he had been awarded the MBE for his contribution to the crossing of the River Rhine, but almost another year was to pass before he was demobilised. During that time Alan

MBE Recommendation.

remembers watching him flying the 'Dickson Pioneer' in an Army firepower demonstration, probably on Salisbury Plain and for years afterwards he kept the message streamer that Lyell had dropped over the spectators. After a final posting to Rolleston Camp at Larkhill, Lyell was released from active service on 30 September 1946.

Lyell left the Army on a standard 'Class A Release', a scheme designed to smooth the transition into civilian life via the Reserve but with a proviso that it could be cancelled in the event of any emergency. He then returned home before going up to Oriel College, Oxford where he was to complete the degree he had started before the war. MT169, the last wartime 'Dickson Pioneer', was sold out of service to the Surrey and Kent Flying Club at Biggin Hill in March 1954, becoming G-ANHO and being repainted in their distinctive blue and yellow markings. Paradoxically, on 9 May 1964, it crashed when taking off from Biggin Hill; one of the two occupants died and on 24 June the aircraft was removed from the register.

It seems surprising that, in January 1947, Lyell wrote to enquire about AOP posts in the Territorial Army. Perhaps he missed the camaraderie, excitement and fulfilment of the war years. However, when a local Yeomanry Regiment offered him a post as an AOP pilot in June, he turned it down to concentrate on his studies. In April 1947, he had married Jean who, after her war service, first in the Voluntary Aid Detachment (VAD) and then in

MT169 Dickson Pioneer in civilian ownership.

the WRENS, was happy to settle down and enjoy a quieter life. In 1948 he successfully completed his degree. At some point, either in 1947 or 1948, Jean and he travelled to France to visit some of the places from where he had flown. They also visited the grave of his friend Geoff Burgess at Le Neubourg, just outside Rouen.

From his letters, it is obvious that the prospect of settling down into a routine job did not appeal to him but at the same time, he felt he was temperamentally unsuited to the life of a peacetime soldier. Of the other options available, he chose the Colonial Office, which held out prospects of travel, challenge and adventure. In 1949, he successfully applied for the post of Assistant District Commissioner in the Central Provinces of Nyasaland (now Malawi). Although life for a colonial official was very much as it had been before the war, it was soon clear that change was inevitable as the peoples of the Empire began to see the possibility of an end to British rule. Lyell was frequently away from home for long periods 'up country' and for Jean this was a difficult time. She was often alone with few, if any, Europeans for company and servants whose English was either rudimentary or non-existent. As a colonial officer's wife, she was expected to manage an often-isolated household and cope with emergencies that could range from invasions by soldier ants, to floods and bushfires. During this time in Nyasaland, Jean and Lyell had two sons: Jim (born in January 1951) and Robert (born in May 1953).

As unrest increased in the surrounding British territories, the security situation in Nyasaland also deteriorated. During his second tour of duty, Lyell and his Askari guards were ambushed while making a trip up country to collect hut tax. A tree was felled which landed on the land rover he was travelling in and the party was pinned down by rifle fire until help arrived. Lyell suffered a broken collarbone and one of the guards was injured by a bullet. The final straw came when a mob attacked the house while Lyell was away and Jean and her two young sons had to flee with an Askari guard and the children's nursemaid. This was Lyell's last tour of duty in Nyasaland and the family returned to Britain towards the end of 1955.

In 1956, after UK leave, he was posted to Cyprus. Compared with Nyasaland, this might have seemed an ideal posting for someone with a young family. Nevertheless, against firm British resistance, Greece was already pressing for an end to British rule on the island. In November 1954, a Greek-Cypriot nationalist, Colonel Grivas, had landed quietly at night on a deserted beach. At the time the authorities paid little attention to his arrival. However in the spring of 1955, Grivas started the group calling itself EOKA whose aim was the union of Cyprus with Greece (Enosis). The organisation recruited from the youth of the island, the school children and students, and instilled anti-British sentiment amongst Greeks. Civil commotion soon escalated into a guerrilla war between the British Army and EOKA (the Turkish population sided with the British). Jean and Lyell's children knew little else besides life in Cyprus and adapted to it, despite the scares and insecurities that represented normality. In March 1957 their third child, Neil, was born in Larnaca. Jean and Lyell did their best to shield their children from the escalating violence in Nicosia and the other towns where EOKA snipers had been targeting British soldiers and their families. However, there were times when the threat came uncomfortably close. On one occasion, Jean and the boys had to leave the car for the shelter of a roadside ditch while Lyell used his pistol to stop an EOKA agent from detonating a bomb in a culvert just ahead.

Lyell's post in Cyprus came to an end after the signing of the complex Zurich-London agreements, under which the island gained an uneasy form of self-government. He had made a considerable success of his assignment on Cyprus and towards the end of his tour in 1960 he became Minister of Defence in the pre-independence transitional government (he spoke Greek well). Later, in recognition of his work, Lyell was awarded the General Service Medal with a Cyprus clasp. Although he had also been offered a senior government post in the Republican government after independence, he turned it down because he had a strong feeling that the new Cypriot government under the Greek-Cypriot President, Archbishop Makarios and Turkish-Cypriot Vice-President Doctor Fazıl Küçük, would be dangerously fragile. Many Greek Cypriots still wanted union with Greece and they now thoroughly detested the Turkish Cypriots whom they saw as traitors and collaborators. Events would soon show that his misgivings were well-founded when, in 1963, clashes between Greek and Turkish Cypriots led to interference from both Turkish and Greek military forces and required the dispatch of 7,000 UN peace-keeping troops. In

1974 an abortive EOKA coup d'etat was followed by a Turkish invasion and the partition of the island.

Lyell, Jean and the boys left Cyprus in 1960 and returned to the United Kingdom where they settled in Leatherhead (then just a small town) on the outskirts of London. Lyell had successfully applied for a post in the Home Civil Service and joined the Ministry of Defence, first as a Principal, then on promotion to Assistant Secretary. It was perhaps to balance the routine of a commuter's life that he now found an interest outside his work.

Whilst he was in Germany after VE day Lyell had been re-introduced to sailing as he describes in a letter to Jean in June 1945:

Meanwhile I am embarking on a nautical life in that elegant vessel the Sharpy. We had a pleasant afternoon knocking about on the Steinhuder Meer (near Hanover) & didn't capsize or break anything. The trouble is we haven't got the nautical gen yet as to the right jargon. Talk of 'sheets', 'jibs' and so on leaves us about two jumps behind. 'That rope' or 'the front sail' slip out in moments of crisis. Anyway, we've got the business buttoned up fairly well so we reckon to spend all our spare time there. It's ten years plus since I sailed a boat so memory is a little halting at first.

Jean had learnt to sail during her time as a Wren and when Lyell left the Army, she and Lyell spent a summer sailing on the River Blackwater on the East Coast. After coming home from Cyprus, they decided that they would take up sailing again when the boys were old enough, and in 1963 they bought their first boat. This began what was to be a lifelong interest that would occupy their spare time and give back to Lyell the challenge and sense of adventure that he enjoyed.

It was also when living in Leatherhead that Lyell also began to consider writing about his wartime experiences. He was a firm believer in the European Common Market as a means of avoiding a repeat of such conflicts and wanted to remind others why it was so important that Europeans should learn to co-exist. He had light-heartedly mentioned the possibility to Jean in a letter from Diest on 18 February 1945:

… until someone bids us go and look for Germans, we're going to get some time to ourselves – first time since last June, not of course that we haven't had quiet spells but never a real period of official idleness before. Shall I write my war reminiscences? A friend, one George Woodman, made a broadcast the other day in a moment of alcoholic rashness while on leave. I believe it was good, but we reckon that if line-shooting is wanted we can think some up and defy all comers. They should earn many a pint in the post-war bars if properly put across.

Now in the late 1960s he began to take the idea more seriously, bought a typewriter and began to put his memories to paper. By 1977, Lyell had retired and he and Jean were living in Essex. It was about this time that they went again to France and began to retrace the journey that 'C' Flight had taken in 1944 and 1945. In anticipation of retirement Jean and Lyell had bought a small cottage in the delightful coastal village of Findhorn in NE Scotland. During the early 1980s, with the help of their sons, they sailed their latest boat – a 6-ton gaff cutter called 'Wendy May' – from her mooring in the Essex backwaters to her new berth beside the Moray Firth. They spent their summers sailing amongst the beautiful islands of the Hebrides and when the autumns came and the boat was laid up for winter Lyell continued working on the book. His son Robert was doing a computer science degree at UMIST and helped him master an early PC he had bought (a Philips!). With Robert's guidance, Lyell enthusiastically took to pre-internet computing and soon began to produce reams of manuscript that he passed out to the family for comment. The book was slowly taking shape.

At the same time, Lyell also began to seek out and contact old comrades from his army days and it was immediately clear that the bond forged during the war was as strong as it had ever been, despite the many years that had passed. At the AOP reunion at Middle Wallop, Jean recalled with amusement that, no sooner had they arrived, than Lyell became the centre of a noisy group who were obviously intent on catching up on forty years of gossip, reminiscence and beer consumption. An extensive correspondence began with the four other surviving 'C' Flight pilots – Ben Hargreaves, Freddie Riding, Bill Turnbull and 'Butch' Pritchard – and with other pilots from 653 including Major Tetley Jones, their first Squadron leader.

The trip to France in the 1970s was followed by several more and including one in 1985 to Germany where Alan's squadron was stationed. Alan recalls:

In the autumn of 1985 Lyell and Jean came to see us in Germany as they retraced his steps. I was stationed at the German Air Force base at Jever in East Friesland, or Lower Saxony. He said that they had driven through Antwerp, in which city he'd had some of his happier wartime experiences. He told me that according to Army intelligence at the time, the British Army had taken Antwerp airfield, so he had landed there to refuel. The garrison came running out with hands held high to surrender to the first British officer that they saw. An official, possibly Belgian, handed Lyell his pistol in surrender and offered him a glass of schnapps in his office. Then, some time later, to Lyell's relief, the first British infantry jeep rolled through the gates. Lyell told me that he wished he had pulled out his own revolver and pointed it at someone. Fortunately his Auster crewman knew the etiquette and had pointed his Sten gun at the garrison while the surrender took place.

Lyell later told me quietly that as he and Jean travelled through Holland he had encountered a church he remembered. In 1945 he had trained his guns on the building when he saw a battalion of German Wehrmacht infantry taking cover inside, and the British artillery had caused terrible damage. At the time there was no alternative but it was typical of the decisions that faced the 'liberators' and it had troubled him ever since. He said he was delighted to see that it been possible to repair the damage and described other such incidents, some of which he mentions in his story.

By the end of 1990, the manuscript was finished and Lyell sent copies to his sons and to Alan. He also sent them to his surviving comrades and others who he felt might be interested. At this stage, he had not planned to publish; it was enough that the story had been set down for his family and comrades so that it would not be lost. He turned his attention to other things, including local politics. He had also become interested in the story of the man after whom the 'Dickson Pioneer' was named. Captain Bertram Dickson really was a pioneer, and he flew the first aircraft to carry out military reconnaissance, during the 1910 manoeuvres on Salisbury Plain. Shortly before D-Day, his sister, Mrs Winifred Gordon FRGS, had donated to the Squadron first an

Auster 3 and later its Auster 4 replacement; apparently, by mere chance, Lyell was the pilot chosen to fly them. After the war ended, Mrs Gordon asked the Army how 'her aircraft' had been used and in response Lyell had written an official account, which he had sent to her. Now, forty-five years later, he at last had the opportunity to find out more about the real life 'Dickson Pioneer'.

Also in 1990, Lyell had flown again for the first time in over forty years. The opportunity came when he and Jean went to stay with Alan who was now retired from the RAF and living in Rutland. Alan recalls

Lyell came to stay with us again in Rutland in the summer of 1990, when I took him flying at the Leicester Aero Club in an aerobatic Cessna 152. He loved the flying, but maybe not the modern metal aircraft with a pilot's yoke in lieu of a stick.

His son Jim visited Lyell soon afterwards and found him thrilled by the experience. It was clear that he had really enjoyed flying and the decision to give it up all those years ago had not been an easy one to make.

In 1992, Jean and Lyell spent the summer as usual sailing around the Western Isles, and then tragically, just after their last voyage on 'Wendy May', Jean unexpectedly died on 14 October aged seventy-five. Lyell was devastated and had to face the problem of how to live his life alone. After a while he sold their boat and although he considered buying another, found that he no longer wished to sail. He threw himself into working on the Dickson project and on another in which Jean had been very interested, the Scottish presence in the Dutch town of Veere. Like many in the same situation, he also started to travel. In 1993 he and Robert went to France and visited Hill 112. Robert remembers that the insignificant looking hilltop had been ploughed and the newly turned earth was still full of steel shards, broken glass and fragments of bone. It was literally a war grave and they left the relics where they lay. Lyell also kept up his links with the remaining pilots of 'C' Flight, now elderly and infirm. 'Butch' Pritchard had died of cancer in Zimbabwe so they were now down to three. He visited the places where he had spent the war prior to D-Day and the places of his youth and his courtship of Jean. He finally arrived at the Army Air Corps Museum at Middle Wallop near Stockbridge in Hampshire (now the Museum of Army

Flying). He found a small museum, desperately needing larger premises, with incredible exhibits packed tightly inside.

The idea of publishing the book came from a chance meeting at the Museum. It had been Lyell's first visit, and he later told Alan that, towards the end, the curator, who was delighted to meet one of the dwindling number of wartime pilots, asked if he had liked the display. Lyell said that it was excellent, but referring to one particular section he said bluntly 'That's not what happened!' The curator, taken aback, pointed out that the narrative accompanying the museum's World War II content was based on the Corps' official history.[1] Lyell replied 'Yes, but I was there, and he wasn't'. Once the curator discovered that Lyell had recorded his experiences he urged him to publish them. Unfortunately, having found a publisher, Lyell was told that, although a good story, it was not long enough for a book. The publisher suggested that he could add some material, for example, telling about how Army aviation developed both before the war and afterwards.

Lyell at the controls of an Auster in 1992.

Lyell was by then already fully occupied in researching Captain Bertram Dickson's career as a soldier and as pioneer of military aviation and so the book was left to take its turn. Meanwhile, from his researches, Lyell wrote a short monograph about Captain Dickson called *Flying Shadow* and also organised a memorial service for him at Achanault on 21 September 1994 at which the AAC provided a flypast by the current 'Dickson Pioneer', by then a Lynx helicopter, and the RAF sent three Tornado aircraft.

Lyell visited Alan again in the December of 1992 when Alan arranged for him to fly a fully aerobatic Auster J5F Aiglet, G–AMTD from the Leicester Aero Club. Alan recalls that 'it took him about ten minutes to re-familiarise himself before flying some very respectable manoeuvres. After that we looked at the Auster factory at Rearsby, and thence to the bar.' It was here that a member asked him if he flew himself. Lyell answered truthfully that he had done some flying on Tiger Moths and Austers.

Member: *Fantastic. Done any good trips?*

Lyell thought about this.

Lyell: *Just the one actually, from East Sussex to the Kiel Canal.*
Member: *Amazing. How long did that take you?*
Lyell: *About eleven months*
Member: *That's a long time*
Lyell: *The Army couldn't go any faster*

During their sailing adventures, Jean and Lyell had often visited the Walcheren town of Veere where they discovered the building that had housed the last Scottish embassy to the Netherlands. Jean had taken a keen interest in its history and presented the town with a Scottish flag that is still flown outside the building to this day. (Lyell also discovered an ancestor, a Colonel Robert Munro, who commanded a Scottish battalion in the Netherlands during the War of the Spanish Succession). He saw that the memories of this ancient link between Scotland and the Low Countries had almost been lost. This neglected part of Scottish history, he firmly believed, could help to inspire the newly flourishing sense of national identity in Scotland. As a great believer in the European Community he also considered that it would highlight and maybe strengthen the ancient links with the rest of Europe, which had characterised Scottish culture for centuries. As a tribute to Jean, he worked with Scottish dignitaries and MPs, such as his friend Winifred Ewing, to organise a commemorative event. At one point there were some tense negotiations with the Dean of Manchester Cathedral about a pair of silver chalices that were kept locked in the Cathedral safe. These were the Veere Cups that had been used during communion in the Scottish Kirk at Veere since 1620. The French inspired revolution in 1795 ended the Scottish presence in Veere and the last Minister's wife was forced to sell the cups. They next appeared in a sale of 'old silver' at the end of the eighteenth century and eventually became the property of the Bishopric of Manchester. In the late twentieth century, as Lyell wrote: 'it was hoped that these cups could be shown at Veere during Veere's seventh Centenary and used in a joint communion service held by the Dutch and Scottish presbyteries.' Sadly the Bishopric did not cooperate and although Lyell was allowed to photograph them, the cups were then returned to the safe in Manchester where no doubt they remain. Nevertheless, the celebrations took place in September 1996 and were a huge success, renewing an old friendship that lasts to this day.

By now Lyell was finding it hard to live on his own in a village where the old residents were disappearing and the newcomers tended to be young commuters who travelled to work in nearby towns. As his health was also failing he took the difficult decision to leave Findhorn and in 1998 he left Scotland to live in York near his son Robert. It was also in 1998 that the surviving members of 'C' Flight met in memory of Captain Burgess who had been killed in the battle to liberate Rouen. A wreath was laid at the Church of Saint John Lee, Hexham where his family worshipped.

Lyell was never to finish the extended book the publisher wanted, despite continuing his efforts to do so. In the autumn of 2001 he underwent an operation to treat a tumour on the brain. When he regained consciousness, we were allowed to visit him. As we entered the room he immediately greeted us, but during our visit it seemed that he had slipped back to that most intense period of his life long ago and his thoughts were of his wartime comrades; very shortly after that he went into a coma and never awoke. On 28 February 2002 he died aged eighty-three. Later, on 11 May, a memorial service was held in Findhorn church. After the service Lyell's ashes were interred with Jean's at Kinloss Abbey, as a piper played and a 653 Squadron Lynx helicopter, the latest 'Dickson Pioneer', flew over in salute to 'C' Flight's last wartime commander.

Findhorn Memorial Service Fly Past, 11 May 2002. Alan and Lyell's grandson Karl, among the onlookers.

Note

1. Farrar-Hockney, General Sir Anthony, *The Army in the Air*, Alan Sutton Publishing, 1994.

Appendix I

The Squadron Leader's Report

In September 1944, 653 Squadron Leader Major Pollitt wrote an objective report on the Squadron's experiences during July and August on the front line that may be of interest to readers. (Major Pollitt left the Squadron early in 1945 to take up a post in the Air Ministry. His successor, Major Newton, commanded the squadron during the subsequent Rhine crossing and occupation of Germany.)

Although part of a Squadron, AOP Flights worked directly with the units or divisions they were allocated to support. Squadron HQ dealt with administration, logistic support – aircraft and other equipment – and later on, resources to support photography.

PART I: <u>GENERAL SURVEY</u>

The Squadron arrived on the Continent on June 27th (Ground Party) and June 29th (Air Party) and went to 12 Corps concentration area where it remained complete until one flight was put under command 8 Corps.

On July 4th a second Flight under command 43 Div. started operations and finally by July 12th the third Flight was operating under command 15 Div. In each case the Flights chose a flight A.L.G. near H.Q.R.A. of Div and worked all four sections from that A.L.G.

From the experience of other squadrons which had been operating earlier it was apparent that the carrying of an observer was an essential and all the available observers were employed.

The large majority of the early work in July was anti – mortar sorties designed firstly to spot the mortars firing (particularly nebelwerfers) and secondly to stop the firing. This latter was successful up to a point – the Bosche thought at first that the Air O.P. could see mortar firing but later discovered that we could not.

Flights remained for the most part on their original A.L.G's. S.H.Q. moved to within two miles of Corps H.Q (Bretteville – l'Orgeuilleuse) on the Caen – Bayeux road and remained there during the static phase on the line of the ODON river.

On July 17th the Squadron had its first casualty – Capt. Watkinson was hit by a 25 pdr shell in mid-air and was killed. He had returned to the gun area to re-net and flew low in front of a troop firing a barrage. As a result of this accident the C.C.R.A. directed that an aircraft was a No's 1 crest responsibility and that great care was to be taken while Austers were flying close to the gun area.

During this period very little enemy activity was experienced against Air O.P's. Two attacks were made by fighters – hits were scored in one case but

'Know your friends'
warning poster.

the aircraft landed safely. Early warning was always given by our Bofors opening up and many times the fighter was never seen but its presence was indicated by our flak.

It was found that the most dangerous aspect of Air O.P. flying on 12 Corps front was the wanton use of small arms fire of every description against any and every fighter that the Bofors engaged regardless of range. It meant that while there was a fighter in the air there was no haven of rest for a pilot to fly to where he could take evasive action until all was dear. It was also very dangerous on the ground particularly in the case of low flying attack. On July 15th however all engagement of enemy a/c by small arms was forbidden and also at the same time engagement of fighters by L.A.A. and H.A.A. situated more than 5000x from. P.D.L's was prohibited. This latter restriction was instituted because of the continued engagement of friendly fighters by our flak.

During the night 17/18th July "B" Flight A.L.G, was bombed and shot up after flares had been dropped over the gun area which included the A.L.G. All four a/c were written off, all the tentage, one pilot received a bullet through his foot and was evacuated to the U.K., – two O.R's received minor shrapnel wounds. As a result of this orders were given that a/c were not to stay in the gun area at night and if necessary flights would have to be withdrawn at dusk. No more trouble has been experienced due to this cause.

During the last part of the month the Squadron started taking photos, first with hand held camera end later with mount held – all were an unqualified success and extremely useful to both us and formations with whom we were working.

The end of the month found the flights one bound of approximately 2000x further forward and S.H.Q. still at Bretteville alongside H.Q.R.A. 12 Corps.

During July the Squadron did 610 sorties of which 128 were shoots and had one flying casualty. For full details see Part II.

August operations have consisted mainly of movement information sorties and intercommunication work. Few normal A.O.P. sorties have been made as the situation has been too mobile.

On August 29th one flight was converted into an intercom flight to cater for the needs of commanders since distance between formations had become very great.

A summary of sorties etc during August will be found in part II. Casualties during August were 1 officer, Captain Burgess, killed – hit H.T. cables during recce and one O.R. seriously wounded by 88mm fire in convoy.

Part III: General Notes.

a) Aircraft

Generally speaking the airframe has stood up well to the conditions obtaining in this theatre with one very notable exception – the windshields and side panels to the rear are extremely unsatisfactory – the perspex rapidly crystallises and becomes opaque in conditions of sunlight. A/c collected from the UK with only a few hours to their credit show signs of the crystallisation. Numerous letters, requests and defect reports have been put forward through RAF channels and nothing yet has materialised.

(b) Engine

The engine has not stood up to the conditions out here – continual loss of compression is experienced – probably caused by using 80 octane MT fuel. Reports on this have been submitted through RAF channels – up to date of writing (Sep 1st) eight engines have had to be changed due to loss of compression.

In the event of an aircraft tipping onto its nose and breaking the propellor – it is more often than not necessary to change the engine owing to the shock load test showing the crankshaft distortion being outside the limits laid down.

This was not the case with either the [Cirrus or?] Gypsy engine and it appears that the Lycoming is weaker in this respect.

*It is still hoped that a more powerful and reliable engine will be supplied as the present Lycoming falls well below the normal requirements and the take – off performance still leaves much to be desired.**

c) The MT generally have stood up to the work well – but careful and regular maintenance is essential. The vehicles in the flights have not been overworked and there has been ample opportunity for maintenance. However

---

* The very reliable de Havilland Gipsy Major engine was replaced with the U.S. built Lycoming simply because U.S. industrial capacity made the latter more available.

in SHQ with large distances to be covered in collecting rations, water, POL, etc, it has been necessary to have vehicles off the road for complete checkover at frequent intervals this applying mainly to Jeeps and 15 cwts., which have had to be heavily overworked. Section Part VII contains recommendations regarding change in establishment.

(d) GENERAL. There is, I consider, an urgent requirement for an Air OP HQ in a theatre of war – some HQ which can co-ordinate ideas, deal with purely Air OP problems and where any experiments can be carried out.

For instance, I have had extreme difficulty in getting replacement pilots. With all the various commitments – photography, intercommunications, and also splitting SHQ into Main and TAC it has been found necessary to have at least two 1st line reinforcements – the present situation in this unit is two pilots under establishment. With a ground unit one officer can do two jobs but, at the risk of being obvious, it is necessary to have one pilot to fly each aircraft and that we have not at the moment got. Had there been an Air OP HQ in France this matter could be taken up through AOP channels.

RECOMMENDATIONS:
PERSONNEL: ARMY.
(i) OFFICERS: In a theatre of war it has been found essential to have at least two additional pilots on Squadron HQ for liaison purposes and semi-intercommunications work. As far as is known all squadrons were allowed to keep their 1st Reinforcements and have found them invaluable and this Squadron is no exception.

OR's [Other ranks, Ed]. It has been found that it is necessary to have one clerk RA and one unit clerk on SHQ to deal with clerical and postal matters (the latter being a full time Job under active service conditions). The present establishment is one clerk RA.

RAF: with the advent of the Lycoming engine the large proportion of maintenance is concerned with the engine. Thus the previous establishment of 1 Sgt. fitter IIE on SHQ and one Cpl. Fitter IIE per flight would now be more appropriate.

No reports are recorded after August.

Appendix II

Jean Munro

On the 18 December 1943, 653 Squadron broke off from their intense training schedule to celebrate Christmas in style. It was a prolonged and lively party – every one believed it would be the last Christmas before crossing the Channel into mainland Europe – and it was celebrated with cheerful optimism. It was also the occasion on which Lyell first met Jean Webster who had been invited with the Volunteer Aid Detachment workers from the nearby Penshurst Hospital.

Jean was the daughter of Thomas Webster, a London silk merchant, and his wife Louise (nee Gawen). She had joined the Volunteer Aid Detachment at the start of the war and, rather unexpectedly, on May 1944 she transferred to the WRNS. Her first Naval posting was to Dover, a town in the front-line, under constant bombardment by German big guns, from 1941 until 24 September 1944 when 3rd Canadian Division drove them out of their gun-positions near Calais. On 17 August 1944, fully trained, she was promoted to Leading Wren (acting) and posted to HMS Flowerdown near Winchester. Flowerdown was a Fleet Air Arm 'Y' Station used throughout World War Two to intercept German radio communications, from as far away as Stalingrad. These intercepts were sent immediately in all weathers via motorcycle dispatch riders (later by teleprinter) to the Bletchley Park

Jean Webster, December 1944.

decoders. The listeners and decoders were sworn to strict secrecy, such that they never divulged what they did until decades had passed. Jean herself never mentioned the stations to which she had been posted let alone anything she knew of the work they carried out. It was only after hers and Lyell's deaths that her service record and some letters were found. In those letters she says that at HMS Flowerdown she was responsible for 'eleven houses' of over 100 personnel and generally describes her life on the 'front line in England' in what turned out to be the last year of war.

In April 1944 with D-Day approaching censorship of communications became rigorous and it was difficult for members of 653 Squadron to obtain leave. It was also during that month that Jean left the VAD and she and Lyell started their correspondence. Her first letter was written to tell Lyell that having resigned from the VAD she would become a Wren.

16/4/1944
14 Queens Gardens
Ealing W5

My dear Lyell,
Thank you for your letter, I was rather surprised to hear from you after all this time. What happened? Did you get writer's cramp?

No, I am not being sent down the mines, perhaps they thought I would stir up the strikers to greater efforts, I don't know. I only hope they are quite as cold as we look like being next winter. I'm not being pushed into anything, being mad as a hatter I volunteered for the Wrens before they had a chance. Somehow or other they (the Wrens) are labouring under the delusion that I've had pre-war experience in catering. I don't know why, I only told the truth. Perhaps it was misleading ...

In the First World War the British Admiralty had benefited by being able to decipher German naval transmissions; unfortunately several historians (including Winston Churchill) later revealed how they had done so. As a consequence, the Kreigsmarine adopted the famous 'Enigma' machines to encrypt their radio transmissions and by the outbreak of the Second World War it was standard practice for German forces to communicate sending strings of letters in morse code that would be meaningless until de-crypted.

A vital (and probably very tedious) role at listening stations was simply to transcribe the strings of letters for the Bletchley Park (otherwise known as Station 'X') decoders to crack. Ironically, having given the game away years earlier, Winston Churchill was a passionate believer in the value of 'Ultra' and the role of those who received and decrypted its secrets:

> 'Make sure they have all they want on extreme priority and report to me that this has been done.'

The planners of the Normandy invasion correctly believed that the Germans were still unaware that their messages could be decoded; no doubt Jean's assignment was part of the build-up of listening capability in preparation for the liberation of Europe:

> "Breaking into these ciphers allowed the Allied staff planning for the invasion of Europe to obtain unprecedented detail of the German defences.
>
> The Codebreakers made a vital contribution to D-Day in other ways. The breaking of the ciphers of the German Secret Intelligence Service allowed the British to confuse Hitler over where the Allies were to land. His decision to divert troops away from the Normandy beaches undoubtedly ensured the invasion's success." [Bletchley Park Trust history]

At Westfield College, where Jean was sent, Wrens were selected to fulfil a wide variety of roles. They were then trained in skills including wireless telegraphy, teleprinter operating, meteorology, coding (e.g. Morse), administration, mass catering, supply work and various technical and transport functions. Unsurprisingly Jean's letters do not reveal exactly what she did although she had an interest in foreign languages and owned some botanical books written in German.

20/5/1944
Westfield College
Kidderpore Avenue,
Hampstead, NW3

My dear Lyell
I think I've more or less got things sorted out now, it's a sort of organised disorganisation that one has to pass through before one is considered fit to 'victual battleships'!

We spend eight weeks here and each week work in a different department. The trouble is that you don't know until Tuesday where you are going to be on Thursday, which is the day we all change round. The crux of the whole matter is this, in some departments you get a half day every day and others none at all. The conclusion seems to be this, if you can phone me between 6.30 and 7.30 on Wednesday evening I can give you the low-down. There is only one phone so it might be a bit tricky.

After training at Westfield, Jean was posted to Dover. Precise details of her role there are not known.

31/7/44
Boys County School
Dover
Kent

My darling,
I'm sitting in the shade with my feet in the sun and my feet are just loving it. Poor dears, they walked all the way up to the castle this afternoon, it was worse than Mayor Pepper's Hill & hot! ..I'd love you to have seen our Quarters Office this morning, imagine a white-washed room with a few oddments of furniture about nine feet square containing eight people all talking about something different, that is they were all trying to do a different section of the monthly returns. Audrey and I were vainly trying to get one column of figures the same twice, 3/o wanted a quarters improvements diary, some-one else was tearing her hair over food order

forms & a foreign body was demanding a registered parcel. It was a riot. I think we do everything as well as sorting mail, operating a switchboard and running a shop. My prayers have been answered, thank goodness, the galley staff are now normally complete & my hands are regaining their normal colour. Always excepting the ink that this pen is pouring on them!

1/8/44

Dearest, I am having a wonderful afternoon playing at being a switchboard operator. Chief has just been up to complain that she got two calls at once & they both thought her quite mad. She was most terribly amused about it, but I feel I shall be teased on it for many days to come.

This letter seems full of interruptions ... everything got so busy that this bit is being written in bed the following night. I've just got back from Canterbury, it's looking very battered but much better than when I saw it last because now the ruins are covered in grass and willow herb, they look rather nice. The Cathedral definitely looks worse, they've blocked all the windows with something like cardboard, I preferred it when the wind and rain whistled in. It was dark last time and most eerie with the banners all blowing in the wind. You felt as if all the old Bishops or Archbishops were watching. Now it looks rather commercial.

7/8/44
Boys County School
Dover

Darling,
Thank you for your letter, I nearly went up in smoke over it! Do you realise that, unsolicited by me, you said you would write directly you got back. I had begun to wonder if you were swimming! I nearly said that I wouldn't write any more until you had written me three letters but then I realised I would have to write and tell you, so that wouldn't work. Anyway, having decided that there may be extenuating circumstances I give you the benefit of the doubt and write again.

Oh gosh, there goes the old wailing winnie, I'm praying its not a double, I just couldn't get out of bed again. I went dancing last night and walking this evening and my legs just give up. The dance wasn't up to much, I spent most of my time parrying and dodging two rather well oiled Yorkshiremen, in the end I am ashamed to say I palmed them off onto an inoffensive friend. By the way, what did you do to the guns? They have been rowdy practically every night since you left!

You are not the only one within a thousand miles of the sea. I went to Deal last night and actually smelt it! The smell made us so hungry that we had to hunt for food, not a café or restaurant open for miles.* In desperation we ended up at a Y.M.C.A. amid cheerful gloom and a gabbling clergyman, even that didn't put us off!

8/8/44 I'm beginning to feel horribly unsettled, I wish I knew where they intend sending me next week or what happens, because I suppose when I get back to Westfield that white paper either begins to operate or drops. I don't know & it's rotten being in such an uncertain state. Like you, I am beginning to feel like a puppet, shoved here there and everywhere…

Your letter spoilt all my pet theories on post by arriving on a Saturday, now I shall have to start all over again, but I still think I am right about letters from here.

I'm not absolutely certain what a crepuscule is, but if it's what I think, then I always thought that they only occurred in the south, apparently misinformed.

Later

I've just seen the news of the battle round Caen, of course 24 hours old by now. It sounds like hell let loose or the sort of thing you don't forget in a hurry. This is an awful letter darling, but there isn't really much uncensorable[sic] news this side of the channel, we've just had a pie-jaw on the enormity of

---

* From early in the war long stretches of UK coastline were treated as off-limits to casual visitors for security reasons; only residents and permit holders were admitted. In 1944 restrictions had eased but seaside towns and beaches remained military areas. The USA imposed no restrictions and no black out. German U boat commanders could see their targets silhouetted against their brightly lit coastal towns and many merchant ships were sunk as a result.

even saying you are going on leave over the phone, so if you can't say that, what can you say?

I'm working under a grand P/O [petty officer] *this week, when I ask what I'm to do she says vaguely 'Oh, just do whatever you think needs doing.' I don't think she'd miss me if I went for a walk. We start punctually for all meals and return hours later, of course strolling in, in the morning at our leisure! Between Wednesday and Sunday I had three half-days two of which she gave me and the other was presented as my natural due. Everything I do she nearly breaks into tears of gratitude, it's all most unusual and will really unfit me for the sterner life to come.*

Oh well Lyell, take care of yourself amidst the dust and noise and take care your terrific stock of beer doesn't get looted in the general scrum.

All my love to you, dearest,

Jean

Having scanned the papers I find that Mackenzie King says the European war will be over by June and the germans* leaving Turkey give it a month, so to take a medium, I'll celebrate peace on my birthday! One day I shall write to W.L.A. (Womens Land Army) by mistake, it nearly always happens.

12/8/44
Boys County School
Dover

Darling,

Do you ever get to the point when you think you've forgotten what it was like to be able to just snap your fingers at everybody and just walk out on them if you wanted to? To travel when, where and how you wished and in fact to be a free agent? What did it feel like when there was no war & no real worries standing behind you? I've forgotten! ... I shall have to go up on The Downs with Kay and the dog, I've tried doing all the horrid jobs e.g. mending and that didn't work, so it's the only cure for this lousy mood on my brain.

---

* Jean often used the small 'g' when typing 'German'.

What a lot of piffle I wrote yesterday. The walk cured it. I don't know if it was a most glorious sunset that did it or the sight of Kay struggling to climb a very rickety fence at the top of the slope. Of course it was topped with barbed wire & of course she sat on it & was too shaken with laughter to get off. I had an awful job to unhook her.

We found some lovely ruins of an old abbey which some bright sole [sic], years ago had made into a farm house, which time and weather had made rather beautiful, rather a change (I'm on the switchboard again, we are having such fun and games, the C.H.2 operator is getting all het-up, we nearly had a fight over the phone.) after the modern type of ruin which is so very definitely hideous as you should know. My family are all going to Cornwall next week thank goodness, they worry me stiff as the jitterbugs* [V1 bombs] seem to be falling all around them. Every time one goes over here I wonder where it's going to land.

Gosh! We've had such a bind in the office this morning, we've been handing out the results of all the complaints we have been treated to recently by various wrens to our own chief, she took them all personally and called in the P.O. Cook who also took them personally so now things are getting really exciting. No doubt Pat and I will end up in a ditch but at least we'll have had a lovely scrap. Aren't people in the mass ghastly!

Evening: most surprising the sweet[sic] that are flying around now after the storm. As you perhaps gathered, I'm back on the job of feeding the flock & as that entails plenty of work, depression has vanished and all in the garden is lovely.

I'm hoping for a letter from you but expect you are hectically busy, so I shan't be surprised if you haven't time to write.

---

* The V1 flying bombs were also called doodle bugs or buzz-bombs. They were Hitler's terror weapon that started to be used a week after D-Day, taking off from the Pas-de-Calais and aimed at London. Quite inaccurate, many fell on the London suburbs, causing thousands of casualties and wrecked dwellings. The London bombardment only ceased when the launch sites were overrun by Allied forces in October.

16/8/44
Westfield College
Hampstead
NW3

Lyell Dearest,

I've just been called conscientious and hard-working, doesn't it sound dull! As you can see the great trek has started and I've achieved half-waydom. Gosh I can't imagine how I stuck this place for nine whole weeks, it seems like a mass of repressiveness now, and like you I find that discipline & I will never manage to live in the same house. The sight of people doing squad drill made me want to run away and hide. I'm so pleased they are sending me to Portsmouth, Audrey is there (not the one you know) and its no longer journey from London than Dover. The trains must be faster! Of course there is always the possibility they might send me on to an inaccessible place. My fingers are crossed. Now I am dying to start off. Wonder if that command has started leave? If so I might get some by the middle of September.

There was a lovely slogan in a window in Folkestone:

'If a doodle dawdles, don't dilly, dive.'

Doesn't it sound good! I am making it almost fashionable around here. I can't write more at the moment, time is short and I can't think straight.

Oh and from now on it's Leading Wren Webster, please!! Pouf…

17/8/1944
Bowlands
Clifton Road
Portsmouth

or

W.R.N.S. Draughting Depot
Girls High School
Kent Road
Portsmouth

Lyell Dearest
The above [Bowlands] is only a temporary address but don't let that deter you from writing to it. It's perfectly good. The great trek continues! I'm feeling rather small, alone and incapable. Like you, I caught an express from Dover that stopped at every station & a few other places as well, the only difference was that mine started twenty minutes earlier than yours. On Wednesday the powers that be in the quarters office decided to make use of me while I was waiting for interviews, until it entered their befogged minds about 6pm that we might possibly have some packing to do and very graciously decided we might go off! So we promptly took ourselves out to supper to celebrate our 'hooks' [promotion to Leading Wren] *and hoped they were wanting us. Sorry, I'm feeling vindictive. Ann and I were blown out of Westfield, we didn't walk. Anyway, we had transport to Swiss Cottage & there we parted and I continued alone. Somehow or other my luggage and I arrived at Waterloo, there were three cases, a tennis racket and the usual impedimenta, including a hat that never stays on. Of course a large patch of the line was under repair & a few extra changes were thrown in just to make life more difficult. Luckily I fell in with an R.A.F. regiment & a G.D.RAF so finished up with only a pair of gloves and a tennis racquet to carry. Arriving at Waterloo we practically discussed and pulled to bits the whole universe over a cup of coffee, it being only ten o'clock, and parted, they on leave & me for the unknown (sounds like Darkest Africa). The train only stopped twice all the way, it definitely shifted. At Portsmouth I looked at my cases, shook my head & got a taxi. How I dislike those cases!*

The first question shot at me when I arrived was have you had any lunch? The answer being "no", a plate containing two lumps of cold fat, a pile of half-cooked sour marrow and the most enormous potato you ever saw! Do I look like a navvy? was presented to me. Having studied it for a while & regretfully chucked it in the swill bin, six of us were taken on a walking tour of the town ...finishing up with the drafting officer who gave the impression that she thoroughly disapproved of your past life, loathed the sight of you & if she had anything to do with it the WRNS would have rejected you. That apparently is her usual attitude, eighteen people deserted from her last ship! ... we finished up by being introduced to our quarters which have a lovely view over the Solent. There I was rudely interrupted as my presence was demanded by the drafting depot, only to learn that my next move will be tomorrow & to a FAA near Winchester. I am quite pleased because a) Lovely country b) Audrey went to the same place & I always thought we'd work rather well together. I'll complete this letter when I arrive so that I can give you my permanent address. I hope.

18.8.44

Having a nice morning doing nothing in particular, meandered around Portsmouth and found it a trifle depressing. I'm so tired of flattened houses, blocked up windows and dilapidated, uncared for shops, it'll be nice to get to a small village like Flowerdown (pretty name, anyway) where everything ought to be whole. Sounds as though I shall have to send for 'Auntie' (my bike) I expect it will be more isolated than Penshurst, however I'll let you know what it's like when I arrive. Meanwhile I think this letter better go off to you in case they have any weird rules and regs at the FAA station.

22/8/44
L/Wren M.J. Webster 93013
D. Block
H.M.S. Flowerdown
C/o G.P.O.
London

My Dearest Lyell,
If you write to me at the above address I'm told it will take 14 days to reach
me. So, as this address was made particularly to annoy people abroad, will
you write to my home address and they will send it on. Every time I've been
to Hampshire before, it's either rained or snowed, this time it hasn't snowed
yet but it's done everything else except sunshine. We slosh around in macs
and large black sou'westers, getting damper and damper, wading through
mud and swimming through puddles. Honestly, I can't think why they don't
provide us with sea-boots!

About ten minutes after I arrived here the quarters officer presented me
with eleven houses to run, also a family, a nice large family, I have over a
hundred children! Ranging in ages from about eighteen to fifty. Makes me
feel quite old! My one sorrow is that someone else feeds them so there is no
victualling to do, not even battle-ships!

Of course the country is heavenly, no bombed houses, no jitterbugs, I
nearly said no sirens but we had one last night of five minutes duration!
Lots of lovely old houses with nice gardens and the usual horde of American
soldiers. Flies and wasps are the chief menace, especially just here, it's a
paddock belonging to a racing stable. I'm sitting on a bale of straw which
will eventually be the bed of some very blue-blooded horse, even now the
flies are waiting and meanwhile practising biting me. Don't imagine I
am sunbathing or anything utopian like that. Oh no! Any moment now
it's likely to pour with rain and my hat which has fallen off will keep one
square inch of my head dry. But I was fed up with the horrible feeling of
being surrounded with barbed wire and strange faces … By the way, will
you describe powdered tea to me in minute detail? I'm sure that is what we
are being poisoned with, it tastes like a muddy puddle well stirred up … I
am feeling terribly triumphant. Having suddenly had a feeling that I must
wash my hair, whatever happens, I discover that the navy with its usual

thoroughness in all things, good or bad, has decided that Tuesday night is fuel economy night and consequently all the boilers are let out, so no hot water ... determined not to be baulked I discovered that shampoo lathers very well in cold water and the deed is done. Voila!, I am thinking of trying to learn Spanish ... There appears to be a terrific educational effort in this camp, they even tried Russian and Polish once!

5th October 1944
Ealing, W5

I've at last found this map for you, it's slightly larger scale than the one you achieved, embracing two-thirds of the world. I was trying to find my way out of a shop and my mother suddenly said, "You know you're going into the basement, don't you?" I didn't and it happened to be an escalator so we just continued and landed in the book dept. So I immediately thought of maps. We had a marvellous shopping day, everything I wanted, just as I dreamed about it. Caution went to the winds, now I shall have to pay my father back! But it was fun, all my coupons gone, shan't have any more until they decide to discharge me.

I'm having lunch with your mother tomorrow and I am feeling awfully nervous. Wish you were here to hold my hand. Looking forward to meeting Alan.

I had my first experience of a warning in a dim-out* tonight; it was rather amusing. I must explain that we possess a Morrison shelter which has displaced most things in the dining room, including the table, so now we use it as a lounge. It's never been blacked out so when the siren goes, off with the light and we sit in the firelight, listening for the nearest klaxon, when that sounds everyone grabs two cushions and queues up at the shelter entrance. It's amazing how safe you feel in the thing. The odd bomb came racketing over our heads but you felt so sure that even if the house collapsed the shelter would protect you!

---

*   On September 1939 a blackout was imposed on the UK. All artificial light had to be concealed from the view of enemy bombers. Streets were dark and hard to navigate and the ban was very unpopular. In September 1944 the ban was eased to a 'dim-out' and lighting equivalent to moonlight was allowed.

"By the way, did you remember to feed the canary". *Second World War Blitz cartoon*

6th October 1944

Darling I've just about returned, I enjoyed myself immensely, your family were terribly kind, I've completely fallen for Alan*. Alison says he told her that he'd invited me to his birthday party. When we first met, he came into the room with his face covered by a painting book. Later on he insisted on 'reading' to your father and kept looking at me out of the corner of his eye to see if I was watching.

I'm feeling awfully pugnacious at the moment, there was a letter waiting for me from K. when I got home. Her fiancé has been killed, it was a pathetic letter. That is the second I've had from friends in five weeks. Lyell darling it makes me feel frightened. She says that the world seems empty and there is nothing much left. I know that feeling from the beginning of the year when you vanished on a course for months. It was partly why I joined the Wrens.

---

* Alan was being looked after by his grand-parents. His father, an RAF pilot, had been killed in 1941. His mother, Alison Munro worked at the Air Ministry for Sir Robert Watson-Watt.

Sorry to be so morbid darling, it was K's letter that rather knocked me sideways. I think I'd better go to bed and sleep it off. I'll try to find a more cheerful note next time.

All my love to you my dearest
Jean

14 Queens Gardens
Ealing
W5
10.X.1944

My Dearest Lyell,

Had a letter from 'Blackie' today, most exciting life she seems to be leading! Her own description is: "get up, go to work, get home, listen to the wireless and sew". She seems completely contented with it, or perhaps not quite, she wants to start a business of her own and is wondering if she will be allowed to. It sounded as though she wouldn't because the Labour Exchange seems to have found her a job as nurse in a factory. It was what she wanted nine months ago but now all she wants is hairdressing.

London is looking just London-ish, very crowded, weather like a Guy Fawkes night & the dim-out doesn't seem much different to a black-out. Our house is the only one with much light & while complying with regulations, we seem to light up the whole road... While I've been at home this leave, several times I carefully walked around a large and nobbly rocking horse in the dark, but my mother gave it away about five years ago. Does that sound sense? What I mean is I must have hit it so many times in my youth that now it's no longer there I still walk round it. But I have never done it before. My case seems to be becoming worse and worse.

Dearest, I'm afraid that was a lousy letter I wrote you last week. I'd like to have got it back as soon as I'd posted it. I'll take jolly good care I don't write to you in that sort of mood again...

Oh dear, the flesh-pots of life are nearly running out, the day after tomorrow at the crack of dawn, Winchester Looms Ahead. Life will be real and earnest again!

Your letters always sound rather like a school picnic with a few hardships thrown in. I can't rise to that happy standard, I should grumble if Utopia was reached, can one ever be perfectly contented? A cabbage-like stagnation from earliest childhood is the answer or else the village idiot.

You see my darling, my letters are either blather or a mass of grumbles. It's disgusting. Shall be impartially watching the newsreels in the next few weeks, do you get a chance of seeing yourselves?

What do you think of this compulsory army education? Do you get included? I'm thinking of putting all the subjects in a hat & then drawing. The result might be staggering; suppose it was art!

All my love to you darling

Jean

13/10/1944

My Darling,

You are a dear old ostrich, but I do know the feeling, it's like knowing your leave is nearly over and that you ought to be looking up trains but putting it off so you can delude yourself that it isn't! Dearest, I don't care a damn what you write to me about, whether it's five years past, future, the last time you saw a phoenix or a soliloquy on the moon if it comes from you.

Well leave has vanished like a dream & now I am chasing non-existent sheets again. It started raining before I'd been back five minutes but now I am prepared for it, my mother insisted on lending me an antique pair of Wellingtons so now like 'John' I'm ready for it. You know 'John'? All good uncles do.

"John has great big waterproof boots on
John has a great big waterproof hat
John has a great big waterproof Mackintosh
And that, said John, is that!"

Yes you are quite right, I am mad, but it is better to take it that way. Oriel now has to move up the wall because my bed has been taken from me & from now on I sleep in the top bunk. The room seemed bare with only me in it but with two there seems hardly room to move. Even the rats welcomed me back last night, I went to sleep with the sound of their dear little feet scampering overhead! I don't mind so long as they don't come any closer.

You don't see many birds sitting talking nowadays they spend their time banking, gliding and hedge-hopping (I can't think of a technical term for the rest of their manoeuvres), soon I suppose there won't be many left.

When I went on leave the country was really only just leaving summer behind, ~~now, they are the~~ (sorry my thought got on too fast) the trees have turned the most glorious colours, the dark green of the pine trees sets them off wonderfully. Some have even lost all their leaves. The berries are lovely this year, hedges smothered with them, I promised I would send some home, I wonder if your mother would like some?! I believe that I told you I met Alan but not that I also made the acquaintance of Alison and your father, oh, and Bill. I ate your share of duck for you and shared the letter they had just received from you. Gosh it's pouring again! The weather creates depression quicker than anything else, even newspaper talk of peace!

Darling I can't be three months away from you now, even if you don't get your leave on time it must be less than that. And the Channel is a mere flea-bite when you fly over it. Oh I admit it usually seems like the Pacific Ocean. I am only trying a bit of my mother's common sense, it won't last long.

Don't you think it would be a good idea if you sent my letters to my home address & then they can forward them, that G.P.O. business is only for the benefit of overseas. Your letters take nearly a fortnight to reach me. I don't know how much of that time is wasted by the P.O.

Oh, I am thrilled to bits, I'm going to learn to play squash! Someone has offered to coach anyone who wants to learn. I never even knew there was a court here. One of my life's ambitions coming to pass.

If it's raining as hard in your part of the world as it is in mine I hope you have more than a tent to shelter you.

To misquote you darling, that is the inglorious present, past and future.

My darling Ostrich,
(forgive the epithet). If this rain doesn't stop soon we'll cease to swim and start sinking … the Romans knew what they were talking about when they said the middle of the road was the safest, both sides of our roads are swollen torrents. We haven't gone in for mud yet but there are plenty of lakes to be

waded through and water coming through the roof, I hope it drowns the rats en route, horrible beasts, they woke me up the other night!.. I have never seen a drowned rat, have you? Someone in this camp has at last accumulated a little sense, they've started running recreational transport from Winchester every night. Now I shan't have to be rude to Americans any more. It was awfully wearing, they are so thick-skinned and I'm not at all good at being rude easily ... You seem to have got your wish for a nice little advance, something seems to have shifted.. By the way I apologise for the vivid hue of this paper, it was either this or a pad with a startling green cover & that hurt far more ... I'll write again shortly if I am not drowned first. Did you see anything of the King? [Lyell: 'No King seen: he didn't get far enough and anyhow we are too busy to bother about visitors – playing cards usually. It's all very busy and so on.']*

D Block
H.M.S. Flowerdown
20/10/1944

Thank you for your letter, I nearly died of shock getting another only a week later, it's so unusual!

Your Germans popping up in the wood near Eindhoven sound just like my rats. They woke me up one night running round the walls, it sounded as if they were playing tag under the bunk. I didn't get out to have a look but assured me that I was much too high up for them to get near me. Now someone has ruined my paradise by assuring me that rats can jump! It will be nice to have Audrey back from leave to share the rats with me. If rats can jump they will reach her first, she sleeps underneath, but I won't tell her so. Nice aren't I!

Things seem to have reached a crisis in our mess while I was on duty there last night; sort of school prefect business. I was amusing myself timing people getting their supper, from the time they took the plates from the hatch, was an average half-an-hour. 3/O wandered in all agitated when the queue reached about 200 strong. Great woman 3/O, she has a wonderful way of stirring up trouble in the right quarter. She soon had all the great panjandrums down to view the queue. I wouldn't have missed it [for] worlds! Now the Captain has issued a memorandum in daily orders which means just nothing at all. I wonder how long it took him to compose so much eyewash!

It was my half-day today so I decided to leave it all behind me. The rain stopped at the right moment & faint patches of sky occasionally tried to struggle through without much success. So I took me for a walk. It was grand, you know what the countryside is like in the autumn when it has been raining hard & it suddenly stops & leaves behind an occasional drizzle more like a mist than anything else. Perfect for walking and I found a lot of ... I can't remember their name, it's something – wood berries. They're pink and divided into four parts and they, the leaves, turn the most glorious colours. Mummy loves them, unfortunately it's Friday and a rotten day for posting things (I've remembered: 'Spindlewood' is the name), if I put them in the sitting room, it's so warm they'll just dry up, my cabin is too small for so many. Shocking quandary!

Still feeling fed up with the mess, I caught the transport and took myself out to supper to eat in a more civilised manner, away from the maddening crowd. I think I'll come and join you, it sounds as if there might be less people and fewer complications.

I spent ages trying to think what a flat earthest was. Did Isaac Newton write a book to prove his theory? If so, shall I send it to you?

We certainly did miss something in Dover, last time I heard from Kay she said that when you went 'on watch' you never knew when you'd come off again; if the shelling warning went they just stayed on the job until the all-clear. Sometimes work started after lunch and they arrived about six the following morning. Think of spending all those hours in those damp, smelly caves! I believe that as a grand climax something happened to the County School boilers (due to the shelling) so the last news we had of them there was no hot water. Seems a terrible hardship to me but I suppose your tent never runs to that luxury. Gosh if the weather is like this in Holland, and I feel sure we aren't the sole recipients, I hope you have more than a tent to live in!

I've just got to the stage now where your next leave is one of those glorious day-dreams that do occasionally come true.

My boots have let me down, I only wore them once and have been trying to get them dry ever since. How are yours? As the Pay bob says rules and regulations forbid Wrens being issued with oil-skins, the mess funds are to have the honour of providing the quarters staff with them. I insist that mine must come down to my feet. There are those beastly stokers in rubber boots while I have to paddle around in shoes, fed up, I am.

If you receive the newspapers you know as much about the war as I do. We are told just so much as is considered right for us to know. What the wireless says one day, the papers confirm the next, so there you are. Nothing seems to move much but there is always fighting. Gosh, I'd like to know what really is happening behind the scenes in Germany. So would a good many people.

All my love my darling,
Jean

PS. I notice you have a new censorship stamp?

Ealing W5
19th December 1944

…my Christmas shopping has been accomplished, heaven knows how.. The crowds were awful … we skipped around the back streets wherever possible & as my brother was with us we had to detour every now and then to examine bomb damage*, especially at the back of Selfridges, horrid mess, not many casualties I believe although the blast blew a taxi through the shop window. What the result was, heaven knows, I don't.** My family insist they had two alerts in one night but I never heard them … one thing I didn't see that I very much wanted to was London lit up but we got home in daylight.

---

* Later to have a successful career in the construction industry.

** *"11 pm on 6 December 1944, a V-2 rocket hit the Red Lion pub on the corner of Duke Street and Barrett Street. A canteen in the SWOD was massively damaged, with eight American servicemen killed and 32 injured, as well as ten civilian deaths and seven injuries.*[17] *In the main building, ruptured water mains threatened SIGSALY, and while the Food Hall was the only department that did not need cleaning, Selfridges' shop-front Christmas tree displays were blown into Oxford Street"*. Ronan Thomas (6 September 2010). "The Blitz: Oxford Street's store wars"

23/12/1944
D. Block
H.M.S. Flowerdown

Dearest,

The German push sounds rather dim*, always when things go well something happens as a sort of dampening influence, maybe it helps to keep us from becoming too cock-a-whoop. Do you think it's a sort of final sting? But 25 miles is such a lump to recover. Perhaps it will help to pull the allies into co-operation again, because they all seem to be drifting apart after their own ends. America still hunting for isolation, Russia fishing in Poland. What are we look [sic] for? I suppose France wants a lump off germany & Italy will consider that after she has fought so nobly (!) she is entitled to something and there will be a wonderful squabble & nothing will ever be done anywhere. I'm sorry darling for this bout pessimism but at the moment I feel as if the war is going on for ever and the rest of my life will be spent living in a herd. Better than mud and water I suppose!

I took two of my stewards out this afternoon to get greenery for decorating, they are both scared of cows and we suddenly found ourselves in the middle of a playful herd of young ones. One of them danced up and began leaping around, whereat one steward threw her mistletoe at him and ran, cow calmly settled down to eating mistletoe and I had to rescue it. So then this cow made a dive for the other steward who threw holly at her and also fled, I had to rescue holly. But it really was amusing to watch.

Holly doesn't seem to be growing berries this year so we had to find other berries and introduce berries to holly at a later day. Most complicated business.

I am glad, darling that you are no longer in danger of drowning in your beds. A roof and four walls must be a great comfort in this foul weather and I don't grudge you the eggs either, we get two a week! I suppose they are chicken's eggs? It sounded as if the house laid them! I feel like a camel, I get

---

* Referring to the Ardennes offensive or 'Battle of the Bulge'.

two letters and a card one week and then have to live on that for the next two or three! I'm afraid that insatiability is my trouble. I'm no camel.

We went carol singing last night, it was great fun, about thirty of us all round the village; only one house refused to even open their doors when we knocked and I am sure we were the best there. We even had a violin and an oboe with us, most highly organised, of course my voice deserted me half way through and I couldn't stop coughing, anyway it gave me a chance to listen to the racket we were making. We found that on the whole the smaller the house the more pleasant the people. Our own collectors were terrific, you'd have thought from the way they carefully fished around all the back doors they'd been at it for years. Perhaps they have!

Hectic afternoon just concluded, putting up all the greenery we collected. I've a lovely mock Christmas tree but it's all gummy where I stuck Epsom salts onto to it and all the cotton wool is guaranteed not to come off. Spent hours sewing cotton wool onto black-out with a steward patiently tearing the blobs for me, I've also sewed mistletoe on, but everyone solemnly assures me that it won't be there tomorrow as we have a dance here tonight and the common idea seems to be to wear it in your hair. Lousy idea, I think, but then I have come to the conclusion that I must be in the wrong place as many of the things that these people do just don't amuse me in the least. Am I a prig? I'm positive the wrens we knew at Penshurst didn't behave like it. Darling, I wish you were nearer and we could have Christmas together, it seems thin somehow, this year. I had a card from Kay today with a Portsmouth post-mark, so I gather she achieved her move, so I hope to see her after Christmas.

I was informed today that the four of us (2.a+s) have to get up the New Year party, happy days! It gives us less than a week to throw a party for about 500! I didn't know they thought so highly of us.(?) Like you, darling, I look forward to your next leave, it can't be long now, there is only six weeks until mine is due, so yours must be. Always supposing you don't get embroiled in this new german offensive and get yours stopped.

We actually awoke to an air-raid warning this morning and I thought I must be at home. My brother looks smaller than ever in longs. I gather that he has been dubbed 'the Cherub' at school but it must be his looks for he certainly doesn't live up to it.

Dearest, have you a photo of yourself? I would like one even if it is only an old snap-shot I don't mind. When I try to visualise you, my memory always begins with you hair and works down to your chin. Don't ask me why, I can't tell. Is your hair your most distinctive feature!

I'm supposed to be duty stooge tonight, but have decided to play truant, no-one will miss me. It usually consists of sitting on a phone in chief's office right down the other end of the camp, it seems an awfully long way and there is a lovely fire in my cabin.

Blessings on you darling, all my Christmasiest love

Jean

A year ago today I went to your squadron dinner with you, remember?

27/1/1945

14 Queens Gardens

Ealing W5

My Darling Lyell

News seems to have practically come to a standstill, nothing much can happen within four walls. Of course our pipes are all froze & there was no hot water for a whole day but that no doubt is absolutely nothing to you nowadays! I believe most people's pipes are frozen & lots of them seem to be coal-less which must be ghastly & for some quite unfathomable reason provokes endless argument between my parents as to whether they could have helped it or not. The result is always the same; they never come to a conclusion, how can they, they don't know the circumstances and Daddy always finishes on an entirely different subject. Just to annoy him, I refuse to argue! Are your family like that?

It's about time I went back, I think, the convalescent is getting extraordinarily impatient. Unfortunately they even disagree with me over that, what can one do with such a family!

My eldest sister is trying to do a slight barter & exchange with me, a length of artificial silk for a pyjama chit, but unfortunately some silly idiot had a father on the Board of Trade & told him what the wrens were doing with their chits, consequently gone are the days when a chit for pyjamas would get practically anything of equivalent coupon value. There are a lot of people who would like to know who it was. Especially as they won't issue chits if the article can be purchased in 'slop'. Well, you know what service clothes are like! The only way out now is to wait until the store has run out & then dash in for a chit. Life gets more and more complicated every day.

It's rather sad, I've missed the first two Spanish classes, so now doubtless my Spanish will always have a strong British accent or remain even more basic than your Dutch. I'd heard german was quite a strong swearing language but no-one would ever reveal the secret to me. Why, I can swear better Welsh than any other language & I never even tried to learn it. It sounded much too hard. One just knew all the usual greetings for courtesy's sake. There was one occasion when an old farmer clambered on the bus going to Cerrigy-druidion [sic] & greeted me in Welsh, I returned it beautifully, whereupon he launched upon a long, long discourse and awaited my reply. It was rather a come down when I had to admit complete bewilderment. Do you know any Gaelic?

Audrey wrote to me while I've been at home, she is still in Oxford on the same job, doing the same things and meeting the same people. In fact hospital life seems to be the same in most places but she seems to enjoy it. Please don't think that I think any the less of her for it, I don't far from it. Audrey has a far higher place in my estimation than a lot of people who left. Blackie for example has gone down several pegs over this business of hairdressing, I don't mean in a snobbish way but because she rather slid off the way she set herself. Perhaps I am too idealistic, too easily disappointed. Kay has come up with flying colours, it can't have been easy taking an exam with the knowledge that your fiancée has been killed.

Gosh, darling what subjects one does wander on to. Your letters manage to stick to the point, how do you do it? When I first read your letters, you don't seem to have said much, but on thinking them over I seem to have an awfully vivid picture of what life is like on your bit of front at that moment. Don't ask me why. You see when I spoke to that guardsman in the train I seemed to know as much about it as he could tell me. I confess I pumped him, not on military affairs but just on general conditions and way of life.

Winchester, I am told has had six inches of snow so perhaps it is a bit warmer now. In my absence Audrey has managed to acquire a poker & a table for our cabin, best not to enquire how, both highly necessary adjuncts. Up till now our pokers have been apt to diminish a little every time they were used being but made of wood. I must now get me up, I've sworn that tomorrow will see me up to breakfast!

Dearest, I live with my fingers crossed in case someone else is on leave when you come over, there is still a leave and a half to go.

Take care of yourself my darling.

All my love

Jean

Monkton House

Crescent Road

Alverstoke

Hants

25/10/45

Sweetheart,

My relief arrives tomorrow & I am to be demobbed on the 1st or thereabouts, so I shall be home for your leave. Isn't it terrific!

Dearest Love darling,

Jean

Monkton House

Crescent Road

Alverstoke

Hants

Lyell, my darling,

Isn't it marvellous, my demob. I'm so thrilled! Now if you get posted to England it will be perfect. My only regret was that the WRNS office had no red pencil, otherwise I would have written it in red too. Now I have a definite date to cling to when my bright specimens get too awful. The duty wren woke me up at 0100 this morning to tell me that two were adrift. The poor girl had waited all that time, luckily she wasn't 'on' until 1300 so she could stay in bed. The other one is under medical observation. Darling what have I done to deserve all this!

Are you having our gale? Lovely wind, we sailed down to the fort this morning & pushed our bikes all the way back. 'The sea was galloping grey and white' & a submarine came in & the ship's company half-heartedly cheered her cold and wet looking crew in the pouring rain. Wonderful weather, it even thundered once; the thought entered my mind that this weather would hold the mails up, I haven't seen any planes flying around.

My fire looks lovely tonight. I admit to using a fire-lighter to get it going & to nearly letting it out during an interesting bit of scandal in the galley! Shocking but quite harmlessly amusing.

I am glad you still have one familiar face at least to hang on to. I wonder if he is at all as I imagine him, you keep on calling him 'my old friend' and the image of a bald-headed and dapper civil servant type intrudes itself. It's your fault for thus describing him.

This is the weather that starts one's weight to increase, too much vested interest in warmth. But various worries maybe will counteract these tendencies. I hope you admire my aptitude for sheer drivel.

The aged dame is looking after your interests, I can't quite work out if she has booked you a complete flat, surely I misunderstood. Only Friday week till I see you my beloved. Just imagine, only 27 more days as a civilian in the wrens!.. Madeleine insists the party on the 5th must be my farewell. Anyway we have the fireworks all tucked up, someone has scrounged them from somewhere. I'm afraid we'll have to pay for the beer, no gash! Au revoir my darling, the last days seem awful long.

All my love darling,

Jean

From RAF Air Observation to Army Air Corps

O nce the frantic pace of war had stilled and the dust quite literally began to settle around them the survivors suddenly became aware of a future more distant than tomorrow's sunrise. Those who joined as 'hostilities only' would probably 'demob' but for professional soldiers it was different. Some looked back at their orderly lives before the war – parades and peacekeeping – and yearned to return to them. The more realistic knew those days were gone and that the changes brought by war were irreversible. In the British army, one such change had been the success of the AOP as a part of the modern battlefield: soldiers had learned to fly in combat and performed their task well.

And the 'peace' was still an illusion: for example there is the story of 656 AOP Squadron which had been in action in Burma since January 1944. Telling their story, EW Maslen-Jones describes listening to the VE day celebrations on the radio: "with shells falling outside our dugout no one spoke. We just sat deep in thought and getting more depressed by the minute until Frank very pointedly got up and switched it off. I thought for a moment he was going to throw the set out of the tent!"

When the fighting in Burma ended, elements of No.656 Squadron took part in a naval landing on the west coast of Malaya, and as Japanese resistance crumbled, they made their way to Singapore, reaching the city by the time of the Japanese surrender. From November 1945, they were heavily involved in Java, supporting the return of Dutch rule. After this, the Squadron was reduced to a single Flight in January 1947 and reformed 18 months later. This was followed by twelve years of operational support to the Army throughout the Malayan emergency.

656 Squadron's story was unusual but not exceptional. Whilst Army flying in post war Europe moved over to a peacetime role of exercises and liaison, in other parts of the world the Army never actually ceased flying combat

operations. After 1945 Britain was faced with a series of uprisings throughout the former Empire and a constant need to commit men and materials to Europe, first as occupiers and then as defenders against the Soviet Union. There were also demands for troops in Korea to meet British commitments to the UN campaign against the Chinese-backed North Koreans. Britain was heavily in debt, money was urgently needed to rebuild the economy and it seemed obvious that the armed forces budget was a good place to make significant savings. The government at first optimistically assumed that the existing massive stocks of war materiel would supply the three Services for years to come, but it soon discovered that these were either inadequate or too outdated to meet the demands made on them.

The Chiefs of Staff began to look for ways to use resources more effectively under the new conditions they faced across the globe and Army aviation came under almost immediate scrutiny. The RAF, anxious to save its front line squadrons, was envious of the funding given to the AOP squadrons and thought it could be put to better use. The Army made the case that the RAF was just as incapable of providing the skills required for the evolving AOP role as it had been in 1939 and 1940. Another issue was that the AOP Squadrons were still technically RAF, but were manned by a mix of Army and RAF personnel and under Army operational control. The consequence of this was that there was no central AOP command unit looking after their interests, particularly where supply and operational issues were concerned. During wartime and post war operations, supplies of spares were often delayed or entirely lacking and aircraft modifications and fault fixing were rarely dealt with quickly by the RAF which gave its own front line squadrons' needs priority and only allowed their technicians to spend "the minimum period in a backwater [away] from the main stream of jet-age technical advancement".

In 1946, the debate between Air Chief Marshal Sir Charles Portal of the Air Ministry, and the Chief of Imperial General Staff, Field Marshal Lord Allanbrooke on ownership of the AOP functions ended inconclusively; other than agreeing to leave things as they were with AOP Squadrons nominally under RAF control but with Army pilots and commanders. In the meantime, the post war cuts to the armed forces had begun. Since 1942, AOP squadrons had formed part of the Army Air Corps, which also included the Special Air Services (SAS), the Glider Pilot Regiment and the Parachute Brigades. By 1947, the number of AOP squadrons had fallen from twelve to four. These were 651 in Palestine, 652 in Germany, 656 in Malaya (disbanded on 15th January 1947 and reduced to No 1914 (AOP) Flight) and 657 carrying out a training and technical development role in the UK. In addition there were several independent liaison flights attached to Army HQs. The Glider Pilot Regiment was also a shadow of its former self, so it was perhaps not surprising that 1949 would see the Army Air Corps disbanded and its components dispersed.

At the same time, another problem had begun to demand attention; the roles that the AOP squadrons were being asked to carry out now exceeded the capabilities of their aircraft. The Auster was still useful for reconnaissance, gunnery control and light liaison work but was inadequate for other duties such as carrying equipment and ammunition or casualty evacuation. Thus it was that the helicopter came under military consideration as a partial or even total replacement for the Auster. The Army was also considering using load-carrying helicopters as 'air lorries' transporting troops and delivering supplies.

Helicopter development arguably goes back almost as far as aeroplanes. The German test pilot, Hanna Reitsch, flew a twin rotor Fa61 helicopter inside the 'Deutschlandhalle' at the Berlin Motor Show of 1938. The development of the early helicopter allowed the Kriegsmarine (German Navy) to deploy the co-axial twin-rotor Flettner Fl282 'Kolibri' (Hummingbird) to fly from the gun turrets of capital ships on anti-submarine patrol duties as early as 1942. The designer in fact went on after the war to design the American 'Kaman' family of naval helicopters.

In the US Navy the Sikorsky R4 had been in service as early as 1941 and in 1944 the YR4B was evaluated by the RAF for all theatres including tropical operations. In fact it made the first ever helicopter casualty evacuation in Burma in 1944. Such developments were closely observed by Army aviation, well aware that the helicopter might bring a vast improvement in the scope and effectiveness of AOP and Army liaison work. The Army had trialled Autogyros at the experimental establishment at RAF Andover but soon recognised that the future lay with the helicopter. 657 Squadron was the first to evaluate the Sikorsky R4B and R6A (known as the Hoverfly 1 and

Hoverfly 2) between 1946 and 1950, with its 'C' flight (renamed 1901 Flight from 1946 to 1947) and then with 1906 Flight in 1950. This Flight was also used as a helicopter training flight for AOP pilots. From that point the eventual transition of the AOP to rotary wing was assured.

The division of responsibility for military transport and liaison flying between RAF and Army was also being very actively considered. In 1949, the Land/Air Warfare Committee of officers nominated by the Air Ministry and the War office had begun discussions on 'Light Aircraft Requirements for the Army'. As a starting point, they assumed that future duties would include reconnaissance, light liaison duties, communications and casualty evacuation. In 1951 the committee produced a set of proposals which set out the type and numbers of light fixed wing (and, later on, rotary) aircraft, which the RAF should supply to the Army squadrons. It proposed the formation of six light aircraft flights with twelve in reserve, and that there should be an established AOP overall command structure within the Army. The Army would provide pilots, signallers and RASC personnel and the RAF would provide tradesmen to carry out servicing and maintenance. The War Office happily accepted these proposals and formally submitted them to the Air Ministry in April 1951.

The RAF delayed looking at the proposals until January 1952. When they did, they immediately balked at the idea of 'light liaison' and casualty evacuation missions being flown by Army pilots. The Air Council counter proposed that RAF pilots should fly these missions and that consequently the Army liaison units in their entirety should be taken over by the RAF. As a result, there would be no need for any changes to the existing Army AOP organisation. One argument put forward in support was the suggestion that Army pilots couldn't fly safely at night and in bad weather. Another was that it was no longer possible for light aircraft to carry out the traditional AOP role over a modern battlefield without total air superiority.

The debate continued for another six months with a succession of counter proposals made by each side. In the process, the Army added a proposal that the RAF should replace fixed wing aircraft used for 'light liaison' purposes by helicopters and that serious consideration should be given to the use of heavy duty helicopters as troop and equipment transports. In this they were drawing on lessons from Korea where British forces had been forced to depend on the US Air Force for vertical take-off transport. The commander of 1913 Flight in this conflict, Major J.H. Hailes, was very clear that he would have preferred helicopters to Austers:

> ... virtually anything that can be done by an Auster can be done far better by a helicopter ... It is a real tragedy that this is yet another place where the Army is losing valuable practical experience with helicopters.

In August 1953 the Air Council accepted a proposal from the Director of Land/Air warfare, General GS Thompson, that the Army should take over full responsibility for flying, maintaining and administering its own light aircraft. It would also set up and maintain at its own expense an experimental unit to investigate the feasibility of operating helicopters as cargo and troop carriers. By this time, the RAF had begun to accept that such a development was inevitable (and they had little interest in helicopters anyway). In 1954, the Chief of Air Staff agreed that it made sense to separate the costs of providing the Army with air services from the air defence budget. The main reason was that the Army's need for transport and mobility were not part of the war in the air and its priorities were therefore completely different from those of air defence. Removing them would simplify air defence planning and budgeting and he felt that the RAF was sufficiently well established to resist any attempt by the Army or the Navy to whittle away its functions.

At this point the debate became bogged down in political wrangling between the respective Secretaries of State. The main problem was lack of funds. Helicopters were expensive – especially those with heavy lift capability and the RAF feared that the cost of establishing an Army fleet of fixed wing and rotary aircraft – and the Army was talking about five hundred aircraft all told - would come out of its budget. So the RAF decided to take the initiative, and in July 1956, Air Marshal Sir Ronald Ivelaw-Chapman proposed that the Army should take over full responsibility for buying, manning and maintaining aircraft used for AOP and light liaison. He stipulated that the aircraft used should be unarmed and have an all-up weight – that is the aircraft loaded to its maximum cargo capacity – of no more than 4,000 pounds (1815 kg). After more debate, both sides agreed although the Army received assurances that they could renegotiate the weight limit if it ever became necessary to do so.

In January 1957, a new Minister of Defence, Duncan Sandys, took office with a brief to fully review the UK defence policy. One of his first acts was to approve the handing over of light aviation to the Army. A new Army Air Corps was formed on 1st September 1957 when the Glider Pilot Regiment finally stood down, and the corps' iconic blue beret was authorised. That date is now the Corps Regimental Day.

In fiction this would be the end of the story, but in reality things are never so tidy. The new Army Air Corps had a base at RAF Middle Wallop Light Aircraft School (soon to be re-christened the Army Aviation Centre) and aircraft. These included Mk6 and T7 Austers, Chipmunk T10s and Skeeter AOP10 and Sycamore HC11 helicopters. It had no budget because it was taken over as a going concern and no-one had any idea what future development and replacement costs would have to cover and how much they would be. Where ground crew and logistics were concerned, REME technicians (Royal Electrical and Mechanical Engineers) started to be trained to take over from RAF engineers and artificers, a move completed in 1958, and Army logistics started to take over their supply chain. The Royal Navy supported them with loan technicians, providing line support for the units reforming in BAOR. On one notable occasion in Germany, a visiting general inspecting an Army squadron was met by a Royal Navy quarter-guard as if he had just stepped onto a ship! Personnel from the Royal Signals, the Royal Army Pay Corps and the Army Catering Corps manned other administrative, technical and supply posts.

The AAC had a small central cadre made up of senior officers and administrative personnel and based at Middle Wallop. As far as pilots and non-technical ground staff were concerned, the Director of Artillery refused to allow Royal Artillery to continue as the main source of recruitment for pilots and non-technical ground staff because of the consequent loss of manpower. The Deputy Chief of the Imperial General Staff, General Hull, also favoured a move away from the Royal Artillery as the sole source because he did not want the AAC to become an Artillery preserve. In the end, a compromise was reached with non-technical ground staff coming from the Artillery and pilots coming from a broader reservoir, either as officer volunteers from the Armoured Corps, the Artillery, the Engineers, Signals and infantry or as warrant officer and sergeant volunteers from any arm of the Service.

For its structure, the AAC drew on World War Two and post war operational experience which had convincingly demonstrated that it was always advantageous for the squadrons and their flights to train with the Army formation that they would be supporting and whose guns would come under AOP direction. The experiences of units such as 653's 'C' Flight also proved that AOP squadrons should always be as close to the front line as possible to provide effective support.

The new AAC organisation allowed for a Wing HQ in each theatre of operations, but Squadrons were assigned as required and were not sub-units of the Wing. Each had three light aircraft Flights and a supporting workshop. Flights would have six aircraft: three fixed wing and three rotaries, and be designated either 'Reconnaissance' or 'Liaison'. Liaison flights were used for communications, personnel transport, transport of stores, signals work and the evacuation of casualties. Reconnaissance Flights supported a Brigade and carried out AOP, reconnaissance, traffic-control and mail services. Independent Flights were expected to cover both areas and be self-supporting in the field. The Army Air Centre provided central control and administration and strategic planning. They had hardly become established when they had to find solutions to several problems that threatened the existence of the fledgling Corps.

The first was aircraft. Discussions on the future of Army flying had included what type of rotary and fixed wing light aircraft the new units would need, but when the AAC was formed there was no helicopter in production which met its needs. The Saunders Roe 'Skeeter' had been undergoing extensive tests at Middle Wallop and at Andover since 1956, but all the early versions were underpowered and it wasn't until August 1958 that a Mark 12 version was accepted for service by the AAC in 1961. It was the first operational helicopter to see service as an army AOP, but it was restricted to European theatres because under tropical conditions it could not generate enough lift to meet the rate of vertical climb required. Between 1958 and 1961, the Army had to buy the French 'Alouette' to fill the light aircraft gap. There was an alternative, the 'Scout' which Saunders Roe produced in 1959 as a speculative development. It fully met the Army's specifications but exceeded the 4,000-pound all-up weight limit imposed in 1956 by the RAF. Nevertheless, the Army decided to accept it, relying on the earlier assurances that the all-up weight limit was flexible!

There was also the question of what should replace the Auster as the fixed wing component of the AAC. The Army's preference was for the de Havilland 'Beaver', a Canadian aircraft with an impressive reputation for reliability and the ability to operate under a wide range of climatic conditions. Unfortunately, the Beaver exceeded the all-up weight limit, but the Army pointed out that it had always reserved the right to set this aside if it had to do so to obtain a satisfactory aircraft. The RAF had already accepted that weight should not be an issue and the Army's decision to take the Scout, but they drew the line at the Beaver. They insisted that it should be flown by RAF personnel because it was able to carry out troop carrying and supply drop duties and under the original 1956 agreement, these were RAF functions. Discussions began in 1959 and were brought to an end by a new Minister for Defence, Harold Watkinson, who ruled that the Army should have the Beaver. Peter Mead, working on the staff of the Director of Land/Air Warfare, wrote of the decision: "It was not the Beaver but the whole of the Army Air Corps that had been saved". Thirty-six Beavers were ordered and they were delivered in 1961.

So far so good, but major changes were looming. The 1957 Defence review by Duncan Sandys had recognised that it was simply too expensive to maintain the existing global military presence given the state of the British economy. It acknowledged the need to counter the Soviet threat in Central Europe (partially addressed by the success of the British nuclear weapons program) and react rapidly to emergencies elsewhere. However, the need to cut costs meant the withdrawal or reduction of overseas garrisons so the RAF would have to transport reinforcements and rapid reaction forces from the UK. This seriously affected the AAC because its light aircraft simply didn't have the range to reach the areas where reinforcements were most likely to be required. Worse still, local commanders insisted that they now needed a permanently attached air reconnaissance and communications capability to compensate for the reduction in their other forces. This meant more aircraft, but the AAC lacked the personnel to fly and maintain them because regiments had become more reluctant to allow personnel to volunteer for AAC service. There was also, once again, a move in Whitehall to 'rationalise' flying and 'hand all flying machines to the RAF'.

In 1960 General Weston, former AAC commander and now Director of Land/Air Warfare, proposed to solve both issues by integrating Army aviation with regular army units. Faced with the prospect of the disbandment of the AAC, its commander, Brigadier Mead, met with General Stockwell the Colonel Commandant of the AAC and General Weston at Middle Wallop. After the meeting, General Stockwell decided that the AAC should remain in existence with some integration to help solve the strategic and manpower problem in the short term at least. In 1964, the AAC began a five-year programme of deploying aircraft at brigade level with regimental air units operating with and considered a part of regular army units. By the time it was completed in 1969, the number of aircraft in operation by the Army had risen from 140 to 356 and 96 per cent of these were helicopters. The Army Air Corps Aviation Centre still existed although the new arrangements meant that it had been relegated to an advisory role. In this capacity it was to spark another argument between the Army and the RAF.

The adoption of the Scout helicopter gave the Army an aircraft which was not only a good workhorse but was also capable of carrying anti tank rockets. The Army Aviation Centre suggested that Army helicopters could become an airborne anti tank system to reinforce the BAOR's ability to deal with Warsaw pact forces whose armoured forces outnumbered them. This idea was greeted with general enthusiasm by Army pilots who looked back with regret to the days when AOP pilots controlled the fire of the guns in action and resented their post war role as airborne messengers, scouts and taxi drivers. It was not welcomed by the RAF which was already unhappy about reports that the Royal Corps of Transport was routinely using Army aircraft to transport troops and freight, and about the Army occasionally using Beavers as light bombers.

The original conditions of the 1956 agreement had been well and truly circumvented or ignored by the Army so in February 1965 the RAF proposed to take back all responsibility for light aircraft operations. This came as a complete surprise to both the Army and to the Navy who promptly formed an alliance to resist the idea. The Army case rested on two arguments. The first was that the history of Army flying had proved that pilots of Army aircraft should be soldiers first and pilots second. This had been the justification for the original creation of an Army piloted AOP in 1940 and was still as valid now as it had been then. Experience since the war clearly showed that ground troops working closely with Army air units were significantly more effective and could deploy much more quickly whether in the plains of central Europe or in jungle and desert terrain. The second was that the Army ran their air services with fewer personnel and at much less cost than the RAF. A committee chaired by Field Marshal Sir Gerald Templar met to consider the RAF's bid and rejected it.

The Army's evidence to the Templar Committee had also shown that although the policy of limited decentralisation had produced good results, it was not sustainable. Army aviation had virtually returned to its wartime position where individual flights and Squadrons operated with minimal centralised control and in close liaison, or as part of, regular army units. However, the new Sud Aviation Lynx and Gazelle helicopters and their weapons and surveillance systems demanded an ever increasing level of technical support which the REME did not have the resources to provide to regimental air units. Without organisational change, the situation could only get worse as new weapons systems and aircraft became more complex and technically demanding. Army resources were being stretched to meet existing and new obligations across the globe and it was most unlikely that more funds would be available in the future. Army Air Corps senior officers suggested that there was only one possible solution, recentralisation. In 1967, the Army Board agreed and decided that this would best be achieved by a staged process which would end with a new Army Air Corps structure.

By 1969, the AAC had been reorganised as a centralised unit with eighteen squadrons and five independent flights divided among the UK, Allied Command Europe, BAOR Near East Persian Gulf and Hong Kong operational areas. To achieve this, they needed more pilots and other personnel so the Army Board required pilots and ground crews from regimental units to join the squadrons on temporary appointments. This annoyed the regiments who strongly discouraged personnel from volunteering for the AAC so again the intake of new personnel declined. The solution was simple; the AAC permanent cadre was expanded to include all army pilots and technical ground crew. It took nearly eight years from first proposal to completion, but in 1979 the Army Air Corps became a Fighting Arm on the same footing as the Royal Armoured Corps and the Infantry.

Since its formation, apart from its Cold War activities in Central Europe, the AAC has been involved in every theatre of conflict in its traditional role of observing, reporting and supporting Army activity on the ground. The arrival of the Scout helicopter led to their starting to carry air-to-ground weapons (leading to the creation of the crewman air gunner). The arrival of the Lynx saw the introduction of the more capable TOW, a wire guided anti-tank missile, and finally the heavily armed Westland/Augusta Apache AH1 effectively replaced the RAF's Harrier as the British definitive front line close air support aircraft. After this the AAC quickly took the Apache into an aircraft carrier capability with naval training on HMS Illustrious. In 2007 the AAC reorganised into single type regiments, each with its speciality including Special Forces.

The Army Air Corps, now distinguished by its sky blue beret, has become a career in itself, worthy of its front line aircraft. It numbers (in 2014) around 2000 full time personnel, with another 2500 within its support from REME (Royal Electrical and Mechanical Engineers) and the Royal Logistics Corps (its support infrastructure). Full time AAC soldiers are now known as 'Airtroopers' and a number of support trades are offered. Today the Army Air Corps enjoys its own distinct culture, as a small combat air force with helicopters and some fixed wing aircraft. The Army also enjoys almost total control of the RAF's tactical transport aircraft. The AAC will receive the Wildcat helicopter totally integrated with Royal Navy operations with a 'sea change' in their attitudes. They are combat ready, belligerent and finely honed.

Annex

653 Squadron post war

After reforming in May 1958, No. 653 Squadron had enjoyed another eight years of mixed operations first in Cyprus and then in Aden before disbanding in October 1967. In 1971 it was remustered at Netheravon, and then on 1st April 1978 the Squadron reformed at Soest (Germany) as part of 3 Regiment AAC. Later equipped with the Lynx Mk.7 and the Gazelle, the Squadron took on a offensive anti-tank role.

In July 1993, 653 moved to Wattisham. They re-equipped with the Lynx Mk.9 Light Battlefield helicopter and were then involved in operations in Kosovo. 2003 saw them in Iraq and then in Bosnia with the Lynx Mk.7. In 2007 they re-equipped with the Apache AH1 and were involved in operations in Afghanistan's Helmand Province. The current No.653 Squadron has named one of their Apaches 'Dickson Pioneer', as they move into an operational training role.

Appendix IV

'The Aeroplane' September 24 1943: The Army's Austers

We recently spent a day with the Austers. We were slightly acquainted with their predecessor, the Taylor-craft Model D, in the days of peace, but meeting them for the first time in their military guise provided a pleasant interlude in a life which circumstances had made all too familiar with aeroplanes of meteoric speed, phenomenal climb, tremendous range, massive size and bristling guns. Here were small aeroplanes which have no pretensions to speed and disdain all forms of armament. Their qualities are the antithesis of those with which the newest fighters and bombers are so liberally endowed.

The Austers work exclusively with the Army. They are the eyes of its artillery and a handy, ever-ready transport. They have been its servants since the earliest days of the War – they went to France with the first British Expeditionary Force in 1939 – and as, with the passing years, the Army has grown, so the demand for them has grown. They have never known the limelight of publicity and their exploits have passed unsung. In Lord Beaverbrook's classic phrase, they have been, until now, the 'backroom boys' of the Air Arm.

They wear camouflage and the circles and 'flash' of the R.A.F., but have different identification marks – usually two letters and a number. For the most part, they are flown by Army pilots of the Air Observation Post Squadrons, trained by the R.A.F. They spend their lives in the open, seldom use aerodromes, and are often kept airworthy in the field by Army mechanics whose skill, by the very nature of their training and duties, must fall far below that of the Flight Mechanics of the Royal Air Force. Yet the Austers contrive to give excellent service in the most difficult conditions. They are serving in many parts of the World and stand up to every kind of weather. Many are still on active service with a thousand hours of flying to their credit. Not one has been withdrawn on the score of decrepitude – a matter of great pride to their makers.

There are two versions now in use, the Auster I and the Auster III. The Auster I has the 90 h.p. Cirrus in-line air-cooled motor and no flaps; the Auster III has the 130 h.p. Gipsy Major and flaps. Both are side-by-side, two-seat, high-wing braced monoplanes, and in normal flight are indistinguishable one from the other. The cabin is roomy and many square feet of 'glazing' allow the occupants to see in many-directions. Only the cockpit floor, the lower sides of the cabin and the motor block the downward view. All the cockpit roof and much of the cabin roof and sides is glazed. The high wing obscures some of the upper hemisphere, but an external mirror on the roof, facing rearwards, partly offsets this blanketing.

We elected, first, to be shown, rather than to test, the flying qualities of an Auster III. The demonstrator proved to be a capable and fearless pilot and gave an exhibition which left us impressed but shaken. We discovered, later, that the pilot's other mount, these days, is the Typhoon.

In a light wind, the take-off run was short and the climb escalator-like. For a time we paraded among white, billowing cumulus at 4,000 ft., for the benefit of a photographer in a Tiger Moth; then returned to the aerodrome for the more intense phases of the demonstration. The pilot dived at a hangar until the Gipsy whined like a Sabre. Then clouds tumbled over the nose in a rapid procession as the Auster sought the zenith of the sky. We fell over on one wing and dived again, seemingly vertical. Once more, the hangar stepped from our path in the nick of time. The trick was repeated several times. Then the pilot flew across the aerodrome, flaps down, at a speed that barely reached 40 miles an hour on the A.S.I. His show ended with a sustained vertical turn a few feet off the ground, and an impeccable landing. We stepped out, full of admiration, but marvelling that so much 'G' could be absorbed in so small a structure.

A thunderstorm prevented us from fulfilling our second intention, but our pre-war experience with the Model D, and the opinions we have heard in sundry places leave no doubt that the Auster is a delight to fly. Although it is so manoeuvrable – the wing loading is only 7 lb. per sq. ft. – it has no vices, will not roll, and comes out of a spin in half a turn when either the stick or the rudder is centralised. The stall hardly deserves the name. The nose drops in the most gentlemanly manner and flying speed is regained in an instant.

In common with all other aeroplanes offered to the R.A.F., the Austers had to pass stern and searching tests. To create the special conditions under which this aeroplane would have to operate, a corner of the aerodrome was covered with rubbish, including bricks. Hundreds of landings were made on this 'treated' area, and hundreds more in odd fields, ploughed and otherwise, up and down the country. In all, more than 1,000 landings were made with each of two Austers, both carrying their maximum permissible load.* Most of them were made, we gather, by Army pilots picked at random from the Air Observation Post Squadrons.

The Structure

The Austers' robustness comes from their simple welded steel-tube structure, which is designed to take loads in compression. The foundation of the structure is a steel shock truss of great rigidity through which all the main flying and landing loads pass. The wing spars are straightforward plank forms in spruce, and the ribs are formed from drawn sections of Birmabrite. Steel-tube drag struts and high-tensile tie rods complete the main wing assembly. The leading edges have a metal sheath and the entire machine is covered with fabric.

Tests made with individual parts have given highly satisfactory results. In one, for instance, a rib did not fail until it had been subjected to a stress – representing 128.5 per cent, of the design load. After four attempts, a shock truss was made to show slight distortion when overloaded by 200 per cent; although the distortion was permanent, it did not make the shock truss unairworthy. We saw these and other parts being made in one of the Taylorcraft factories. Some of them seemed almost frail to look at, but attempts to bend or distort them were largely unavailing. The rudder frame resisted the efforts of two strong men to twist it.

The simplicity of the Auster's design is reflected in the low proportion of skilled to semi-skilled labour needed to build it. In the factory we visited, half the labour force appeared to be youths and young girls. A good percentage of the welders, we noticed, were women and to our amateur eye their work looked as good as that of the men. Only thirteen different sizes of tube are used, and assembling is done on swivelling steel jigs. Each part is cut to its correct length and seldom requires filing to ensure a perfect fit before the riveting or welding is done. On the compact assembly line, each framework is one stage in advance of its neighbour. The jobs to be done at each point are so timed that the whole line can be moved every three hours or so. This applies to wings and fuselage.

The Cockpit

An unusual feature in the cockpit is the design of the controls for ailerons and elevator. The 'stick' is carried by a bar cranked at each end and running in bearings. The bar runs across the cockpit past both seats, and moves backwards and forwards to work the elevator. The stick moves laterally in roller bearings and works the ailerons. Another stick can be fitted for the passenger. Two rudder bars are standard. The control surfaces are connected by cables, and the rudder is mass balanced.

"Aeroplane" photograph

COCKPIT LAYOUT.—Among the cockpit details shown in this photograph are the instruments, the throttle lever, the wide doors and the bar which works the elevator and carries the "stick." The small pedals on the floor operate the wheel brakes.

The dashboard has all the essential instruments, which can be read with ease from both seats. They include a three-lingered sensitive altimeter, turn-and-bank indicator, air-speed indicator and rev. counter. The throttle lever is in the centre of the dashboard, where it can be reached with equal ease from either seat. A simple, stick-type fuel-contents gauge projects a short distance beyond the dashboard and gives a clear reading.

On the Auster III, the long flap lever – the flaps are manually operated – is set near the roof of the cockpit above the pilot's left shoulder. When the lever is fully raised the flaps are closed. There are three open positions ; the first is for take-off, the second for normal landings and the third for use in an emergency. In the extreme open position, the flaps make an angle with the wing of about 70 degrees.

Another unusual feature is the elevator trimming device. This is not attached to the elevator, but takes the form of a small control surface at the extreme end of the fuselage. The tail skid is a multi-leaf cantilever spring. To counter-balance the additional weight of the Gipsy Major motor, a 26 lb. weight is carried in the tail of the Auster III.

To the best of Taylorcraft's knowledge, only one of the many Austers delivered to the Army is not now in service. We were shown one of the original contingent which accompanied the British Expeditionary Force in 1939 [April 1940]. Its log book recorded nearly 900 hours of flying, and a preliminary examination in the repair shops had suggested that only the most superficial work would be needed to restore it to service. The greater part of its life had been spent in the open.

Though unarmed, the Austers are not the easy prey for enemy fighters which the "Art. Obs." machines were in the last War. Several have had encounters, but all have escaped. One was attacked by 13 Messerschmitt Me109s, but the pilot flew into a hollow between two hills, where by tight turns and skilful manoeuvres, he defied the enemy until rescued by Spitfires called to the scene over his radio. When it was examined, not one bullet mark was found.

Another Auster brought back valuable information which no other aeroplane could secure. Under an umbrella of Spitfires, it cruised round Long Stop Hill early in the Tunisian campaign and plotted the position of enemy guns which were holding up the Allied advance. Faster aeroplanes had tried in vain to locate and plot them.

Now that the Auster has been unveiled, the World may perhaps be told more of its exploits. Its work is unspectacular, but as the land fighting grows in scale and scope it will become increasingly important. Though tanks and aeroplanes have tended to steal the picture in this War, artillery is still an essential force in any land campaign. Other and faster aeroplanes may find the targets for the guns, but the crews must rely on the Auster to tell them where their shots are falling. There should be many a good story to tell. – s.v.

PERFORMANCES Auster I (90 h.p. Cirrus motor)

Maximum weight for straight and level flight	1,400 lb.
Maximum weight for all forms of flying	1,200 lb.
Maximum permissible speed (AS.I.j	144 m.p.h.
Maximum speed, level flight (A.S.I.)	118 m.p.h.
Cruising speed (A.S.I.)	100 m.p.h.
Stalling speed (A.S.I.)	36 m.p.h.
Take-off run (no wind)	90 yards.

Auster 111 (130 h.p. Gipsy Major Motor)

Maximum weight (aerobatics not permissible)	1,550 lb.
Maximum permissible speed (A.S.I.)	144 m.p.h.
Maximum speed, level flight	126 m.p.h.
Cruising speed (A.S.I.)	100 m.p.h.
Stalling speed (flaps fully open)	25 m.p.h.
Take-off run (no wind)	65 yards
Rate of climb (sea level)	1,040 ft. per min

Editor's note: The above article was reproduced here as it gives a very readable contemporary view of the Auster and its role. This despite some errors, either journalistic, in the cause of misinformation or simply in the turn of events.

Bibliography

For the 1990 unpublished version
'Hill 112', J.J. How, 1984
'North-West Europe 1944-45', North, J., 1977
'Long Left Flank: The hard Fought Way to the Reich 1944-1945', Williams, Jeffery, 1988
'Overlord', Hastings, M., 1985
'Decision in Normandy', D'Este, C., 1983
'Caen - Anvil of Victory', McKee, A., 1977
'The Battle for Normandy', Belfield and-Essame, 1975
'History of 15th (Scottish) Division', Martin, H.H., 1948
'The Big Show', Pierre Closterman, P., 1951
'The Eye in the Sky', Mead, P. HMSO
'Monty - Master of the Battlefield', Hamilton, N., 1984

for the 2016 extended, edited version
'Army Wings', Jackson, R., 2006
'Fire by order', Maslen-Jones, E.W., 1997
'Germany puts the Clock Back, Edgar Mowrer, 1933, 1937
'The Struggle for Europe', Wilmot, Chester, 1952
'Unarmed into Battle', Parham, H.J & Belfield, E.M.G., 1956

Acknowledgements

for the 1990 unpublished version
Major John Cross at the Museum of Army Flying, Middle Wallop, for general help and advice
Lambert Munro, Findhorn, for help with photocopying
Alec Fraser, Forres, for help with reproducing old photographs
Lynne Donaldson, Forres, for expert word processing and advice

for the 2016 extended, edited version
The curator and staff of the Museum of Army Flying for their continued support, access to their archives and inexhaustible patience in dealing with our requests for information, documents and advice

Lieutenant General Sir Gary Robert Coward KCB, CB, Lieutenant Colonel Andrew Simkins OBE and Major Stewart Pearce for their enthusiasm and encouragement.

Mr Guy Warner, aviation expert and author of 'From Auster to Apache' for his expertise in assisting us in our summary of post-war development of the Army Air Corps. Any errors are our doing and not his.

Index